Dimensions of United States-Mexican Relations

Volume 3

Mexican Migration to
the United States

Dimensions of United States-Mexican Relations

a series

Volume 1. *Images of Mexico in the United States*, edited by John H. Coatsworth and Carlos Rico, with contributions from Christine E. Contee, John Bailey, Carlos E. Cortés, and Gerald Greenfield.

Volume 2. *The Economics of Interdependence: Mexico and the United States*, edited by William Glade and Cassio Luiselli, with contributions from Barry Bosworth, Francisco Gil Díaz, Rosario Green, Luis Bravo Aguilera, Guy Erb, Joseph Greenwald, Manuel Armendáriz, and B. Timothy Bennett.

Volume 3. *Mexican Migration to the United States: Origins, Consequences, and Policy Options*, edited by Wayne Cornelius and Jorge Bustamante, with contributions from Wayne Cornelius, Manuel García y Griego, Marta Tienda, Kitty Calavita, and Jorge Bustamante.

Volume 4. *The Drug Connection in U.S.-Mexican Relations*, edited by Marta Tienda and Guadalupe González, with contributions from Ann J. Blanken, Miguel Ruiz-Cabañas I., Richard B. Craig, and Samuel I. del Villar.

Volume 5. *Foreign Policy in U.S.-Mexican Relations*, edited by Rosario Green and Peter H. Smith, with contributions from Guadalupe González, Lars Schoultz, Jorge Chabat, Carlos Rico, Cathryn L. Thorup, Claude Heller, and William H. Luers.

**Series editors:
Rosario Green and Peter H. Smith**

Mexican Migration to the United States
Origins, Consequences, and Policy Options

edited by
Wayne A. Cornelius and Jorge A. Bustamante

Dimensions of U.S.-Mexican Relations, Volume 3
papers prepared for the
Bilateral Commission on the Future of United States-Mexican Relations

Published by the
Center for U.S.-Mexican Studies
University of California, San Diego
1989

ISBN # 0-935-391-90-8

Table of Contents

Dimensions of United States-Mexican Relations: ix
Series Introduction
Rosario Green and Peter H. Smith

1   Mexican Migration to the United States: 1
     An Introduction
     Wayne A. Cornelius

SECTION I
THE MIGRATION PROCESS

2   The U.S. Demand for Mexican Labor   25
     Wayne A. Cornelius

3   The Mexican Labor Supply, 1990-2010   49
     Manuel García y Griego

| 4 | Measuring the Flow of Undocumented Immigrants
Jorge A. Bustamante | 95 |

SECTION II
CONSEQUENCES

| 5 | Looking to the 1990s:
Mexican Immigration in Sociological Perspective
Marta Tienda | 109 |

SECTION III
POLICY OPTIONS

| 6 | The Immigration Policy Debate:
Critical Analysis and Future Options
Kitty Calavita | 151 |

| About the Contributors | 179 |

Dimensions of
United States-Mexican Relations:
Series Introduction

Rosario Green and Peter H. Smith

This volume is part of a five-volume series, *Dimensions of United States-Mexican Relations,* consisting of selected background papers originally prepared for the use of the Bilateral Commission on the Future of United States-Mexican Relations.

Appreciation of the series must begin with an understanding of its origin. The Bilateral Commission was formed in 1986 as an independent, privately funded group of prominent citizens who were seeking to make a contribution to the improvement of U.S.-Mexican relations. Early in its deliberations the Commission agreed to produce a book-length report in time for consideration by incoming presidents to be elected in 1988.

With a two-year schedule, the Commission decided to seek the opinions of expert analysts on a variety of issues—specifically, on economics (including debt, trade, and investment), migration, drugs, foreign policy, and cultural relations. In addition, of course, Commissioners read a great deal of already published material and heard testimony from numerous government officials in both Mexico and the United States.

As staff directors for the Commission, the two of us assumed responsibility for coordination of the research activity. With the assistance of an Academic Committee,[1] we organized an intensive series of workshops and solicited papers from leading experts on each of these broad topics.

Our principal purpose was to provide the Commission with a broad range of informed perspectives on key issues in U.S.-Mexican relations. We wanted to introduce its members to the terms of current debates, rather than buttress conventional wisdoms; we sought to acquaint them with the broadest possible range of policy alternatives, rather than bias the discussion in favor of any particular view.

As a result, many Commissioners do not agree with the opinions expressed in these papers—just as some of the authors may disagree with parts of the Commission's report, published in English as *The Challenge of Interdependence: Mexico and the United States* (University Press of America, 1988).[2]

Accordingly, the publication of this series does not necessarily represent the viewpoints of the Commission or its members, and the papers herein do not simply provide supporting documentation for positions and recommendations of the Commission. The *Dimensions of United States-Mexican Relations* series represents an outgrowth of the same initiative that resulted in the Commission's report, but in other senses it is separate from it.

As we developed our research program on behalf of the Bilateral Commission, we nonetheless sought to make useful contributions to scholarly discourse on U.S.-Mexican relations. In this regard we had three goals:

One was to encourage the application of *comparative perspectives* to the study of U.S.-Mexican relations. Much of the work in this field has tended to concentrate on properties of the bilateral relationship alone and to assume, and often to assert, that the U.S.-Mexican connection has been "unique." It goes without saying, however, that you cannot determine the uniqueness of a relationship without comparing it to others. This we invited our authors to do.

Second was to encourage appropriate *attention to the United States*. We believe that much of the literature tends to concentrate

---

[1]The members were: Jorge Bustamante, John Coatsworth, Wayne Cornelius, William Glade, Guadalupe González, Cassio Luiselli, Carlos Rico, and Marta Tienda.
[2]The Spanish-language version appeared under the title *El desafío de la interdependencia: México y Estados Unidos* (Mexico: Fondo de Cultura Económica, 1988).

too much on Mexico, on Mexico's problems, and on Mexican contributions to the state of the relationship. We wanted to correct that imbalance and, at the same time, to promote the study of the United States by Mexican students and scholars.[3]

Third was to encourage analysts to spell out the *policy implications* of their work. Academic investigation and primary research have enormous value, of course, but we hoped to provide an opportunity for scholars to speak as directly as possible to the policy-making community. Accordingly, we asked each contributor to provide practical policy recommendations; in addition, we obtained some papers from specialists with policy experience and authority.

With such criteria in mind we solicited and obtained forty-eight papers that were presented at about a dozen workshops in 1987 and early 1988.[4] These presentations proved to be of great use to the Bilateral Commission. With the aid of the Academic Committee, we then defined a set of topics for the volumes in this series. We selected papers for inclusion in the series primarily on the basis of their relationship to these particular subjects. This led us, regrettably, to exclude many fine papers from this collection. But our purpose has been to produce anthologies with thematic coherence as well as substantive originality, and we hope to have achieved that goal.

We conclude with an expression of thanks to all of our authors, especially to those whose papers are not in these volumes; to members of the Commission and its co-chairmen, Hugo Margáin and William D. Rogers; to our colleagues on the Academic Committee; to officers at the Ford Foundation who made possible this enterprise. Sandra del Castillo, Lee Dewey, Will Heller, Blanca Salgado, Gerardo Santos, and Arturo Sarukhan all made invaluable contributions to the editing and production of these volumes; to them our heartfelt gratitude.

Mexico City

La Jolla

---

[3]Indeed, one of the most alarming findings of the Commission relates to the decline of U.S. studies in Mexico. See *Challenge*, ch. 6.
[4]A complete listing of all papers appears in Appendix II of the Commission's report, *The Challenge of Interdependence*. Papers not included in this series may be published elsewhere and are available upon request; please send written inquiries to the U.S. Office of the Bilateral Commission, Institute of the Americas, 10111 North Torrey Pines Road, La Jolla, CA 92037.

1

Mexican Migration to the United States: Introduction

Wayne A. Cornelius

Immigration is one of the most enduring sources of both conflict and cooperation in the U.S.-Mexican relationship. For more than a hundred years, Mexican migrant workers have been alternately welcomed and persecuted in the United States, and sometimes both simultaneously. Widely divergent U.S. and Mexican definitions of "the immigrant problem" have often contributed to bilateral tensions, and have tended to obscure the convergence of objective U.S. and Mexican interests in this area of the relationship.[1] Within the United States, public controversy over the rapidly expanding presence of Mexican workers in U.S. labor markets in recent decades has pitted entrenched economic interests (e.g., agribusiness) against labor unionists (some—not all), environmentalists, cultural conservatives (e.g., the "English only" movement), taxpayers' lobbies, and other special interests.

The enactment of the Immigration Reform and Control Act (IRCA) in 1986 represents the culmination of the most recent phase of this debate. Approved in Congress by the narrowest of margins and only after several previous, similar legislative proposals had failed to attract sufficiently broad support, its primary objective

---

[1]This point is developed further in Wayne A. Cornelius, "México y Estados Unidos en la década de los ochentas," *Nexos* 89 (May 1985): 15-27; and Cornelius, "America in the 'Era of Limits': Migrants, Nativists, and the Future of U.S.-Mexican Relations," in *Mexican-U.S. Relations: Conflict and Convergence,* edited by Carlos Vásquez and Manuel García y Griego (Los Angeles: Chicano Studies Research Center and Latin American Center, University of California, Los Angeles, 1983).

was to curb the flow of illegal (undocumented) immigration into the United States, mainly from Mexico. But the passage of IRCA has only opened a new debate over the efficacy and appropriateness of restrictive immigration legislation—one destined to continue for many years. At the same time, IRCA's creation of opportunities for more than three million undocumented immigrants to legalize their status and integrate themselves more fully into the U.S. economy and society has aroused new concern in Mexico about the permanent loss of valuable human capital.

The purpose of this introduction is to provide a general context for the essays that follow, and to highlight the specific migration-related issues most in contention today between Mexico and the United States—and within the United States itself.

FRAMING THE ISSUES

The Mexican Presence in U.S. Labor Markets

Much research conducted in the 1980s shows that, for all intents and purposes, labor markets for some industries, in some regions of the United States, are already transnational in character. Businesses in these sectors of the U.S. economy are linked, through family networks and sometimes labor contractors, to "sending" communities in Mexico. The labor pools upon which these firms draw to fill lower-level production jobs and some skilled-worker positions are replenished primarily through migration from these Mexican communities. The source communities function mainly as nurseries, rest-and-recreation centers for migrants temporarily worn out by their labors in the United States, and nursing homes for "retired" migrant workers and their spouses who did not opt to settle permanently in the United States.

While the movement of Mexican labor to the United States long ago acquired a social dynamic of its own,[2] it still responds to changes in employer demand and, to a much lesser extent, changes in U.S. immigration law and policy. On the demand side, various

---

[2]Excellent recent case studies of the "social process" of Mexican migration to the United States are: Douglas Massey, Rafael Alarcón, Jorge Durand, and Humberto González, *Return to Aztlán: The Social Process of International Migration from Western Mexico* (Berkeley, Calif.: University of California Press, 1987); and Roger C. Rouse, "Mexican Migration to the United States: Family Relations in the Development of a Transnational Migrant Circuit" (Ph.D. dissertation, Stanford University, 1989).

changes in the U.S. economy and society have increased the attractiveness or necessity of Mexican immigrants as a labor source. Economic restructuring has yielded millions of "deskilled" assembly jobs that can easily be filled by immigrant workers. Rapid expansion of service industries ranging from building maintenance to convalescent care to fast-food restaurants has generated additional millions of low-wage, manual-labor jobs that are unattractive to U.S.-born workers. Moreover, the diminishing interest in blue-collar work among young people in the United States has produced shortages of *skilled* workers, in industries ranging from shoe manufacturing to masonry to ornamental metal work. For such industries, workers trained in Mexico provide skills and experience that are in short supply among the U.S.-born population.

The strength and persistence of the demand for Mexican labor in the U.S. "post-industrial" economy is one of the most impressive features of the contemporary immigration phenomenon. Even the sharp recession of the early 1980s—the most severe contraction of the U.S. economy since the Great Depression—failed to reduce that demand appreciably. And field studies suggest that the robust growth in employment opportunities in the United States in the second half of the 1980s has been the key factor fueling the current wave of emigration from Mexico—more so even than the effects of Mexico's lingering economic crisis.[3]

The changing U.S. demographic profile is beginning to be an important contributing factor as well. Low birthrates since the mid-1960s have resulted in a shrinking and aging U.S.-born labor force. In the 1970s, the U.S. work force grew by 5 percent. In the 1980s, total work force growth has been just 1.5 percent, despite the greatest wave of immigration since the first decade of this century. The U.S. Census Bureau projects that the work force will grow by less than 1 percent in the 1990s. Clearly, the United States has entered an era of growing labor scarcity, which will be felt most acutely in precisely those Sunbelt cities where Mexican immigrants are already clustered, and where new migrants will continue to arrive. Economic growth in these areas during the 1990s and beyond is expected to be far more vigorous than in the United States as a whole. In southern California alone, an estimated 7 million new jobs will be created during the next two decades.

---

[3]See, for example, Rafael Alarcón, "'Gracias a Dios y al Norte': Tlacuitapa, Jalisco y su relación con los Estados Unidos," paper prepared for the Commission for the Study of International Migration and Cooperative Economic Development, August 1989.

It is popularly believed that undocumented immigrant workers toil in the informal or "underground" economy, where employers pay sub-minimum wages and escape government regulation of labor standards. Some immigrants do—especially recent arrivals who lack social networks in the United States that can assist them in job-seeking. But field research in California and Illinois[4] has found that most *indocumentados* work in relatively small or medium-sized "formal sector" firms that are very much part of the mainstream economy. They tend to concentrate in firms and industries that are under intense foreign and/or domestic competitive pressures and that suffer from sharp fluctuations in demand for the goods or services they produce.

For such firms, the principal advantage of undocumented immigrant labor is not its cheapness but its *flexibility* (or *disposability*, in the more critical view of many academics and labor-union leaders). The immigrant work force is more willing than U.S.-born workers to accept high variability in working hours, working days per week, and months per year, and low job security. These same conditions, combined with relatively low wage scales, make employment in such firms unattractive to U.S.-born workers. Immigrant workers are ideal "shock absorbers," enabling businesses to adapt more quickly and easily to rapidly changing market conditions and consumer preferences. They can be brought on board quickly when needed, in periods of peak product or service demand, and disposed of just as easily when demand slackens.

Thus, the U.S. labor markets in which Mexican undocumented workers typically participate are not so much *illegal* as they are *fluid* and *volatile*. Mexican labor gives U.S. employers the flexibility they need to cope with an increasingly competitive, frequently global market. For many firms and industries affected by restructuring in the U.S. and world economies, the availability of immigrant labor has had a cushioning effect, helping them adjust to changes in production techniques and spreading the costs of adjustment over a longer period of time.

In recent decades there has been a trend toward greater sectoral and geographic dispersion of the Mexican immigrant work force

---

[4]See Barry R. Chiswick, *Illegal Aliens: Their Employment and Employers* (Kalamazoo, Mich.: W.E. Upjohn Institute for Employment Research, 1988); María de Lourdes Villar, "From Sojourners to Settlers: The Experience of Mexican Undocumented Migrants in Chicago" (Ph.D. dissertation, Indiana University, 1989), pp. 100-103; and several of the chapters in Wayne A. Cornelius, ed., *The Changing Roles of Mexican Immigrants in the U.S. Economy: Sectoral Perspectives* (La Jolla, Calif.: Center for U.S.-Mexican Studies, University of California, San Diego, forthcoming).

within the U.S. economy. According to the best-informed estimates, agriculture now employs no more than 15 percent of Mexican labor in California, Texas, and Arizona. Between 1981 and 1987, the percentage of farmworkers among the total of "deportable Mexican aliens" located by the U.S. Immigration and Naturalization Service averaged only 7 percent.[5] Most Mexican immigrants—both legal and undocumented—are now being absorbed into the labor-intensive urban service and retail sector, light manufacturing, and construction. In short, the U.S. demand for Mexican labor has become much more diversified, and this trend is likely to persist. Agriculture will continue to be a major employer of Mexican labor (mainly in the Southwest and the Pacific Northwest); but in relative terms, Mexican migrants will find far more employment opportunities in the nonagricultural sectors of the U.S. economy. The service sector—where Mexicans now work primarily as janitors, dishwashers and busboys, gardeners, hotel workers, maintenance and laundry workers in hospitals and convalescent homes, car washers, house cleaners, and child-care providers—will be particularly important in absorbing future migrants.

While the destinations for Mexican migrants to the United States are increasingly dispersed—extending from southern California to the Pacific Northwest, Chicago, the New York City metropolitan area, and the deep South—most Mexicans continue to gravitate to the same places favored by their fathers and grandfathers. California alone absorbs at least half (and perhaps as much as 60 percent) of the total flow of both legal and illegal immigrants from Mexico.[6] It is highly probable that the distribution of undocumented Mexican immigrants is very similar, since most are part of extended family networks "anchored" by legal immigrants with long residence in the United States.

Impacts on U.S.-born Workers

Are U.S.-born workers helped or hurt by the availability of Mexican immigrant labor—especially undocumented workers? What impact does the immigrant presence in U.S. labor markets have on wages and working conditions? These are the questions

---

[5] U.S. Immigration and Naturalization Service, *Statistical Yearbook, 1987* (Washington, D.C.: U.S. Government Printing Office, 1988), table 72, p. 126.

[6] See James P. Allen and Eugene J. Turner, "Where to Find the New Immigrants," *American Demographics*, September, 1988, pp. 74-77; and Jorge Bustamante's chapter in this volume. The Los Angeles-Long Beach metropolitan area receives two and one-half times more legal Mexican immigrants than any other metropolitan area in the country.

concerning Mexican immigration that have been debated most intensely in the United States since the early 1970s.

Virtually all available evidence suggests that the *macroeconomic* impact of Mexican immigration—and of immigration more generally—on the United States is positive.[7] The availability of this labor source helps to hold down prices of many consumer goods and services, makes it possible for labor-intensive industries to expand more rapidly, and stimulates employment growth through consumer spending by the immigrants themselves and their families. But the *microeconomic* impacts of undocumented immigration—particularly on U.S.-born minorities and other disadvantaged workers—have been the subject of considerable controversy.

The deceptively simple questions about "labor market impact" require complex answers, which fail to satisfy either politicians or the general public. In-depth field studies of specific industries and labor markets have found that the impact of undocumented Mexican immigration on U.S.-born workers varies widely. Undocumented immigrants can be either substitutes (competitors) or complements for U.S.-born workers, depending on the industry, the region, type of firm, vigilance of government agencies (in regard to wage and labor standards), and other conditions.[8] Some domestic workers—particularly those employed in "immobile" industries where large numbers of undocumented immigrants have clustered, such as agriculture and building maintenance—are adversely affected. Other U.S.-born workers are benefited, especially in potentially mobile or "footloose" industries that face strong foreign competition, such as garment and shoe manufacturing, and electronics. For firms in these industries, the availability of Mexican labor to perform lower-level production jobs or to fill jobs in the firm's subcontractors (resulting in lower-cost inputs) enables management to keep at least some production operations in the

---

[7]See, for example, Council of Economic Advisors, *Economic Report of the President, Transmitted to the Congress, February 1986* (Washington, D.C.: U.S. Government Printing Office, 1986), chapter 7 ("The Economic Effects of Immigration"); and Division of Immigration Policy and Research, Bureau of International Labor Affairs, U.S. Department of Labor, *The Effects of Immigration on the U.S. Economy and Labor Market*, Immigration Policy and Research Report, no. 1 (Washington, D.C.: U.S. Department of Labor, May 1989).

[8]For a summary of the relevant evidence, see Richard Mines, "U.S. and Mexican Workers: Complements and Substitutes," in Cornelius, ed., *The Changing Roles of Mexican Immigrants in the U.S. Economy*. See also Richard Mines and Michael Kaufman, "Mexican Immigrants: The Labor Market Issue," in *Mexico and the United States: Studies in Economic Interaction*, edited by Peggy B. Musgrave (Boulder, Colo.: Westview, 1985).

United States rather than moving them "offshore," thereby preserving jobs for U.S.-born workers.

Other industries (e.g., full-service restaurants) that provide jobs for large numbers of U.S.-born workers could not have expanded so rapidly in recent years without the immigrant labor pool.[9] In some firms and industries, Mexican immigrants play a "key ingredient" role: Even where they do not constitute a majority of the work force, they perform key tasks in the production process, and their removal would force drastic restructuring and cause significant employment losses for U.S.-born workers.

Considerable evidence contradicts the simplistic notion of one-to-one job competition between Mexicans (especially the undocumented) and U.S.-born workers. When immigrants displace native workers, such displacement usually occurs *indirectly*—not as a result of direct competition between natives and migrants for the same jobs. For example, firms that hire mostly undocumented Mexican workers can often underbid firms (especially unionized ones) that hire mainly U.S.-born workers; as a result, immigrant-using firms expand while other firms in the industry lose business and lay off U.S.-born workers. It is through this mechanism—the expansion of some types of (immigrant-dependent) firms and the contraction of other kinds (low or non-users of immigrant labor)—that "displacement" most commonly occurs.

Today, competition for jobs in industries where Mexican immigrants cluster most often pits one subclass of immigrants against another segment of the immigrant population (e.g., newly arrived "illegals" vs. long-staying undocumented immigrants, or those who have legalized themselves through IRCA-mandated "amnesty" programs). U.S.-born workers no longer seek these jobs; and most employers who now rely on immigrants to fill them—tired of extremely high turnover among the very few non-immigrants who apply for such jobs—have given up on recruiting U.S.-born workers.

Real wages in many immigrant-dependent industries have not risen in recent years, and wages for low-skill jobs in some sectors (e.g., Los Angeles manufacturing industries) have declined in relation to national and other regional averages, leading researchers

---

[9]See Rick Morales, "The Utilization of Mexican Immigrants in the Full-Service Restaurant Industry: The Case of San Diego County," in Cornelius, ed., *The Changing Roles of Mexican Immigrants in the U.S. Economy*.

to conclude that the influx of undocumented immigrants is depressing wage scales in these sectors of the economy.[10] It is true that immigrant workers—especially those most recently arrived and those still lacking any kind of legal status in the United States—are usually willing to accept wage scales lower than the average U.S.-born person would demand for similar work. However, the weight of the evidence suggests that immigration per se is not the most important factor affecting wages and labor standards in these and other sectors of the U.S. economy. Far more influential are technological changes affecting the labor content of products, foreign competition (the changing international factor price of labor), and the declining strength of the U.S. labor movement—a decline which is largely unrelated to the growing presence of immigrant workers.[11]

In most parts of the United States that are impacted by immigration from Mexico, the objective complementarities between the Mexican labor supply and U.S. needs probably increased during the 1980s. These complementarities are likely to be strengthened in the 1990s, as the U.S. "baby bust" and the restructuring of the U.S. and global economies continue. This does not mean, however, that public perceptions will mirror the realities of the situation. On the contrary, recent public opinion polls and a rising chorus of protests from residents of urban neighborhoods close to the street-corner labor markets where recently arrived undocumented migrants congregate suggest that a majority of Americans will continue to view Mexican immigrants as having a net negative impact on the U.S. economy and society.[12] And some U.S. politicians and other opinion leaders will continue to insist that, despite a looming domestic labor shortage, there are still substantial pockets of unemployment in the United States (e.g., legally admitted refugees living on welfare), and such people can fill jobs now being taken by undocumented immigrants.

---

[10]See, for example, Thomas Muller and Thomas J. Espenshade, *The Fourth Wave: California's Newest Immigrants* (Washington, D.C.: Urban Institute Press, 1985), pp. 103-123.
[11]See Thomas R. Bailey, *Immigrant and Native Workers: Contrasts and Competition* (Boulder, Colo.: Westview, 1987), especially pp. 141-142; and Héctor L. Delgado, "The Unionization of Undocumented Workers: A Los Angeles Case Study," in Cornelius, ed., *The Changing Roles of Mexican Immigrants in the U.S. Economy*.
[12]For example, in a national sample of 1,418 people interviewed in September 1988 for the *Los Angeles Times* Poll, 64 percent believed that "immigrants get more from the United States through social services and unemployment [than they] contribute to the U.S. economy through taxes and [higher] productivity" (*Los Angeles Times*, 19 September, 1988.) See also Daniel Wolf, *Undocumented Aliens and Crime: The Case of San Diego County*, Monograph Series, no. 29 (La Jolla, Calif.: Center for U.S.-Mexican Studies, University of California, San Diego, 1988).

Impacts on Mexico

The impacts of U.S.-bound migration upon Mexico are still concentrated in eight key sending states (Michoacán, Guanajuato, Jalisco, Zacatecas, Durango, San Luis Potosí, Baja California, and Chihuahua), which account for an estimated 70 percent of all undocumented migration. Together, these states contained slightly more than one-fourth of Mexico's total population in 1980. Impacts of U.S.-bound migration are further concentrated in a subset of regions, *municipios*, towns within *municipios*, and families within particular localities. Most of these key sending units have a long (50-60 years or more) tradition of sending workers to the United States. Nevertheless, a trend toward greater diversity and geographic dispersion of points of origin became evident in the 1980s.

Mexico's urban areas are the source of an increasingly large proportion of migrants to the United States.[13] On a per capita basis, cities in Mexico are relatively less dependent on income earned in the United States than are rural sending communities, but their populations have been hard hit by the economic crisis of the 1980s. This is particularly true of the Mexico City metropolitan area, where nearly one of out of every four Mexicans now lives. It is clear that in those parts of Mexico most severely affected by high inflation, unemployment, and deteriorating living conditions since 1982, migration to the United States has been embraced increasingly as a household survival strategy. Thus, states, localities, and families that lack a long tradition of U.S.-bound migration have been propelled into the migratory stream.

The high fluidity and volatility of the U.S. labor markets in which Mexican immigrants are clustered causes a steady stream of return migration to sending areas. Returning migrants sometimes face formidable problems of "reinsertion" into local economies.[14] But for most of those who intend to continue migrating to the

---

[13]In one sample of 834 immigrant workers employed in nonagricultural firms in California in 1984, more than 60 percent had originated in urban areas of Mexico. In another sample of 200 unemployed, recently arrived undocumented migrants interviewed in southern California in 1988-89, the Mexico City metropolitan area was the single most important point of origin. See Wayne A. Cornelius, "*Los Migrantes de la Crisis*: The Changing Profile of Mexican Labor Migration to California in the 1980s," in *Población y trabajo en contextos regionales*, edited by Gail Mummert (Zamora, Mich.: El Colegio de Michoacán, forthcoming). Rural-origin Mexican workers continue to predominate in California's agricultural sector, however.
[14]Guillermo de la Peña, "Social Change and International Labor Migration: An Overview of Four Agrarian Regions in Mexico," paper prepared for the migration workshop of the Bilateral Commission on the Future of United States-Mexican Relations, 1987.

United States, little or no effort is made to secure an economic base in the community of origin. Jobs in these places simply pay too little, and are too insecure, to be an acceptable alternative to international migration.

As long as traditional local economic structures remain unaltered, and in the absence of some collective effort to invest capital accumulated by migrant workers in the United States, "remittance" income typically does not stimulate economic development in the sending communities.[15] Income earned in the United States is used mostly to finance personal consumption and housing construction. Consumer goods and inputs for construction typically are purchased outside of the migrants' home community (most commonly in a nearby city that serves as a regional marketing center and offers lower prices), so the multiplier effects of consumer spending by returned migrants or their dependents are not experienced by the labor-exporting communities.

Effects of Changes in U.S. Immigration Law

The changes in U.S. immigration law enacted by Congress in October 1986 opened a new era in Mexican migration to the United States. The "employer sanctions" provision of the Immigration Reform and Control Act sought to deter illegal border crossings and curb the hiring of undocumented immigrants, by imposing fines ranging from $250 to $10,000 per alien on employers who "knowingly" hire them. At the same time, IRCA created opportunities for millions of long-staying undocumented immigrants already in the United States, as well as agricultural workers still in Mexico, to legalize their status.

These were the most sweeping changes in U.S. immigration law since 1952. But the new law has not proven as disruptive, either to immigrant-dependent sectors of the U.S. economy or to the established rhythms of Mexican migration to the United States, as many had anticipated. Three years after IRCA's passage, businesses traditionally dependent on undocumented immigrant labor report

---

[15]Numerous studies have reached this conclusion. See, for example, Merilee S. Grindle, *Searching for Rural Development: Labor Migration and Employment in Mexico* (Ithaca, N.Y.: Cornell University Press, 1988); and Richard Mines, *Developing a Community Tradition of Migration: A Field Study in Rural Zacatecas, Mexico, and California Settlement Areas*, Monograph Series, no. 3 (La Jolla, Calif.: Center for U.S.-Mexican Studies, University of California, San Diego, 1981).

no difficulty in obtaining sufficient numbers of workers—from the usual sources—and only a tiny minority are making plans to do without Mexican workers. Agricultural employers have switched easily from undocumented migrants to migrants who legalized themselves in 1987-88 through IRCA's Special Agricultural Workers (SAW) program.[16]

In the urban sector, Mexican immigrants—both undocumented and newly legalized—continue to hold onto jobs in those subsectors of the labor market that they had long ago "conquered." Even though they may consider their economic hold in the United States to be less secure as a result of the new immigration law, most undocumented Mexicans already established in the United States seem determined to remain, believing that there is a permanent niche for them in the U.S. labor market.

The vast majority of newly-arriving undocumented migrants are still finding work of some kind, even though some must search longer than their predecessors and may have to settle for very short-term employment—day labor or jobs that may last a month or two—rather than regular jobs with some security. New migration networks—anchored in regions of Mexico that have not previously sent migrants to the United States—are being formed, despite the 1986 law.[17]

Mexico has not had to cope with massive return migration by long-absent workers who suddenly found themselves jobless in the United States as a result of employer sanctions. On the contrary, recent field studies have found that migratory flows from traditional sending communities in Mexico remain unchanged or may actually have increased since IRCA's passage.[18] In communities that

---

[16] A February 1989 survey of California farm employers found that about half of their seasonal workers during 1988 were SAW permit holders, one-fourth were "green-card" (permanent legal) immigrants, and one-fourth were U.S. citizens. Fewer than one-fifth of the respondents planned to make any labor-saving changes or modify their labor-recruitment practices. See Philip L. Martin and J. Edward Taylor, "Immigration Reform and California Agriculture: One Year Later," unpublished paper, (Davis: Department of Agricultural Economics, University of California-Davis, June 1989).

[17] See Cornelius, "Los Migrantes de la Crisis"; and Michael Kearney and Carol Nagengast, "Anthropological Perspectives on Transnational Communities in Rural California," Working Paper no. 3 (Davis, Calif.: California Institute for Rural Studies, February 1989).

[18] Wayne A. Cornelius, "Impacts of the 1986 U.S. Immigration Law on Emigration from Rural Mexican Sending Communities," paper presented at the XV International Congress of the Latin American Studies Association, Miami, Florida, December 4-6, 1989, p. 10; and Douglas Massey, Katherine M. Donato, and Zai Liang, "Effects

have long depended on income earned in the United States, most people continue to have an essentially positive view of the U.S. opportunity structure: not as wide open as before IRCA's passage, but still accessible to those with determination and, even more importantly, family contacts in the United States.[19]

Nevertheless, INS statistics on apprehensions of illegal entrants along the U.S.-Mexico border show a 40 percent drop compared with the 1986 fiscal year, before enactment of IRCA. INS authorities consider this decline indisputable proof of IRCA's deterrent effect on would-be illegal immigrants. Researchers at the Urban Institute, reporting the results of a sophisticated though technically flawed regression analysis of the INS statistics, have argued that "the new legislation *has* slowed the rate of undocumented migration across the southern border of the United States, but this reduction is not as large as many have claimed."[20] Meanwhile, another team of researchers, based at the Rand Corporation, analyzing the same data base, conclude that IRCA did cause a significant decline in illegal entries in Fiscal Year 1987 but had little or no impact on illegal border crossings in Fiscal Year 1988, after the effects of legalization programs and enhanced border enforcement by the INS are taken into account.[21]

Resolving the conflicting claims and evidence concerning the deterrent impact of IRCA's employer sanctions is beyond the scope of this essay. Interpreting changes in INS apprehension statistics has been rendered vastly more complicated and ambiguous by IRCA's amnesty programs, which have made it possible for more than three million persons to cross the border legally, no longer at risk of being apprehended by the Border Patrol.[22] Similarly,

---

of the Immigration Reform and Control Act of 1988: Preliminary Data from Mexico," paper presented at a conference on "Illegal Immigration Before and After IRCA," The Urban Institute, Washington, D.C., July 21, 1989, p. 13.

[19]Cornelius, "Impacts of the 1986 Immigration Law"; and Jesús Arroyo Alejandre, "Algunos impactos de la ley de reforma y control de inmigración (IRCA) en una región de Jalisco de fuerte emigración hacia Estados Unidos de Norteamérica," paper presented at the conference on "International Effects of the Immigration Reform and Control Act of 1986," Rand Corporation, Guadalajara, Mexico, May 3-5, 1989.

[20]Michael J. White, Frank D. Bean, and Thomas J. Espenshade, "The U.S. Immigration Reform and Control Act and Undocumented Migration to the United States," Research Paper No. PRIP-UI-5, Program for Research on Immigration Policy (Washington, D.C.: The Urban Institute, July 1989), p. 23.

[21]Presentation by Beth Asch, Program for Research on Immigration Policy, the Rand Corporation, at the West Coast Workshop on Immigration Research, El Colegio de la Frontera Norte, Tijuana, Baja Calif., June 22, 1989.

[22]The Rand Corporation's researchers estimate that 135,000-400,000 of the border apprehensions made annually in the pre-IRCA period involved persons who have now legalized themselves under IRCA.

employer sanctions, coupled with stepped-up border enforcement, undoubtedly have made some heretofore "short-stay" undocumented migrants already in the United States reluctant to leave, for fear that they will find it too difficult to come back or to find regular employment in the United States again. These temporarily or permanently grounded "shuttle" migrants are no longer at risk of being apprehended at the border either. Clearly, several more years of data—collected through different methodologies—will be needed before any definitive assessment of IRCA's efficacy in halting new illegal migration can be made. In any event, it is premature to conclude that the employer sanctions component of the law is "working"—at least in the way the U.S. Congress intended.

Today, the vast majority of U.S. employers are complying with their legal obligation under IRCA—a relatively simple paperwork requirement.[23] But quite obviously, the supply of jobs available to undocumented Mexican immigrants has not dried up. Most critics of employer sanctions legislation predicted that its principal consequence would be to create a bonanza for false document makers, and gradually this prophecy is coming to pass. Field research findings reported elsewhere in this volume suggest that large numbers of undocumented migrants are successfully using bogus documents—purchased or borrowed—to gain employment in the United States. And employers, not required by IRCA to verify the authenticity of documents presented by job applicants, are either unable or unwilling to go beyond their obligations under the law.

While IRCA may not, in the long run, drastically reduce the overall *level* of Mexican migration to the United States, its effects on the *social composition* and *dynamics* of the flow could be both significant and enduring. The sudden legalization of a large portion of the migratory flow from Mexico to the United States has shifted it toward greater permanence: relatively less short-term, shuttle migration; more "settling out" in the United States. The migration of women and children has increased since IRCA's enactment, both to take advantage of the amnesty programs and for family reunification. Male family heads who secured amnesty for themselves quickly began sending for their wives and children in Mexico,

---

[23]Employer surveys conducted by the U.S. General Accounting Office and several independent research groups have found very high levels of "voluntary compliance" with IRCA—in the 90-95 percent range. The INS itself reports that 91 percent of a nationwide sample of employers, randomly selected for INS checks through April 30, 1989, were in compliance with the law, while 59 percent of 13,840 employers whom the INS has investigated based on specific "leads" were found to be in compliance (James L. Buck [Acting Commissioner, INS], "Amnesty Law Cut Illegal Border Crossings," *New York Times*, 5 August 1989).

whether or not these dependents themselves could qualify for legalization, using *coyotes* to guide them across the border.

Given the increased problems associated with crossing the border,[24] there is now a stronger incentive for whole family units to migrate together. The presence of more complete immigrant families in U.S. receiving communities will inevitably be reflected in heavier utilization of education, health care, and other social services. On the Mexican side, it will mean fewer dollars remitted by migrants employed in the United States. More generally, to the extent that IRCA's legalization programs reduce shuttle migration and encourage permanent settlement in the United States, the law is likely to have a negative impact on remittance flows in the long term.

POLICY OPTIONS

Precisely because Mexican migration to the United States is inherently a *social* process, with deep roots in both the sending and receiving societies, many aspects of this migratory movement are not amenable to government intervention or manipulation, at least at this time.[25] Exaggerated public expectations about "immigration control" measures like IRCA may become politically inflammatory when they are (inevitably) disappointed. The *limits* of government intervention in this phenomenon—on either side of the border—must be clearly recognized, as well as the narrowness of the range of desirable and politically feasible policy options. Among those options, for the United States, are the following:[26]

---

[24]IRCA authorized a 50 percent increase in Border Patrol strength, beginning with the 1987 fiscal year. This build-up has occurred, though it has taken nearly three years to complete.

[25]The United States is not alone in this regard. The experience of France, West Germany, and other West European countries since the early 1970s suggests that industrialized democracies are experiencing increasing difficulty in regulating immigration. The West European experience also shows that social and economic conditions in the labor-exporting and labor-importing countries have a greater impact on outcomes (i.e., the behavior of migrants and employers) than government actions. See James F. Hollifield, "Immigration Policy in France and Germany: Outputs versus Outcomes," *Annals of the American Academy of Political and Social Science*, 485 (May 1986): 113-128; and Hollifield, "Immigration and the French State: Problems of Policy Implementation," *Comparative Political Studies*, forthcoming.

[26]The policy options outlined in this section emerge from the discussions of the working group on migration, a binational group of scholars—including the contributors to this volume—assembled in 1987 and 1988 to advise the Bilateral Commission on the Future of United States-Mexican Relations. Several of these options were recommended by the commission in its final report, *The Challenge of*

- *Target immigration law enforcement more selectively.*

As long as employer sanctions legislation is on the books, enforcement efforts should be carefully targeted at those sectors of the U.S. economy where complementarities between U.S.-born and undocumented immigrant workers clearly do *not* exist. Some of these sectors are already known, and others could be identified through further research. Enforcement strategy should be informed by an accurate understanding of labor market dynamics in specific industries.

- *Significantly expand opportunities for legal permanent immigration from Mexico.*

This was not accomplished by the 1986 revisions of U.S. immigration law, which focused on measures to reduce illegal immigration and to legalize undocumented workers already settled in the United States. Subsequent legislation, approved by the U.S. Senate in 1989 but still pending at this writing in the House of Representatives, would amend the law regulating legal immigration in ways that would make it more difficult for certain classes of Mexicans to migrate legally on a permanent basis. The goal should be to establish a more realistic equation between objective demand for Mexican labor in the U.S. economy and opportunities for permanent legal immigration, and thereby to shift the ratio of legal to illegal Mexican workers in immigrant-dominated firms and industries toward greater legality.

The nature of contemporary U.S. demand for Mexican labor must be recognized. Most jobs for which Mexican workers are now sought by U.S. employers are full-time, year-round jobs rather than temporary ones. Therefore, temporary legal worker ("guest-worker") programs are increasingly inappropriate, except for seasonal agriculture, which already has access to legal temporary workers through the RAW (Replenishment Agricultural Workers) program authorized by IRCA.

It must also be recognized that raising the ceiling on permanent legal immigration from Mexico is not a panacea. Even with a major increase in the current quota, there would still be a substantial

---

Interdependence: Mexico and the United States (Lanham, Md.: University Press of America, 1988), at pp. 108-112. Neither the commission nor all members of the commission's academic working group necessarily endorse all of these policy options.

flow of undocumented migrants, which will continue to generate political pressure in the United States for more restrictive measures.

- *Encourage a more positive, activist stance by organized labor toward the Mexican immigrant work force.*

U.S. labor unions should play a more active role in defending labor standards in immigrant-dependent firms and industries. The U.S. labor movement must be convinced that they have something to gain from getting involved with undocumented immigrants and with former *indocumentados* who have legalized their status through the IRCA amnesty provisions. The symbiosis between Mexican immigrants and U.S.-born workers—in industries where immigrants can help to preserve or enlarge overall employment opportunities—should be recognized.

U.S. labor unions could also help Mexican workers negotiate contracts with their employers that improve living standards in migrants' communities of origin, following the successful model established by the Arizona Farmworkers Union. In this model, contractually mandated employer contributions are made to development and infrastructure improvement projects in the home communities of Mexican union members, based on the number of hours worked by the members in the United States.[27]

On the Mexican side, the following policy options merit consideration:

- *Develop mechanisms for harnessing the capital being generated through the labor of Mexican nationals in the United States, to promote broadly based economic and social development in migrants' places of origin.*

New micro-level (region- and local community-focused) opportunities for investment of U.S. earnings in productive activities could be created. Optimally they would take the form of grassroots development projects based on local *asociaciones civiles*, rather than vertically organized government programs. Possibilities for technology transfer from the United States to sending communities in Mexico should also be explored. For example, Los Altos de Morelos is one of the few central plateau regions that has stopped exporting labor to the United States. In the 1960s, returning braceros from

---

[27]See Guadalupe L. Sánchez and Jesús Romo, *Organizing Mexican Undocumented Farm Workers on Both Sides of the Border*, Research Report Series, no. 27 (La Jolla, Calif.: Center for U.S.-Mexican Studies, University of California, San Diego, 1981).

the United States introduced new production techniques for tomato growing, which stimulated the local economy and stabilized the work force.[28]

There is a need for realism in gauging the capacity of sending area-based development schemes to retain would-be migrant workers in these places. A recent study of high-emigration *municipios* in the state of Jalisco, for example, found that commercialization of agriculture and nonagricultural development in relatively underdeveloped areas where demographic pressure on land and other local resources remains strong tends to *promote* emigration of labor.[29] The outlook for retaining workers in such areas is bleak, whatever governments choose to do.

- *Press for an enforceable bilateral accord guaranteeing the labor and human rights of migrant workers.*

Negotiations leading to such a treaty must involve the U.S. and Mexican governments, U.S. employer associations, and labor unions. The agreement could serve to implement provisions of the forthcoming United Nations resolution on human rights of migratory workers. Mechanisms and sanctions to ensure U.S. employer compliance with the terms of any such accord must be devised. This is a key problem, given Mexico's frustrating experience with the bracero program of contract labor importation (1942-64), which provided numerous worker protections and guarantees that proved unenforceable.[30] The problem is complicated by the fact that most U.S. small businesses—the heaviest users of undocumented Mexican labor—do not belong to any employer organization that could work to insure members' compliance with a bilateral immigration agreement. Nevertheless, as Jorge Bustamante points out in his contribution to this volume, the deepening shortage of native-born labor in the United States may open new possibilities for the negotiation of a bilateral accord.

---

[28]For a detailed analysis of this case, see de la Peña, "Social Change and International Labor Migration."
[29]See Jesús Arroyo Alejandre, *El abandono rural: un modelo explicativo de la emigración de trabajadores rurales en el Occidente de México* (Guadalajara, Jal.: Universidad de Guadalajara, 1989).
[30]See Manuel García y Griego, "The Bracero Policy Experiment: U.S.-Mexican Responses to Mexican Labor Migration, 1942-1955" (Ph.D. dissertation, University of California, Los Angeles, 1988); and García y Griego, "The Importation of Mexican Contract Laborers to the United States, 1942-1964: Antecedents, Operation, and Legacy," in *The Border That Joins: Mexican Migrants and U.S. Responsibility*, edited by Peter G. Brown and Henry Shue (Totowa, N.J.: Rowman and Littlefield, 1983), pp. 49-98.

- *Develop an explicit national policy on emigration.*

Since 1974, when President Luis Echeverría suspended efforts to conclude a new bilateral agreement with the United States on contract labor importation, Mexico has pursued a strategy of *not* having an explicit, publicly stated policy regarding the emigration of its citizens.[31] Routine statements by a succession of Mexican presidents and legislative leaders concerning the need for greater protection of the human and labor rights of Mexican nationals employed in the United States have been the only indications of the Mexican government's position on emigration.

The absence of an explicit policy has been politically convenient, enabling the Mexican government to distance itself from immigration policy debates within the United States, and to avoid being "used" by the various contending parties in those debates. But it has also reduced Mexico's capacity to influence the terms of those debates, as well as the shape of the U.S. policy decisions and legislation that emerged from them—actions that have potentially significant consequences for millions of its citizens.

An explicit Mexican policy on emigration could, among other things, spell out the specific interests of Mexico that are at stake in this area, articulate Mexico's views and preferences regarding the future supply and demand for Mexican labor in the United States, and specify Mexico's plans for increasing the labor-absorptiveness of its own economy. Such a policy statement would help to combat widely held U.S. perceptions that Mexico has no interest in reducing the exportation of its "surplus" labor, and lacks realistic plans and programs that address the root causes of emigration to the United States. Such notions have been used in recent years to justify unilateral U.S. actions to restrict the migratory flow.

IN THIS VOLUME

This collection of papers does not seek—nor achieve—"closure" on the difficult research and policy issues outlined above. The contributors synthesize and identify major points of consensus in

---

[31]See Manuel García y Griego, "Hacia una nueva visión del problema de los indocumentados en Estados Unidos," in *México y Estados Unidos frente a la migración de los indocumentados*, edited by M. García y Griego and Mónica Verea Campos (México, D.F.: Coordinación de Humanidades, Universidad Autónoma Nacional de México/Editorial Miguel Angel Porrúa, 1988), pp. 145-152.

the scholarly literature, but they emphasize presentation of fresh data, projections, and hypotheses to stimulate future research and public debate.

The first section of the volume examines the migration process itself, from three different perspectives. Cornelius focuses on the demand side, developing a profile of the archetypical "immigrant-dependent" firm in the United States. Drawing on data collected through field studies in California since 1982, he explains the growing employer demand for Mexican labor as a response to the need to maximize flexibility and reduce costs in the face of an increasingly competitive domestic and world economy. He argues that greater attention to the determinants of employer demand is necessary if we are to understand more fully the difficulties encountered by the United States in restructuring its labor markets so as to reduce dependence on foreign-born labor.

Manuel García y Griego analyzes the supply side of the migration phenomenon. He uses an innovative demographic projection model to estimate upper limits on migration from Mexico to the United States in the period from 1990 to the year 2010, based on anticipated changes in the size and structure of the population in high- and low-emigration regions of Mexico. In essence, what are the demographic limits on the future flow of Mexican migrants to the United States?[32] To what extent is the supply of potential migrants likely to be reduced by the sharp drop in Mexico's overall fertility rate since the late 1960s? García y Griego's meticulously derived answers to these and other questions help to establish scientific parameters for public debates in both the United States and Mexico concerning the magnitude of migration flows and their social and economic consequences.

Jorge Bustamante's contribution illustrates the utility of direct, systematic observation of illegal border crossings via Tijuana and other Mexican border cities, supplemented by personal interviewing of clandestine border crossers. Most analyses of changes in the

---

[32] A recent national survey of the Mexican population conducted for the *Los Angeles Times* Poll suggests that the *potential* reservoir of would-be U.S.-bound migrants remains quite large. Almost 6 percent of the respondents said they were "very likely" to take up residence in the United States within the next twelve months, and another 16 percent said they were "fairly" likely to move to the United States during the same period (Marjorie Miller, "Despite New Laws, U.S. Still a Lure in Mexico," *Los Angeles Times*, 21 August 1989). While such expectations may represent little more than wishful thinking for many of the interviewees, they are nonetheless a reminder of the powerful attraction of the U.S. labor market, even in the post-IRCA period.

migratory flow rely on apprehension statistics compiled by the U.S. Immigration and Naturalization Service. The apprehension data have numerous inherent deficiencies,[33] and recent attempts to use them to assess the efficacy of IRCA have raised more questions than they have answered. The methodology pioneered by Bustamante and his associates offers not only an alternative, continuous indicator of the volume of illegal border crossings but a means to detect short-term changes in the socioeconomic profile of undocumented immigrants.

The second section of the volume deals with social and economic consequences of transborder labor migration. Marta Tienda's wide-ranging sociological analysis argues that the scope and nature of the social impacts associated with Mexican immigration have as much or more to do with settlement patterns and with the complex social arrangements that organize the migratory flow as they do with sheer numbers of immigrants. She traces the evolution of Mexican immigration from a population movement motivated by narrowly economic considerations to one propelled and sustained by broader social processes, including family reunification and the expansion of transnational social networks linking sending and receiving communities. Like most of the contributors to this volume, she questions whether it is even possible to devise a viable public policy to regulate such complex, well-institutionalized social processes. Tienda also calls attention to the growing diversity of Mexican migration to the United States, and the consequent need for policymakers to differentiate among social impacts according to the type of immigrant—temporary and permanent immigrants, legals and illegals, those belonging to various visa admission categories, etc.

Kitty Calavita concludes the volume with a penetrating, critical analysis of the evolution of U.S. immigration policy from the eighteenth century to the present. She blames the lack of consistency and coherence in U.S. policy in this area fundamentally upon the absence of a commonly accepted definition of what the "immigrant problem" *is*, which in turn reflects the wide range of conflicting interests involved in the U.S. immigration policy debate. She also calls attention to the pervasiveness in the United States

---

[33]See, for example, Gilbert Cárdenas, "Public Data on Mexican Immigration into the United States: A Critical Evaluation," in *Current Issues in Social Policy*, edited by W. Boyd Littrell and Gideon Sjoberg (Beverly Hills, Calif.: Sage, 1976); and Daniel B. Levine, Kenneth Hill, and Robert Warren, eds., *Immigration Statistics: A Story of Neglect* (Washington, D.C.: National Academy Press, 1985).

of a series of myths about immigration, such as the "myth of unilateral benefits"—accruing only to the immigrants themselves and their home country. Against this background, Calavita assesses the merits of a variety of immigration policy proposals—ranging from maintaining the status quo to militarizing the U.S.-Mexico border—and offers her own alternative.

SECTION

I

THE MIGRATION
PROCESS

2

The U.S. Demand for Mexican Labor

Wayne A. Cornelius

Mexican migration to the United States has usually been analyzed and debated from a "supply-side" perspective. There has been much less attention to the demand side of the migratory phenomenon. While U.S. officials and other opinion leaders often acknowledge that the lure of higher-paying job opportunities in the United States is the critical factor underlying the migratory phenomenon, very little effort has been made to document and explain the large and growing demand for Mexican labor in the U.S. economy. As a result, we know far more about the migrants themselves (their individual characteristics) and the conditions that impel them to leave Mexico than we do about the U.S. employers who hire them and the dynamics of the U.S. labor markets in which Mexican migrants are entrenched.

This neglect of the demand side can be explained at least partly by the way in which U.S. political leaders and much of the general public choose to view the migratory movement from Mexico. Mexican workers—and unskilled immigrants in general—are

---

I am indebted to Carol Dudziak, James F. Hollifield, and Marta Tienda for comments on an earlier version of this paper, and to Richard Mines, Kitty Calavita, Anna García, Jeffrey Weldon, and other members of the field research team for interpretive insights into the data. The research reported here was supported by grants from the Ford, Rockefeller, Rosenberg, and Sloan Foundations; the University of California Pacific Rim Research Program; and the University of California Consortium on Mexico and the United States.

seen as superfluous to the "real" needs of the U.S. post-industrial economy. In this view, the United States has not become structurally dependent on Mexican and other immigrant labor to fill low-skill, low-paying, low-status jobs. Such labor is regarded simply as a windfall to a greedy minority of U.S. employers intent on protecting or enlarging their profit margins; a subsidy to middle-class U.S. consumers who do not want to pay more for their restaurant meals, clothing, agricultural produce, and personal services; and a social safety valve—an employment-welfare program—for Mexico. It is often pointed out that Japan, the new powerhouse among the world's advanced industrial countries, has a negligible foreign-born work force. The implication is that the United States is absorbing immigrants from Mexico at levels that greatly exceed the actual requirements of our own economy. From this perspective, the presence of a large, predominantly undocumented Mexican labor force in the United States is an artificial and pathological phenomenon: a cancer that can and should be cut out of the economy, through government actions (e.g., employer sanctions legislation) designed to make it much more difficult for undocumented migrants to find jobs. The excision of the cancer may produce some short-term disruptions and unpleasant side effects; but U.S. employers and consumers will adjust quickly, according to the conventional wisdom, and many disadvantaged U.S.-born workers will benefit from the forced restructuring of low-skill, low-wage labor markets.

The empirical evidence summarized in this paper is not consistent with this view of the role of Mexican labor in the U.S. economy. It suggests a very different conception—one in which the "Mexicanization" of certain jobs, firms, and industries in recent decades is an integral part of much more fundamental processes of economic and social change in the United States and in the U.S. role in the global economy. Large-scale immigration from Mexico during this period has not been a primary cause of these changes. It may, however, have delayed some adjustments and served to cushion the impact of these changes on certain sectors of the U.S. economy and society.

The available data also suggest that reliance upon Mexican labor to fill low-skilled, manual-labor jobs is not simply a matter of U.S. capitalism seeking to protect its profits. The demand for Mexican labor in the U.S. economy is selective. Not all U.S. capitalists need Mexican labor, and those who do utilize this labor source usually need Mexicans to fill only a few (but essential) categories of jobs in their enterprises. The selectivity of the U.S.

demand for Mexican labor, as well as the lack of a uniform immigrant impact on labor standards and other conditions in the industries where they cluster, are just two of the "demand-side" phenomena that require better explanation.

METHODOLOGY

This paper relies primarily on data gathered through a long-term field study based in the Center for U.S.-Mexican Studies at the University of California, San Diego. The project began as an attempt to gauge the impact within California of a specific government intervention in immigrant-dominated labor markets—namely, the INS's "Operation Jobs," a well-coordinated, highly publicized national sweep of work places during the last week of April and the first week of May 1982. Our interest was in how patterns of labor recruitment, hiring practices, and labor force composition in immigrant-dominated or immigrant-dependent firms might have been altered by this government effort to reduce the utilization of undocumented immigrant labor and, in the absence of any durable impacts, to explain the lack of change.

Our interests quickly broadened, however, beyond the realm of government attempts to regulate the use of immigrant labor. It became apparent that such a focus was too narrow; that there were some basic transformations underway in many sectors of the U.S. economy and society that were generating an increased demand for Mexican and other foreign-born labor; and that these change processes and their consequences for the organization of production, labor/management relations, and the mobility of capital were of far greater significance in understanding the role being played by Mexican labor in the state's economy than anything that federal or state government agencies were doing—or might conceivably be doing in the future. We therefore came to focus more on the conditions within various industries and different types of firms within them that affected the hiring of Mexican and other foreign-born workers, the terms of their employment, and more generally the ways in which labor was being utilized by businesses that have depended heavily on immigrant workers.

The original universe for the study was defined as all firms in California's three largest metropolitan areas (San Diego, Los Angeles-Orange County, and the San Francisco Bay area) with ten or more employees that make substantial use of Mexican and other foreign-born labor. "Substantial" users were defined as firms where at least 25 percent of the jobs in production were filled by Mexicans. The actual average proportion of Mexicans in these jobs among our 177 firms, as revealed by our interviews with workers, was 65 percent as of 1983-84.

In each metropolitan area, we attempted to contact all firms that had been raided by the INS during Operations Jobs in 1982. Lists of these firms were compiled both from INS sources and from newspaper reports on Operation Jobs. We then randomly sampled the more comprehensive lists of firms in each of the three metropolitan areas that the INS had already raided or had enlisted in its "voluntary" job applicant screening program, Operation Cooperation. Access to these lists was provided by INS officials. About half of the 177 firms in our sample were chosen in this way.

We wanted to capture a wide range of dependence on Mexican labor, particularly on undocumented Mexicans. Therefore it was important to expand our sample of firms beyond those that could be identified through INS enforcement activities, which were presumably targeted at the most intensive users of illegals. There are several other important biases in INS enforcement practices: concentration on larger, higher-wage, frequently unionized firms; on sites where substantial concentrations of illegals could be found and easily rounded up (factories, for example, rather than office buildings being cleaned by undocumented workers employed by a particular company); on work places that could be raided on a 9:00-to-5:00 schedule; and so forth. In order to gain a more comprehensive view of the role played by Mexican labor in the California economy, we took care to include in our sample representatives of certain types of firms that, by their very nature, are not cost-effective targets of the INS, and therefore were not well represented on the lists of firms that have been raided by the INS. Examples would be building maintenance firms, construction firms, and restaurants.

The half of our sample firms that had not been targeted by the INS were identified in various ways. During interviews with unionized employers, we asked them to name their principal nonunion competitors, who were subsequently interviewed. Other firms were identified in our interviews with labor union officials in each metropolitan area. Some firms were selected at random from industry and telephone directories. In San Diego, several employers who had been identified in a 1980-81 study of health service utilization by 2,100 Mexican immigrants in San Diego County were selected for inclusion in the new study.[1] Several of our Mexico-origin interviewers also used their personal contacts to tap into immigrant networks for assistance in identifying firms that might be appropriate for inclusion.

This eclectic set of purposive sampling techniques limits the generalizability of our results in a strict statistical sense. However, considering the impossibility of sampling the universe of immigrant-dependent firms in California (no such sampling frame exists) and the limitations of a random sampling approach relying on populations that may have been significantly biased in various ways (e.g., firms that have been raided by the INS, or apprehended illegals who identify their employers on INS forms), we opted for eclecticism. Our goal was to study a cross section of immigrant-dependent firms that would be as representative as possible of the universe, excluding only the smallest employers (family-owned and operated business, household employers, etc.). Agricultural employers were also underrepresented in our sample because of the limitation of our study to the state's three principal metropolitan areas.

The first stage of the study consisted of very detailed interviews with employers and labor union representatives (if they were present) in each firm. In the second stage, we selected for more intensive study firms in seven nonagricultural industries that make heavy use of Mexican labor. They include construction (including roofing and construction site cleanup), food processing, shoe manufacturing and tanning, high-tech electronics, building and landscape maintenance, hotels, and restaurants. We chose to concentrate on these nonagricultural sectors of the economy because so much less is known about how they use Mexican labor than about agricultural employers, and because urban employers are considerably more important as sources of jobs for Mexicans and other immigrants in California today than are agricultural firms.

In this second stage of the project, we interviewed 834 workers employed in the 94 firms that fell into our seven "intensive-study" industries. So, for example, we interviewed no workers employed in agriculture, which had been excluded from the second stage of the study. We attempted to interview ten workers in each firm,

---

[1]Wayne A. Cornelius, Leo R. Chávez, and Oliver W. Jones, *Health Problems and Health Service Utilization among Mexican Immigrants: The Case of San Diego* (La Jolla, Calif.: Center for U.S.-Mexican Studies, University of California, San Diego, 1984).

chosen at random from the workers in all job categories in which Mexicans were employed. If non-Mexican workers (Anglos, Chicanos, Blacks, Asians) were also found to be employed in those same job categories, we interviewed several of them in each firm as well. Interviewers were instructed to choose a cross section of production workers in a given firm: some young, some older, some undocumented immigrants, some legal immigrants, and (if present) some non-Mexican workers. One-fifth of the resulting worker sample consisted of U.S.-born workers, the majority of them second-generation Mexican-Americans (Chicanos). Our interviewers made initial contact with them at the work place—sometimes inside the plant, sometimes outside the gates; sometimes with the knowledge of management, sometimes not. But all interviews with workers were conducted in the privacy of their homes, rather than at their work place. Most of these interviews lasted from 90 to 120 minutes.

In the third stage of the project, from May 1987 to June 1988, we returned to a subsample of the original 177 firms, to conduct new interviews with management and with a new sample of workers employed in each firm. These employer interviews were done in 105 nonagricultural firms located in southern California (San Diego, Orange, and Los Angeles counties), 71 of which were included in the earlier stages of the project. These 71 firms represent all of the original-sample firms that were located in southern California *and* were still in business by May 1987.[2] Firms in the San Francisco Bay area could not be included in this last phase of the project, due to financial constraints. Thirty-two firms not represented in earlier stages of the project but belonging to the same industries we have been studying were selected for inclusion in the 1987-88 fieldwork. Detailed, in-person interviews were conducted with 105 employers or managers, 500 workers employed in their firms (an average of 5 workers per firm, interviewed, as before, in their homes), and 200 recently arrived undocumented immigrants—interviewed mostly in street-corner labor markets and public parks—who were still seeking steady employment in southern California. In this last phase of the project, particular attention was devoted to the impacts of the 1986 Immigration Reform and Control Act (IRCA) on the behavior of U.S. employers and immigrant workers.

---

[2]We "lost" only nine of the eighty-five original-sample firms that had been located in southern California, due to closure or movement of the firms outside of the region during the 1984-87 period. An additional eight original-sample employers declined to be interviewed a second time.

Immigrant-dependent Firms in California: A Profile

The demand for Mexican labor in the California economy is highly diversified—much more so today than it was ten or fifteen years ago. As table 1 shows, more than 60 different types of goods and services were being produced by the 177 firms we studied in 1983-84. The sector that used to absorb the majority of Mexicans arriving in the state—agriculture—has lost ground continuously to manufacturing, construction, and the rapidly expanding urban service sector (including retail trade). The explosive growth of industries like construction and building maintenance in California's major urban centers in recent years has been made possible, in no small measure, by the ample supply of Mexican labor. While there is no way of estimating with precision, it is unlikely that more than 15 percent of the undocumented Mexicans working in the state today are in agriculture. However, California fruit, vegetable, and horticulture producers remain highly

---

Table 1. Goods and Services Produced by 177 Immigrant-Dependent Firms in California

Aircraft parts	Hospital
Animal feed	Hospital services
Apparel and accessories	Hotel
Avocados	Hotel services
Bakery goods	Household appliances
Batteries (rechargable)	Iron & steel foundries
Building alterations	Labor contracting
Building construction	Landscape maintenance
Building demolition	Laundry
Building site cleanup	Leather products
Building maintenance	Leather tanning
Candles	Medical equipment
Candy	Metal product fabrication
Canned fruit)	Mexican foods (processed)
Canned vegetables	Mobile homes
Car washing	Mushrooms
Chicken processing	Picture frames
Communications equipment	Plastic products
Computers	Radiators
Computer chips, circuits	Roofing
Convalescent home	Rubber products
Duck processing	Ship building & repair
Electrical machinery	Soft drinks
Electricity (public utility)	Table-service restaurant
Fish processing	Take-out restaurant
Flowers	Textile products
Footware	Turkey processing
Fresh fruits and vegetables	Vinyl products
Frozen vegetables	Water (bottled)
Furniture and fixtures	Wood products
Giftware	

Source: Center for U.S.-Mexican Studies survey, 1983-84.

dependent on Mexican labor—far more so than any other sector of the state's economy—followed by food processing, hotels, and garment and shoe manufacturing (see table 2, entry for "Monolingual Spanish-speakers as a percentage of work force").

The typical immigrant-dependent firm is a small or medium-sized business—the median size in our 1983-84 sample was 85 employees; in our 1987-88 sample of southern California firms, it was 103 employees. Such firms are often thought to be in precarious financial shape. While most of the firms we studied were not highly capitalized, only one out of ten appeared to be in serious financial difficulty (defined as operating at a loss or just breaking even) at the time of our 1983-84 fieldwork. The majority of these firms are financially sound and some are leaders in their respective local markets. A large portion of them have low profit margins, however. The less profitable enterprises tend to rely more upon undocumented immigrant labor.

Many immigrant-dependent firms suffer from marked seasonal or business-cycle fluctuations in the demand for their product or service. Many of them are also subject to strong foreign and/or domestic competition. Most depend on relatively unskilled workers in certain portions of the production process (in our sample of firms, unskilled workers comprised a third of the total work force, on the average). Their level of technological sophistication varies tremendously. The firms included in our study range from antiquated foundries and plants that process fish using kitchen knives, to high-tech firms manufacturing diamond-turned substrate memory discs and other state-of-the-art computer hardware.

About 15 percent of the firms we studied were primarily subcontractors, reflecting a growing trend in the California economy. Virtually all of these subcontracting firms operate in highly competitive arenas and are subject to dramatic swings in demand for their products or service. Their work force typically includes a substantial portion of temporary "on-call" workers (sometimes called "contingency workers"), who tend to be recently arrived Mexican immigrants.

We found that one out of five employers in these immigrant-dependent industries are, themselves, first- or second-generation immigrants who started their own small businesses. The work force in these "immigrant enclave" firms is almost entirely foreign born (Mexican or Asian), and the employer's own extended family and friendship network is usually well represented.

Table 2. Characteristics of Immigrant-dependent Firms in California

Firm characteristic	ALL FIRMS	Agriculture, Horticulture	Construction	Food Processing	Garment, shoes, leather	High-tech electronics	Other manufacturing	Building/ landscape maintenance	Other services	Hotels	Restaurants
Total number of employees (median)	85	65	38	90	83	88	100	71	87	628	46
Volume of annual sales (in thousands)	$4,000	$3,750	$2,250	$8,000	$3,800	$5,000	$10,000	$2,000	$1,500	$22,000	$625
Average profitability: high (%)	41	27	50	26	36	58	43	31	50	54	33
Breaks even or operates at a loss (%)	10	9	0	16	7	8	13	0	19	15	33
Subject to seasonal variation in demand (%)	42	50	86	37	50	17	25	19	35	64	56
Age of firm (years)	15	21	14	22	22	12	25	9	20	10	4
Does subcontracted work (%)	15	0	50	5	31	25	9	19	6	7	11
Is unionized (%)	41	33	50	65	44	0	39	44	29	92	11
Subject to foreign competition (%)	20	36	0	16	86	36	25	0	13	0	0
Unskilled workers as percent of total work force	33	40	34	50	20	5	38	58	37	42	18
Annual turnover among unskilled workers (%)	20	25	11	10	14	10	10	20	5	45	25
Hourly wage for unskilled/semi-skilled workers	$6.00	$5.25	$8.50	$7.00	$4.25	$5.50	$6.00	$7.39	$5.50	$7.12	$4.25
Hourly wage for entry-level workers	$4.00	$3.85	$5.00	$5.42	$3.35	$3.68	$4.25	$4.00	$3.68	$4.25	$3.35
Days needed to learn job (entry-level)	7	1	68	5	7	14	14	30	14	52	5
Average age, unskilled/semi-skilled workers (years)	28	25	25	30	30	27	30	27	30	32	24
Females as percent of total full-time work force	35	17	5	45	55	50	27	11	73	54	45
Monolingual Spanish-speakers as percent of workforce*	50	80	40	63	53	29	50	48	45	61	29
Blacks as percent of work force	1	0	0	0	1	2	1	0	6	11	0
Asians as percent of work force	2	0	0	0	2	8	2	1	4	10	0
Provides health insurance for unskilled work force (%)	78	100	73	88	77	100	86	69	77	100	24
Has pension plan for unskilled workers (%)	45	56	46	71	39	36	52	50	54	42	6
Has difficulty recruiting suitable workers (%)	11	0	14	10	25	0	5	13	13	29	6
Employer is Hispanic (%)	21	33	54	14	0	20	11	23	0	14	38
Has been raided by the INS at least once (%)	50	83	14	75	60	20	68	31	50	39	22
No change in hiring practice after raid (%)	61	80	100	60	50	33	32	86	57	88	100
Prefers hiring referrals from employees (%)	69	82	69	73	87	58	71	81	60	36	69
Ever inspected by Labor Department (%)	39	67	14	38	42	8	39	31	50	80	35
Ever fined for labor stds. violations (%)	7	25	0	15	6	0	8	13	6	0	0
Couldn't raise wages and stay profitable (%)	42	25	36	75	21	60	55	43	33	58	8
Could raise wages by less than 25% and stay profitable (%)	43	0	46	8	71	40	35	36	50	33	92
Could not survive removal of undocumented workers (%)	31	50	14	20	69	17	27	50	24	0	44
Will stop hiring illegals if law passes (%)	35	25	43	35	25	50	41	25	53	36	11

*Best indicator of percent of undocumented workers in the firm's work force.

Source: Employer interviews in 177 firms, Center for U.S.-Mexican Studies survey, 1983-84.

In California, even firms that are not run by ethnic entrepreneurs frequently rely on immigrant family networks as their principal means of labor recruitment. Sixty-nine percent of the employers whom we interviewed in 1983-84 preferred to hire referrals from their current employees. Hiring "walk-ins"—people who simply show up at the door—was the second most common means of recruitment. No significant changes in recruitment practices were detected in our 1987-88 employer interviews. Not surprisingly, when a job becomes available at one of these firms, word spreads quickly through the immigrant networks from which the employer has previously hired, enabling him to choose from among several immigrant job aspirants.

The predominance of Spanish in many immigrant-dependent firms is virtually guaranteed by the large numbers of monolingual Spanish-speakers that they employ. They constituted 50 percent of the total work force, on average, in the businesses that we studied in 1983-84 and 1987-88. The percentage of monolingual Spanish-speakers rises to 80 percent or more among unskilled and semi-skilled production workers in industries like food processing and shoe manufacturing. In heavily immigrant-dominated firms, the vast majority of foremen or supervisors are native Spanish-speakers. These "Hispanic intermediaries" are often recruited specifically by Anglo management to enable the firm to effectively utilize the pool of Spanish-speaking immigrant labor. Nearly half (45-46 percent) of the workers whom we interviewed in both 1984 and 1987-88 had a Spanish-speaking boss (supervisor or employer).

Our research shows that, once established, this ethnic distribution pattern is highly resistant to change. Only 4 out of 177 firms where we interviewed in 1983-84 reported a decline in the proportion of Hispanics in their work force during the last 5-10 years; nearly a quarter of the firms reported an increase in the Hispanic presence. In only one firm had the proportion of white workers increased. Among the southern California employers interviewed in 1987-88, three-quarters anticipated no change in the ethnic composition of their work force, at least as a result of the 1986 immigration law. For U.S. non-Hispanic workers, the Spanish-speaking culture of the work place becomes an additional disincentive to seeking employment in such firms.

Forty-one percent of the firms included in the first stage of our project—encompassing both southern California and the San Francisco Bay area—were unionized. Among the firms surveyed in 1987-88, 28 percent were unionized. The lower proportion of unionized firms in the 1987-88 sample, which was limited to southern California, primarily reflects the historically lower level of unionization in that region as a whole, as compared with the San Francisco Bay area. Even 28 percent is higher than we expected to find, considering that much of the growth of immigrant-dependent firms in California during the last fifteen years has occurred in sectors of the economy that were not highly unionized to begin with: restaurants, electronics manufacturing, janitorial services, and so forth.

It is clear that in some industries (e.g., construction) non-union firms relying primarily on undocumented Mexican labor have proliferated during the last ten years, often at the expense of unionized firms. But our research has found that in most cases the growing presence of undocumented immigrant workers in the labor market was only a secondary factor contributing to this change. More important were changes in the macroeconomic environment in which firms and unions must operate that have weakened the unions' bargaining power. Undocumented workers can typically be found in both unionized and non-union firms in a given industry, including construction. Since the passage of IRCA, the work force of the average immigrant-dominated firm in California has been a mixture of permanent legal immigrants ("green-carders"), amnesty applicants ("Rodinos"), and undocumented aliens.

Are immigrant-dependent firms more likely to form part of the underground economy? Firms that rely heavily upon undocumented immigrant labor are frequently portrayed as clandestinely operated sweatshops that continue to exist only because they avoid making employee-related payments to the government (by paying their workers in cash), violate minimum wage and labor standards laws with impunity, fail to pay for overtime, and deny their employees standard fringe benefits. The data gathered from our worker samples forcefully contradict this impression. Only 3 percent of the workers in 1984 and 5 percent in 1987-88 told us that they were typically paid in cash rather than by check. Ninety-four percent reported that they had been required to give a Social Security number when they were hired, and 99 percent reported regular employer withholding of Social Security and federal and state income taxes. We found that only 2 out of 177 original-sample firms, and none of the firms surveyed in 1987-88, paid their entry-level workers below the legal minimum wage. Only 1 percent of the workers who worked overtime were not being compensated for it. Seven percent of the firms acknowledged that they had been fined at least once by the Labor Department for violation of labor standards laws, although there is undoubtedly some under-reporting reflected in the responses to this question. Fringe benefits provided by these employers are not very generous, but they are standard for the industries of which they are a part. Seventy-eight percent of the firms in our original sample offered health insurance plans, for example, but only 16 percent of their production workers had opted to participate in them, usually because a substantial contribution was required from the employee (see table 3).

These results may understate the actual extent to which California employers of undocumented immigrants form part of the "informal sector" or underground economy. Our worker data come exclusively from *non*agricultural firms. Our study also excludes the smallest employers (those with a work force of under ten, and household employers) who make use of immigrant labor. We could expect to find a higher incidence of payment in cash, wage and labor standards violations, and other indicators of participation in the underground economy among the smallest employers and in the agricultural sector. Such practices appear to be rare, however, among larger, nonagricultural users of Mexican labor in California.

Explaining the Growing Demand for Mexican Labor

The central objective of our research since 1982 has been to explain the development of dependence on Mexican immigrant labor, at the industry and firm level, over time. How did such dependence occur? And what factors continue to increase the demand for immigrant labor in the U.S. economy? These questions can be addressed most effectively with the qualitative, case-study material gathered for our project. This section attempts only a broad-brush summary of our findings, which greatly understates the complexity of the processes that we encountered.

We find that there is not one but many distinct paths to reliance upon Mexican immigrant labor. Mexican immigrants are hired for many different reasons, under widely varying circumstances. One category of firms consists of those that are growing at least partly because of the availability of relatively low-cost Mexican labor. These are enterprises that are, in essence, "following the immigrants," relying upon them both as a labor source and, in some cases, as consumers. Perhaps the best examples are firms started by Mexican immigrants themselves or by second-generation Mexican-Americans, who have continued to "hire their own." In California, the expansion of this ethnic enclave accounts for a nontrivial portion of the growth in demand for Mexican labor.

Table 3. Characteristics of Workers in Immigrant-dependent Firms in California

Worker characteristic	ALL FIRMS	Construction	Food Processing	Shoes, leather	High-tech electronics	Other manufacturing	Building/ landscape maintenance	Hotels	Restaurants
Age (median # of years)	29	32	29	32	27	28	30	35	29
Sex (% of males)	72	97	64	82	40	84	83	49	73
Marital status (% married)	58	76	62	63	53	59	64	68	35
Education (# of years completed)	8	8	6	6	9	11	7	8	11
Place of birth:									
Mexico (%)	65	69	80	83	66	60	73	43	54
United States (%)	20	31	17	6	29	25	8	19	32
El Salvador (%)	8	0	1	7	0	4	10	25	11
Other (Guatemala, Nicaragua, Viet Nam, etc. (%)	6	0	2	4	5	11	9	13	3
Years of residence in U.S. (if Mexico born)	7	8	8	7	4	9	8	8	5
Number of jobs held in U.S.	3	3	3	3	2	3	3	3	3
Number of years in current job	2	1	3	2	2	1	2	4	2
Migrated from urban area in Mexico* (%)	61	78	46	89	69	58	58	38	64
Intends to remain in U.S. (%)	62	59	67	41	77	67	63	61	64
Was undocumented when first entered U.S. (%)	71	65	72	83	64	68	76	62	73
Is currently undocumented immigrant (%)	51	33	52	64	49	50	64	41	49
Ever apprehended by the INS (%)	37	32	54	30	6	39	35	27	43
Asked for SS# when applying for a job (%)	94	92	95	98	97	96	91	95	92
Asked to show SS card when applying (%)	42	34	48	85	29	45	38	41	20
Employer or supervisor is Hispanic (%)	46	65	41	40	29	64	62	35	37
Worker understands English instructions (%)	53	57	39	19	55	61	51	63	73
Hourly wage (median)	$5.63	$6.25	$6.24	$5.00	$4.38	$5.55	$5.56	$6.00	$5.00
Gets paid for overtime (%)	99	100	99	100	100	100	99	97	97
Employer withholds taxes and social security (%)	99	98	100	100	100	100	97	100	97
Employer provides health insurance (%)	16	0	2	12	27	49	10	13	14
Employer provides pension plan (%)	88	100	93	80	88	77	93	84	67
Belongs to labor union (%)	44	52	56	66	3	24	46	73	11
Job is very hazardous (%)	15	39	22	15	3	33	6	11	3

*Urban area is defined as a locality having 15,000 or more inhabitants in 1980.

Source: In-home interviews with 834 workers employed in 94 firms, Center for U.S.-Mexican Studies survey, 1984.

Another category of immigrant-dependent firms consists of those who rely upon the immigrant labor pool for skills and experience that are simply not available in the U.S.-born work force. The clearest example is the shoe and leather industry, whose continued existence in California is due primarily to its ability to import skilled workers from Mexico—mostly from the cities of León and Guadalajara, where Mexico's shoe and tanning industries are concentrated. Since the 1950s, practically all new hires in Los Angeles shoe factories have been Mexicans who had previously been employed in the Mexican shoe industry. Despite mechanization that has deskilled some aspects of the production process, most jobs in the U.S. shoe and leather industry—even entry-level jobs—require more than two years of training. The continued demand for Mexican labor in industries like shoe manufacturing reflects the failure of the United States to train an adequate supply of skilled manual labor for these industries. Moreover, few U.S. citizens are willing to invest much time training for a career in a dying industry.

In other industries, technological change has been the driving force promoting increased utilization of immigrant labor in recent years. The automation and fragmentation of production has broken down every possible operation into simpler, more routinized tasks, making it possible for employers to use unskilled immigrant workers to perform them. Such workers can often be taught in a week or less to operate one specialized machine on an assembly line. They need to know little or nothing about the rest of the production process. Similarly, in the construction industry, the standardization of many on-site tasks, the shift to prefabricated components manufactured off site, and the introduction of new techniques like "cold-process" roofing have reduced the number of skilled craftsmen required and increased the demand for unskilled laborers. In the poultry processing industry, advancements in mechanization have left many unskilled and semi-skilled jobs that are extremely unappealing. Over the next ten to fifteen years, we can anticipate that continued deskilling of production tasks in many sectors of the U.S. economy will generate a great many more so-called "bad jobs" that will be unattractive to most native-born workers.[3]

---

[3] See, for example, M. Patricia Fernández-Kelly and Anna M. García, "Economic Restructuring in the United States: The Case of Hispanic Women in the Garment and Electronics Industries in Southern California," in *The Changing Roles of Mexican Immigrants in the U.S. Economy: Sectoral Perspectives*, edited by Wayne A. Cornelius (La Jolla, Calif.: Center for U.S.-Mexican Studies, University of California, San Diego, forthcoming).

For some industries, changes in attitudes toward work, higher educational levels, and rising job aspirations among the U.S.-born population have made it desirable or necessary for employers to recruit primarily from the immigrant community. An example is the hotel industry in Los Angeles. Our research shows that until the mid-1960s, many unskilled hotel jobs in that city were filled by U.S.-born workers. By the 1980s, only the least mobile native-born workers (older minority women and uneducated minority men) were still occupying such positions. Other U.S.-born workers had moved on to better jobs, and the majority of minority children have chosen to avoid this sector of the economy altogether. The voluntary out-migration of Blacks and other U.S.-born minority workers from unskilled hotel positions forced hotel managers in Los Angeles to search for new unskilled labor sources—workers who would not be discouraged by low wages and degrading tasks. Undocumented Mexican immigrants provided the solution.

In some firms and industries, employers seem to have substituted Mexican- for U.S.-born workers *against* the preferences of the domestic workers who remained. This is particularly common among employers who have had negative experiences in attempting to use alternative labor sources (usually Blacks or Anglo teenagers). Such employers develop an active preference for Mexican workers, believing them to possess highly desirable working traits (punctuality, reliability, loyalty to the firm, low propensity to complain, etc.) that they see lacking in most potential substitutes. Asian immigrant workers—imbued with the same strong "work ethic"—are perceived by some California employers as an acceptable alternative to Mexican labor, although few firms have seriously considered such a substitution. One employer whom we interviewed expressed the prevailing view:

> Mexican aliens have a strong work ethic. They need the job; they are good workers. If you can't hire them, other workers that you might hire will be less motivated. If enforcement [of the 1986 immigration law] gets tougher, then it may be hard to get motivated workers.

In other sectors of the U.S. economy, employers have shifted toward greater reliance on immigrants as part of an overall strategy to cut costs and reduce the risks of doing business. For some of these employers, the pursuit of a low-wage, high-productivity, more flexible work force, with a higher ratio of part-time and temporary workers to full-time and permanent workers, has been considered a matter of survival. Many firms—especially in labor-intensive industries using conventional technology—have found themselves confronted in recent years by much stiffer competition from both foreign and domestic firms.

Foreign competition has been a particularly important factor explaining the Mexicanization of the work force in the garment, electronics, furniture, rubber products, and even food processing industries. Some large electronics and automotive firms suffering from intense foreign competition have opted to subcontract their labor-intensive assembly work to firms with predominantly immigrant labor forces. For some of these firms, the use of immigrant-dominated subcontractors represents a transitional strategy of cost reduction, which will be followed eventually by the transfer of production operations overseas.[4]

In less mobile urban service industries like building maintenance, domestic competitive pressures have had similar consequences. Even employers who had no particular desire to shift to an immigrant-dominated work force have found it impossible to resist the general trend in their industry, as their principal competitors made the shift.

The wage bill savings that can be achieved by substituting immigrant workers—especially the undocumented—for U.S.-born workers have often been overestimated. For example, in the firms that we have been studying, entry-level unskilled immigrant workers typically earn $4-5 per hour, while skilled workers receive $6-8 per hour. California employers do tend to pay their undocumented workers less than legal-resident workers performing similar jobs, but immigration status per se does not seem to be a significant cause of these wage differentials. It is much less important than job seniority, union membership, the particular sector of the economy in which the worker is employed, and the ethnicity of one's employer. In short, it is simplistic to argue that undocumented immigrants are hired preferentially just because they are cheaper.

Paradoxically, the substitution of lower-wage, non-unionized Mexican workers for unionized U.S.-born workers in some industries seems to have been accelerated by the successes of the labor movement in the 1970s. Complicated union work rules and wage rigidity—the persistence of high, rigid union wage scales that have

---

[4]See, for example, Rebecca Morales, "Transitional Labor: Undocumented Workers in the Los Angeles Automobile Industry," *International Migration Review* 17 (Winter 1983).

proven resistant to downward pressures in the market and to cyclical slumps in demand for goods or services—have encouraged the proliferation of non-union firms that have more flexible work rules and which rely on the lower-wage immigrant labor pool. We have documented this phenomenon most clearly in California's construction industry, where even unionized firms frequently must now subcontract to non-union firms in order to remain competitive. Another example is provided by the janitorial service industry, where union victories in the 1970s created such a huge differential between union and non-union wage scales that unionized firms were highly vulnerable to cost-cutting when the economic recession of the late 1970s and early '80s hit. Newly cost-conscious building managers flocked to non-union maintenance firms, many of them run by ex-employees of large unionized firms.

We have found that in many industries in California, a two-tier structure of firms has emerged in recent years. In each of these industries there is an "upper tier" consisting of primary, relatively high-wage, unionized firms; and a "lower tier" made up of small, non-union firms, often operating as subcontractors and relying almost exclusively on undocumented immigrant labor. The relationship between upper- and lower-tier firms in an industry can be either competitive or complementary. Many of the lower-tier firms, in direct competition with the upper-tier firms in their industry, use their lower labor costs to underbid the high-wage, unionized firms. But other lower-tier firms—those functioning as subcontractors to upper-tier firms—have a symbiotic relationship with them. In fact, the competitiveness of many large, upper-tier businesses in which immigrants comprise only a small portion of the work force depends heavily upon their ability to subcontract work to smaller firms that are immigrant dominated.

As international competitive pressures increase, well-paying unionized jobs in "mainstream" firms are being protected by a buffer of non-union, immigrant-dominated firms. Because of the increasing fragmentation of the production process on a global scale, it is likely that the upper tier in manufacturing industries will continue to shrink as time goes on. This has already happened in the garment industry, where firms with large work forces have virtually disappeared since the mid-1970s.[5] But this would happen

---

[5] See M. Patricia Fernández-Kelly and Anna M. García, "Economic Restructuring in the United States: The Case of Hispanic Women in the Garment and Electronics Industries in Southern California," paper presented at the Research Workshop on Changing Roles of Mexican Immigrants in the U.S. Economy, Center for U.S.-Mexican Studies, University of California, San Diego, August 26-27, 1987.

even faster in the absence of the Mexican immigrant labor force and the lower-tier firms that make heaviest use of this labor source.

Small, immigrant-dominated firms offer a number of advantages beyond lower labor costs. Firms in the most competitive consumer-goods sectors and those responding to highly volatile consumer preferences (e.g., electronic games, personal computers, apparel) must have very quick turn-around time on subassembly and prototype work to ensure that their products reach the market before those of their competitors. The small firms with their more flexible (not just "cheap") immigrant work forces can produce new items virtually overnight. Needless to say, such firms cannot offer their employees much in the way of job security or steady income.

The increasing presence of Mexican immigrants in U.S. labor markets appears to be an effect or concomitant of many of the change processes just described, rather than a primary cause. For some U.S. firms and industries affected by economic restructuring, the availability of immigrant labor has a cushioning effect, helping them adjust to changes in production processes and spreading the costs of adjustment over a longer period of time. These fundamental change processes are likely to persist in the foreseeable future, and the demand for Mexican and other immigrant labor in the state's economy will continue to grow. The main questions for the future relate to how that demand will be satisfied, particularly in the new regulatory environment created by the Simpson-Rodino legislation.

IMPACTS OF THE IMMIGRATION REFORM AND CONTROL ACT OF 1986

Most immigrant-dependent employers in California have adjusted easily to their new obligations under IRCA, without having to give up their traditional labor source. The overwhelming majority of firms—95 percent in our 1987-88 survey—are requesting the documents and filling out the I-9 forms required under IRCA, attesting that they have examined a job applicant's documents and found that each document "reasonably appears on its face to be genuine."[6] Most employers are even going beyond

---

[6] Over two-thirds of the California employers in our 1983-84 sample were already asking job applicants for documentary proof of legal-resident status *before* the Simpson-Rodino law was passed. They erroneously believed that it was illegal to hire undocumented immigrants, even before Congress actually made it a crime to do so.

the requirements of the law, by photocopying the documents presented by job applicants and keeping the copies on file.

Simultaneously, false documents—whose authenticity the employers are not required by IRCA to verify—are proliferating among the migrant population, especially in the urban sector. Forty-one percent of our sample of urban undocumented workers employed in southern California in 1987-88 had gotten their jobs using bogus or borrowed documents. And 25 percent of recent migrants to the United States whom we interviewed in three traditional labor-exporting communities in rural Mexico in 1988-89 had used false documents to gain employment during their most recent trip to the United States, purchasing them for an average of $50.[7] And although it is not common, some undocumented migrants have been told by employers to *get* fake papers.

When we asked California employers in 1987-88 what they would do if they suspected that a document presented by a job applicant was fraudulent, the answers were very illuminating. Here are a few representative responses:

> I'd put it in the file and say, I hope it's not [fake].

> If it's a flagrant fake I.D., then we obviously would turn it down; but we're not responsible for being professional identification checkers.

> I would just try to get them to get something that wasn't so fraudulent looking. If it doesn't look right, go get a right one for me.

> It's not our business [to check]. We're an employer, not a policeman. Blatantly fraudulent documents we don't accept—and we've had some miserable reproductions. Some of the forgeries are absolutely magnificent, however, and we don't question them.

> The technology of falsification is far more advanced than the technology of detection.... They show me the stuff, and it's wrong, and there's nothing I can do about it.

---

[7]These figures are probably underreports of actual behavior, because many Mexican migrants regard the use of bogus documents as an unsavory business, and the majority are aware that they are subject to criminal penalties under IRCA if they attempt to use such documents to gain employment in the United States.

> The compliance procedures are not that difficult. You don't have to verify the person's documents are valid, so there's no hazard in hiring someone with fraudulent documents.
>
> It's so easy for these guys to get the fake IDs.... I think that's one of the reasons we haven't had any problems getting employees. You ask them for IDs and they don't have any. Three days later, they do.

Not surprisingly, for most U.S. nonagricultural employers, the 1986 immigration law does not pose a credible threat to their operations. Among our sample of southern California firms, only 7 percent anticipate having to close all or parts of their business because of the law. The vast majority do not anticipate having to use various strategies—like leasing workers from another firm, or subcontracting work, or transferring assembly work abroad—in order to circumvent the law. While more than half of the employers in our sample—especially smaller firms—expect IRCA to reduce the pool of job applicants for their firm eventually, only one out of four has made any plans to offset potential labor shortages.

Of course, the simplest way of adjusting to a tighter labor market would be to raise wages. But California employers tell us most emphatically that they have not and will not raise wages. Only 38 percent would even consider it, and 50 percent say "absolutely not." There is, in fact, no evidence that IRCA has placed upward pressure on wage scales in immigrant-dominated sectors of the U.S. economy. A recent Rand Corporation study comparing pre- and post-IRCA wage rates found that wages for low-skilled "immigrant" jobs in U.S. cities with large numbers of undocumented aliens have not risen in the post-IRCA period—one indication that the law thus far has failed to reduce the undocumented immigrant labor supply.[8]

While more than 15 percent of our 1987-88 sample of workers in immigrant-dependent firms claimed to know at least one person in their work place who had been laid off or fired since IRCA's passage because the employer suspected that they were

---

[8]Presentation by Beth Asch, Rand Corporation, to the West Coast Workshop on Immigration Policy Research, El Colegio de la Frontera Norte, Tijuana, Baja Calif., June 22, 1989.

undocumented, there has been no pattern of mass layoffs by employers fearful of violating the new immigration law.[9] Nearly four out of five employers in our 1987-88 sample knew that they were not required to lay off undocumented workers who were on the payroll prior to November 6, 1986.

Nor has there been a mass exodus of undocumented workers, fearful of becoming unemployed and unemployable in the United States because of the new immigration law. Indeed, the overwhelming majority seem committed to remaining in the United States, even though they see their future job mobility as more limited than before, due to employer sanctions. Only 15 percent of the employed undocumented workers whom we interviewed in southern California in 1988 were considering leaving because of the immigration law.

Prospective migrants still in Mexico remain optimistic about their chances of finding a U.S. employer who will hire them, with or without papers. Among a sample of would-be, first-time migrants to the United States whom we interviewed in three rural Mexican communities, 71 percent believed that it was still possible to get a job in the United States without valid immigration documents, despite the employer sanctions law.[10]

Among a sample of two hundred recently arrived undocumented migrants whom we interviewed on southern California street corners in 1988-89, nearly two-thirds were in the United States for the first time. Over half of them had heard about the employer sanctions provision of the Simpson-Rodino law. Many were having a difficult time finding regular, permanent jobs; they were relying on casual day labor to survive. But these recent arrivals obviously were not deterred by the 1986 immigration law from trying their luck in a more uncertain, more problematic U.S. labor market.

---

[9] IRCA does not require employers to dismiss any undocumented worker who was on the payroll prior to November 6, 1986, the law's enactment date. There are hundreds of thousands of such "grandfathered" workers in the U.S. labor force today, which helps to explain the absence of severe dislocations in immigrant-dependent industries since IRCA's passage.

[10] See Wayne A. Cornelius, "Impacts of the 1986 U.S. Immigration Law on Emigration from Rural Mexican Sending Communities," paper presented at the XV International Congress of the Latin American Studies Association, Miami, Florida, December 4-6, 1989.

A LOOK AHEAD

Firm conclusions about the long-term efficacy of the Simpson-Rodino legislation are obviously premature at this juncture. There are still many unanswered questions concerning the enforcement of employer sanctions that could affect the outcome. But barring the kind of massive and intrusive enforcement effort that would be highly disruptive in the relatively open, liberal U.S. political economy,[11] the Simpson-Rodino law in its present form is unlikely to compel enough users of undocumented immigrant labor to switch to another labor source, or reduce their overall labor requirements, to significantly diminish the immigrant presence in U.S. labor markets.

Weaning the U.S. economy of its dependence on foreign labor will be especially difficult over the next fifteen years, when the effects of the "baby bust" of the 1970s and early '80s will be strongly felt in many parts of the country. The members of the post-World War II "baby boom" generation tended to postpone marriage and/or childbearing. Most wives entered the labor force to supplement family incomes, and "baby boom" couples eventually had only about half as many children as their parents. Because of this sharp change in reproductive behavior, the number of young adult Americans will shrink, in absolute terms, by 10-15 percent between 1985 and 1995. Simultaneously, the number of prime-age (35-45 years) workers and consumers will increase by 35 percent.[12]

These demographic shifts will result in a major increase in consumer demand and a shortage of workers available to fill low-skill jobs. The effects will be particularly acute in regions of the United States where vigorous economic growth can be anticipated. In California, for example, it is expected that over three million new jobs will be created between 1985 and 2000 in the state's five largest metropolitan areas alone.[13] The bulk of these will be rela-

---

[11]Evidence that the 1986 law is failing to reduce significantly the immigrant presence in the U.S. work force is generating pressure to amend the law, by creating a new, more "secure" national worker identification card coupled with a computerized verification system. See, for example, Roberto Suro, "Immigration Chief Proposes National Computer Screen," *New York Times*, 23 June 1989. The idea of a "national ID card" was hotly debated during the early 1980s and ultimately was dropped by both the Reagan administration and congressional supporters of new immigration legislation, because of objections from civil libertarians and the enormous cost of implementing such a system.

[12]Projections by Kevin F. McCarthy, the Rand Corporation.

[13]Projections by the National Planning Association. The metropolitan areas are Los Angeles-Long Beach (1,032,000 new jobs), Anaheim-Santa Ana (701,500 jobs), San Jose (539,200 jobs), San Diego (422,400 jobs), and San Francisco (360,400 jobs).

tively low-paying jobs in services and retail trade. The shortage of young, U.S.-born workers willing to take low-paying, entry-level jobs is already evident in places like California and New York, where employers have been struggling in recent years to fill such jobs even at $4 or $5 an hour.[14]

There is little likelihood of a swift reversal of these trends. In June 1987, the U.S. Census Bureau announced that the country's birth rate, declining since 1957, had reached an all-time low: "Fertility seems relatively stable now at a low level," a Census Bureau official concluded. "There is no particular reason to expect, in the near future, a turnup."[15] Under these demographic conditions, with an increasingly competitive, global market for most products and services, the pressure on many employers to circumvent legislative restrictions on their use of immigrant labor may become overwhelming in the 1990s. We can therefore expect the U.S. demand for Mexican labor to remain strong, diversified, and increasingly impervious to government regulation.

---

[14]See, for example, William E. Schmidt, "Growing Job Problem: Finding People to Work," *New York Times*, 28 October 1984; Dirk Johnson, "Youth Labor Scarcity Forcing Up Low-Level Pay in New York Area," *New York Times*, 17 March 1986; Tim Schreiner, "California's Future: Shortage of New Young Workers," *San Francisco Chronicle*, 28 March 1986.
[15]Statement by Donald E. Starsinic, Chief, Population Estimates Branch, U.S. Bureau of the Census, as reported by the Associated Press, 10 June 1987.

3

The Mexican Labor Supply, 1990-2010

Manuel García y Griego

For the remainder of this century and part of the next, Mexican migration to the United States will probably constitute a recurring and pressing policy issue both in the sending and the receiving country. In large part this reflects the increasing demand for Mexican labor in the United States and intensifying economic pressures to emigrate in Mexico.

To be sure, the Immigration Reform and Control Act of 1986 (IRCA), intended to reduce illegal entries and diminish the presence of undocumented workers in the U.S. labor market, undoubtedly will deter—though perhaps only slightly—future undocumented flows. However, it is unrealistic to assume that undocumented migration will disappear in the 1990s merely because of the adoption of a law whose enforcement, incidentally, will be problematic. Estimates of future flows which are based on projected supply and demand are likely to yield a more accurate assessment of possible

---

The author gratefully acknowledges the suggestions and materials provided by Virgilio Partida and Sergio Camposortega during the preparation of the population projections presented here, and the use of an unpublished tabulation from the 1980 Mexican census made available by the Instituto Nacional de Estadística, Geografía e Informática. Many thanks also to three groups whose comments, suggestions and editorial work improved the paper: the participants of the research seminar of the U.S.-Mexico Program (Center for International Studies) the participants of the seminar of the Center for Demographic and Urban Development Studies, both of El Colegio de México; and the editorial staff associated with this volume. Their suggestions are greatly appreciated; any remaining errors are the responsibility of the author.

migration flows than estimates which assume that IRCA will completely suppress illegal entries and unauthorized employment.

This essay examines the supply side of this estimation problem. It undertakes a demographic exercise rarely attempted: a regional projection of Mexico's population for the period 1980-2010 which takes into account migration within Mexico and between Mexico and the United States.[1] Two projections are presented which focus on alternative hypothetical scenarios of future flows to the United States for the period 1990-2010. Both assume a level of migration during the 1980s which approximates the higher end of empirical estimates for the decade. The numbers of Mexican emigrants in the United States refer to all Mexican-born persons, with no distinction between legal immigrants and persons subject to deportation.

These estimates of the supply of emigrants *do not* forecast the magnitude of migration from Mexico to the United States between 1980 and 2010. A forecast is a prediction of future events based on assumptions expected to hold. Future changes in demand for Mexican workers, such as a possible labor shortage in the United States or a decline in demand for Mexican labor due to IRCA enforcement, are likely to affect significantly the volume of migration. These projections do not explicitly account for these changes. Rather, this exercise examines the supply-side (i.e., demographic) constraints on emigration, assuming two different emigration rates. It also estimates hypothetically possible magnitudes of future flows. However, were a prolonged recession to occur in the United States, the net flow could reverse direction.[2]

The estimates presented are approximate measures of supply which permit examination of how expected changes in the size and demographic composition of the Mexican population might affect the supply of future migrants and identification of the demographic variables that participate in determining the dimensions of supply of migrants to the United States.

---

[1] A projection of regional population which did not explicitly consider international migration was undertaken by José B. Morelos and Susana Lerner and published as "Proyecciones de población activa de México por regiones, 1960-1985," *Demografía y Economía* 4:3 (1970): 349-363.

[2] The Great Depression of the 1930s provoked a large-scale, sustained repatriation of Mexicans that resulted in a net flow towards Mexico larger than the net migration to the United States of the 1920s. Manuel García y Griego, "Migración Internacional; Cifras Pequeñas, Retos Grandes," *Demos; Carta Demográfica sobre Mexico* 1 (September 1988): 10.

The regional population projections upon which this paper is based divide the Mexican population into three regions. Region 1 comprises eight states in Mexico in which outmigration rates to the United States are highest or which contribute the highest proportions of emigrants: Baja California, Chihuahua, Durango, Guanajuato, Jalisco, Michoacán, San Luis Potosí, and Zacatecas. These eight states were home to approximately 26 percent of the national population in 1980 and provided about 70 percent of the total emigrant population that left for the United States during the late 1970s. They will be referred to as the "traditional core sending region" in Mexico. (A justification for the selection of states that comprise region 1 is presented below.) Region 2 constitutes the balance of Mexico—twenty-four states, comprising 74 percent of the 1980 population and 30 percent of the emigrant flow in the late 1970s. Region 3 is the United States. Only the Mexican-born population habitually resident in the United States is included.

Attempting to estimate the magnitude and growth of the supply of Mexican migrants to the United States between 1990 and 2010 leads to specific questions based on the results of the two regional population projections.

- How fast will the working-age population grow in the traditional core sending region, and will this influence the growth of the supply of emigrants?

- Could the decline in fertility observed in Mexico since the 1970s slow the growth of the supply of migrants to the United States before the year 2000? Conversely, to what extent could high hypothesized emigration levels constrain the growth of the number of births in Mexico?

- What would be the impact of constant age-specific emigration rates and return-migration rates on the magnitude of the net flow to the United States?

- And finally, are there constraints on the supply of temporary migrant workers, i.e., on the number of persons who work temporarily in the United States but maintain their habitual residence in Mexico?

This study offers tentative answers to these questions and suggests their interrelationships.

THE PROBLEM

Observers of Mexican migration to the United States commonly assume that Mexico has a virtually inexhaustible supply of migrants, limited only by the size of Mexico's national population. Experience does not support this view, however. Whatever the theoretical supply of migrants to the United States may be, the total emigrant population outside of Mexico has, in fact, always been a small proportion of the national population. The peak was probably reached in 1930, when about 5.7 percent of Mexico's national population resided in the United States. At no other census year between 1920 and 1980 has Mexico's emigrant population in the United States exceeded 3 percent of Mexico's total population—even when corrections are made for known instances of underenumeration of the Mexican born in past U.S. censuses.[3] In view of the large and persistent economic disparities between the two countries and the long tradition of mass labor migration from Mexico to the United States, the compelling question is why so few Mexicans have emigrated. The answer may be on the demand rather than on the supply side. That is, the relatively small volumes of observed migration may reflect real limits to the size of the labor market that can absorb them in the United States rather than a shortage of workers in Mexico.

I define the supply of migrants to the United States, or the population exposed to the risk of emigrating, as the stock of Mexican-born persons which could be expected to change residence to the United States. Changes in the size of the stock are due to net flow.

The Constant Rates Hypothesis

The existence of emigration rate differentials makes it possible to talk about limits on the supply of emigrants. The differentials are based on demographic characteristics, of which age is the most important, and geographic characteristics—habitual residence inside or outside of the traditional core sending region. To take advantage of what is known about these differentials it is first assumed—in what I term the constant rates hypothesis—that emigration rates observed during 1975-80 hold constant across age-sex groups for the two regions in the country and the Mexican-born population in the United States until 2010. It is quite possible

---

[3]Mexican-born population totals recorded in past U.S. censuses, and some of their corrections, are summarized in García y Griego, "Migración Internacional," 10.

that this approach may weigh inertia too heavily and change too lightly. But in the absence of a theoretical model, it is one of the few approaches which account for the large number of Mexicans that do not migrate.

The Drastic Change Hypothesis

An alternative hypothesis simulates a sharp break from established patterns, an unprecedentedly large rise in the rates of emigration to the United States from areas outside the core sending region, and also a sharp increase, though proportionately smaller, in the emigration rates from areas within the traditional core sending region. This translates to a sharp growth of emigration to the United States during the 1990s and early twenty-first century and reflects a supply of emigrants only partially constrained by historically established demographic and geographic migration patterns. Thus the drastic change hypothesis simulates a sharp departure from long-established trends and patterns.

One of the most remarkable but least examined characteristics of Mexican migration to the United States is its concentration in a small proportion of the national population and in certain Mexican states. Table 1 illustrates this point by identifying the eight states which most contributed to emigration at various times since 1924.

In 1924 these eight states provided 79.2 percent of the flow and in 1984, 68.7 percent. This stability is all the more remarkable because the eight states constituted only 33 percent of Mexico's 1924 population. The eight states that sent 68.7 percent of the emigration in 1984 comprised only 26 percent of the national population. Thus, the demographic concentration of emigration has hardly changed at all.[4] The similarity is especially striking given the different sources of data employed; only in 1977 and 1984 are the categories of migrant population strictly comparable.

---

[4]Similarly, table 1 shows that in 1957 eight states contributed 74.3 percent of the emigrant flow; those states constituted about 31 percent of the population at midyear. Table 1 shows eight states contributing 71.1 percent of the flow in 1977; these states were about 26 percent of the population. Estimates of total population by state for April 1924, June 1957 and November, 1977 were obtained as logarithmic interpolations based on state populations reported in the appropriate censuses. The December 1984 population for the eight states was estimated in the same manner utilizing INEGI-CONAPO's projections by state for the years 1980 and 1985. These projections, discussed below, appear in Mexico, Instituto Nacional de Estadística Geografía e Informática y Consejo Nacional de Población, *Proyecciones de la Población de México y de las Entidades Federativas: 1980-2010* (Mexico City: INEGI-CONAPO, 1983).

Table 1. Distribution of Mexican Migrants to the United States by Top Eight States of Origin in Mexico, selected years (shown in percentages)

	1924	1957	1977	1984
Total, top 8 states	79.2	74.3	71.0	68.7
Baja California	—	—	17.0	10.2
Coahuila	9.2	5.5	—	—
Chihuahua	—	6.9	7.7	15.7
Durango	5.8	8.6	3.9	—
Guanajuato	10.8	13.2	9.0	7.7
Guerrero	—	—	—	4.4
Jalisco	20.0	10.8	13.7	10.0
Michoacán	14.5	11.8	11.5	11.1
Nuevo León	5.8	—	—	—
San Luis Potosí	—	5.6	3.7	—
Sonora	4.1	—	—	5.2
Zacatecas	9.0	11.9	4.5	4.4

—Indicates state not among top eight during that year.

Sources: 1924: Robert F. Foerster, *The Racial Problems Involved in Immigration from Latin America and the West Indies to the United States: A Report Submitted to the Secretary of Labor* (Washington, D.C.: U.S. Government Printing Office, 1925): 51. Refers to legal immigrants admitted by Los Angeles, California, El Paso, and San Antonio, Texas, immigration district offices, during April 1924.

1957: Moisés González Navarro, *Población y Sociedad en México (1900-1970)*, 2 vols. (Mexico City: UNAM, Facultad de Ciencias Políticas y Sociales, 1974): 1462. Refers to contract laborers admitted during 1957.

1977: México, Secretaría del Trabajo y Previsión Social, Centro Nacional de Información y Estadísticas del Trabajo, *Análisis de Algunos Resultados de la Primera Encuesta a Trabajadores Mexicanos No Documentados Devueltos de los Estados Unidos, CENIET, octubre 23- noviembre 13 de 1977* (Mexico City: CENIET, 1979): 20. Refers to undocumented Mexicans expelled by INS in twenty-one day period in October-November 1977.

1984: México, Consejo Nacional de Población, *Encuesta en la Frontera Norte a Trabajadores Indocumentados Devueltos por las Autoridades de los Estados Unidos de América, diciembre de 1984 (ETIDEU); Resultados Estadísticos* (Mexico City: CONAPO, 1986): 53. Refers to undocumented Mexicans expelled by INS during ten-day period in December 1984.

To be sure, the proportions of migrants from individual states went up and down erratically over this period. Nuevo León and Coahuila—both border states—constituted a significant source of emigration in the 1920s, but neither provided a large proportion of emigrants by the 1970s. Four states—Guanajuato, Jalisco, Michoacán, and Zacatecas—consistently appear among the top eight states sending Mexican migrants to the United States since the 1920s. It would not be venturesome to suggest that these same states will continue to be major providers of emigrants in the coming years.

The age-sex emigration rates in this study were calculated such that during 1975-80, 70 percent of the migration flow departs from the eight traditional core sending states and 30 percent from the balance of the country. This serves as a starting point, notwithstanding a December 1984 border survey of expelled migrants which could be interpreted to suggest that Guerrero and Sonora had displaced San Luis Potosí and Durango among the top eight states, dropping the core's contribution to 68.7 percent. However, the difference between 68.7 and 70 percent is small if we take into account possible estimation errors. And the geographical distribution recorded by the 1984 survey may be spurious, since it was based on interviews generated by migrants expelled during a short period—ten days—at a time of the year when the flow ebbs. Taking this into account, the estimates that identify our eight traditional sending states are a more certain guide. Even so, assuming that some of the top eight states that send emigrants to the United States had changed definitively, a like proportion (26-27 percent) of the national population would still be sending an almost identical proportion (68.7 to 70 percent) of emigrants.

Two additional reasons justify the current definition of region 1 and the assumed 70/30 split in migration to estimate base emigration rates for 1975-80. First, the "new" states identified in the 1984 survey, Guerrero and Sonora, are not new. Their rise to the top eight states could be the result of a fluctuation of migration volumes among states that contribute intermediate proportions of emigrants. The other reason requires distinguishing between a change in the geographical origin of migrants and geographic dispersion or deconcentration. Table 1 suggests that fluctuations have occurred in the principal areas that send migrants without substantial deconcentration of emigration.

Other data corroborate that Durango and San Luis Potosí have high incidence of emigration. A border survey of about 25,000 expelled migrants conducted during August 1978 showed that these eight states provided 73.6 percent of the migrants; a national household survey of 62,500 households conducted in 1979 generally corroborates this proportion approximately.[5] On the basis of these data we can be reasonably certain that the eight states in region 1 provided 70 percent of the emigration flow to the United

---

[5]For the 1978 border survey data, see Jorge A. Bustamante and Gerónimo Martínez G., "Undocumented Immigration from Mexico: Beyond Borders but Within Systems," *Journal of International Affairs* (33), p. 268. The national survey referred to (Encuesta Nacional de Emigración a la Frontera Norte del País y a los Estados Unidos, ENEFNEU) found that 71 percent of the migratory workers living in Mexico and working in the United States resided in a geographic area somewhat larger than the previously mentioned eight states. This geographic area is the sum of

States during the late 1970s and are likely to remain the principal source regions for the next few years.

One of the two sets of projections takes into account explicitly the possibility of a more rapid increase in the rates of emigration from the balance of Mexico than from the traditional core sending states. Geographical dispersion results to the extent that this occurs. That is, less than 70 percent of the emigration flow will originate in a region, such as region 1, with approximately 26 percent of the population. There is apparently little empirical basis for projecting a future deconcentration of emigration. The proportion of emigration of the top eight states has declined slowly (table 1), roughly concurrent to a decline in their combined relative demographic weight. Here the drastic change hypothesis assumes a rapid deconcentration of emigration—not because there is any basis to expect such a change, but because the estimation of the supply of migrants requires that we consider it an extreme case.

Projection Method

The regional population projections prepared for this paper are based on the component method. Fertility, mortality, and emigration rates or probabilities were estimated for both sexes, each age group, and each region, and then applied to a 1980 base population by five-year intervals until 2010. Emigration rates are region specific; i.e., estimates were made of the probability of emigrating from each region to the other two. These probabilities are estimated on the basis of 1975-80 data and a 1975 base population. The two different regional population projections adopted a single set of migration estimates during 1980-90. They adopted two different sets of assumptions regarding emigration to the United States during 1990-2010.

Both regional population projections were based on the same mortality and fertility assumptions of the population projections

---

regions I, II and III, as defined by in the ENEFNEU, and includes: all *municipios* (counties) that border the United States; the entire states of Jalisco, Michoacán, Colima, Guanajuato, Durango, Zacatecas, San Luis Potosí, Querétaro, Nayarit, and Aguascalientes; parts of the states of México, Guerrero, Hidalgo and the *municipio* of Ensenada, Baja California. It includes states and areas not contained within the eight states of our region 1, but excludes the nonborder *municipios* of Chihuahua. From: México, Secretaría del Trabajo y Previsión Social, Centro Nacional de Información y Estadísticas del Trabajo, *Los Trabajadores Mexicanos en Estados Unidos; Resultados de la Encuesta Nacional de Emigración a la Frontera Norte del País y a los Estados Unidos* (Mexico City: STyPS), p. 90.

prepared as a joint effort by INEGI and CONAPO for the period 1980-2010.[6] This effort took into account state variations of mortality and fertility and adopted assumptions regarding net migration between each state and the rest of the country. Though these projections present population estimates by age and sex for each Mexican state, they are not regional projections in the sense used here since the individual state totals are ex post facto distributions of a national projection. Nor was any effort made to project emigration among the various states. These population projections do, however, constitute the point of departure for the effort presented here and provide a useful basis of comparison.

For the entire 1980-2010 period, INEGI and CONAPO assumed a constant level of net emigration from Mexico of about 525,000 emigrant survivors at the end of each five-year projection period. (The term "emigrant survivors" is used to refer to the number of migrants estimated to have moved, taking into account mortality during the five-year period.) The estimate incorporates the net effects of the international migration of nationals and foreigners to and from Mexico. The precise estimate of the net migration of foreigners is unknown, but it is quite small relative to the net migration of Mexicans. This procedure thus implies a gradually declining age-specific emigration rate from Mexico to the United States and does not reflect foreseeable regional differentials in demographic composition and dynamics over the period. Similarly, it neglects to incorporate explicitly the foreseeable effects of changing volumes of return migration to Mexico as a result of the growth of the emigrant population in the United States. Though the authors of the INEGI-CONAPO population projections were aware of these limitations, they assumed that the effects of international migration on Mexico's national demography would be sufficiently small so that these assumptions would have little effect on the total population and its age-sex composition.

This paper does not assume a constant level of migration because it has different objectives. The intent of the INEGI-CONAPO projections was to forecast Mexico's population as accurately as possible. To that end, assuming similarity between the absolute volume of past and future net migration may be proper. (According to findings obtained subsequent to INEGI and CONAPO's study,

---

[6]México, Instituto Nacional de Estadística Geografía e Informática y Consejo Nacional de Población, *Proyecciones de la Población de México y de las Entidades Federativas: 1980-2010* (Mexico City: INEGI-CONAPO, 1985).

however, the numbers of the 1970s only serve as a rough approximation of the lower end of the estimates of net migration experienced during the 1980s.) In our regional projections, there is no intention to forecast. Rather, our intention is to analyze the effects that Mexico's demography might have on the supply of emigrants. Nevertheless, estimates from the constant rates hypothesis may provide a more accurate forecast than the INEGI-CONAPO projection upon which it is based.

INEGI and CONAPO assumed that the component of change most likely to affect population size is fertility. They adopted two fertility schedules: one low, the other high. The low fertility schedule, also referred to as the "planning hypothesis," assumes a drastic decline of fertility between 1980 and 2010 and reflects government targets regarding Mexican fertility behavior as a result of more extensive family planning and pressures toward smaller families. Accordingly, Mexico's national population reaches the target of slightly over 100 million by the year 2000.

A more realistic alternative is the high fertility schedule, which assumes a continued decline in fertility but slower than that in the "planning hypothesis." This projection, referred to as the "alternative hypothesis," results in nearly 104 million people by 2000. Both hypotheses employ the same mortality schedules. The regional population projections prepared for this paper adopted the mortality and fertility schedules of the "alternative hypothesis" because they are considered to be the more accurate estimate of components of change over the three-decade projection period.

Table 2 summarizes the fertility and mortality assumptions developed for the "alternative hypothesis." The total fertility rate for the 1980-85 interval was estimated at 4.4 for region 1 and 3.85 for region 2. These rates decline gradually to 2.81 and 2.68, respectively, and converge in the final projection interval, 2005-2010. Female life expectancy at birth was estimated at 70.86 years for region 1 and 70.34 for region 2. These expectancies were estimated to rise slowly to 76.78 and 77.06, respectively. A similar pattern of rising and converging life expectancies was estimated for males (table 2). Mortality for region 3 was assumed to be identical to that of region 1, in large part because precise levels of mortality of the Mexican-born population are unknown and also because the two levels are not likely to be very different.

As in the case of the fertility and mortality assumptions, our regional population projection adopted without modification the

Table 2. Summary of Fertility and Mortality Assumptions Used in Projection, 1980-2010.

	1980-85	1985-90	Projection Interval 1990-95	1995-00	2000-05	2005-10
Total fertility rates						
Region 1	4.402	3.520	3.053	2.875	2.827	2.807
Region 2	3.845	3.182	2.849	2.727	2.700	2.679
Life expectancy at birth (females)						
Region 1	70.86	72.48	73.85	75.01	75.98	76.78
Region 2	70.34	72.22	73.80	75.10	76.17	77.06
Life expectancy at birth (males)						
Region 1	65.14	66.36	67.89	68.95	69.02	70.57
Region 2	63.72	65.57	66.89	68.14	69.74	70.07

Source: Calculated by the author from: México, Instituto Nacional de Estadística, Geografía e Informática and Consejo Nacional de Población, *Proyecciones de la población de México y de las Entidades Federativas: 1980-2010* (Mexico City: INEGI-CONAPO, 1983); Sergio Camposortega Cruz, "Estimación de la mortalidad en México" unpublished manuscript, Consejo Nacional de Población, 1987.

INEGI-CONAPO estimates of the base 1980 population for regions 1 and 2. These population totals appear in the column for the year 1980 in table 9 and table 14, which summarize the results of our two regional projections.

Given that these regional population projections adopt the same 1980 base population and the same mortality and fertility schedules as the INEGI-CONAPO "alternative hypothesis" projection, any differences between the results obtained here and INEGI-CONAPO results are attributable to the effects of employing the regional population projection method and to the higher emigration rates that I adopt which translate into higher levels of net emigration.

The population estimate of region 3—the Mexican-born population resident in the United States, both documented and undocumented—is drawn from estimates of Robert Warren and Jeffrey Passel, who base their figures on 1980 U.S. census and INS data.[7] The corrections made on the U.S. census and INS data assume that nativity and citizenship misreporting understate the number of Mexican-born. A total of 2.5 million Mexican-born persons were estimated to reside in the United States in 1980 (see tables 20 and 21, below).

---

[7]Robert Warren and Jeffrey S. Passel, "A Count of the Uncountable: Estimates of Undocumented Aliens Counted in the 1980 United States Census," *Demography* 24 (August 1987): 375-393.

Six emigration schedules cover the permutations of emigration from each of the regions to the other two.

Assumptions Regarding Emigration to the United States

First we shall consider the data utilized to calculate forward emigration rates from regions 1 and 2 to region 3 during 1975-80. The Warren and Passel data used in table 3 is an acceptable estimate of Mexican-born residents that entered the United States during 1975-80. However, because these data do not tell us where these individuals resided in Mexico before emigrating, we allocate 70 percent of these to region 1 and 30 percent to region 2 (see table 3).

Table 3. Mexican-Born Immigrant Survivors in the United States (Region 3) Who Changed Residence during Previous Five Years (1980)

Age	\multicolumn{4}{c}{Absolute Number}	\multicolumn{2}{c}{Proportion}
	\multicolumn{2}{c}{Region 1}	\multicolumn{2}{c}{Region 2}	\multicolumn{2}{c}{Both regions}
	males	females	males	females	males	females
Total	328,916	268,648	140,963	115,136	1.0000	1.0000
0-4	23,222	22,411	9,952	9,605	0.0706	0.0834
5-9	31,469	29,975	13,487	12,846	0.0957	0.1116
10-14	27,499	26,912	11,785	11,534	0.0836	0.1002
15-19	50,614	37,893	21,692	16,240	0.1539	0.1411
20-24	78,086	53,180	33,466	22,791	0.2374	0.1980
25-29	49,011	36,300	21,005	15,557	0.1490	0.1351
30-34	27,623	22,337	11,839	9,573	0.0840	0.0831
35-39	15,198	12,345	6,514	5,291	0.0462	0.0460
40-44	9,817	8,101	4,207	3,472	0.0298	0.0302
45-49	6,208	5,625	2,660	2,411	0.0189	0.0209
50-54	3,947	4,550	1,691	1,950	0.0120	0.0169
55-59	2,764	3,162	1,184	1,355	0.0084	0.0118
60-64	1,453	2,092	623	896	0.0044	0.0078
65-69	861	1,471	369	631	0.0026	0.0055
70-74	546	987	234	423	0.0017	0.0037
75-79	341	641	146	275	0.0010	0.0024
80-84	167	389	71	167	0.0005	0.0014
85 +	90	277	38	119	0.0003	0.0010

Source: Robert Warren and Jeffrey S. Passel, unpublished tables, foreign-born counted in the 1980 census (documented and undocumented), 1987 and "A Count of the Uncountable."

Forward emigration probabilities from regions 1 and 2 to region 3 are thus calculated with these allocations in the numerator and the base age-sex populations of regions 1 and 2 in 1975 in the denominator. To arrive at the 1975 populations we took the 1980 population aged 5 and over, "revived" the 1975 population on the basis of 1975-80 mortality, and "returned" interregional migrants to their place of origin in 1975. To avoid underestimating emigration rates—given that the numerators are unadjusted estimates of emigration—the denominators similarly employed unadjusted census-based population estimates.

The first projection, based on the constant rates hypothesis, assumes that the age-sex-region specific emigration probabilities observed in 1975-80 remain constant between 1980 and 2010. This has the effect of estimating supply-driven interregional migration since the size of the regional populations and their changing age-sex composition determines the magnitude of the flows. Significantly, upper estimates of net Mexican migration to the United States during the 1980s are consistent with the results obtained holding the 1975-80 emigration rates constant during the decade.[8]

The second regional population projection, based on the drastic change hypothesis, adopts a number of assumptions regarding the future course of emigration to the United States during the interval 1980-2010. First, the observed emigration rates of 1975-80 are held constant during the decade of the 1980s, for the same reason stated for the constant rates hypothesis. This produces identical results for both hypotheses during 1980-90.

Second, the five-year period 1990-95 is treated as a transitional period of rapidly rising emigration probabilities from Mexico to the United States. The same rates held to apply between 1975 and 1990 are increased by 50 percent from region 1 to the United States and doubled from region 2 to the United States. This produces the beginnings of a hypothetical and rapid deconcentration of emigration toward region 2. The final emigration rates are held constant during the interval 1995-2010. Emigration probabilities from region 1 to the United States are double those observed or estimated for 1975-90. Emigration probabilities from region 2 to the United States are triple those observed during 1975-80. All other emigration rates (from the United States to regions 1 and 2 and between regions 1 and 2) are held at 1975-80 levels for the 1980-2010 period.

---

[8] In 1989 Karen Woodrow and Jeffrey Passel estimated the total of Mexican-born residing in the United States at 4,085,000 individuals, based on the Current Population Survey of June 1988. This unpublished estimate suggests that the rate of emigration from Mexico to the United States held practically constant throughout the 1980s. An extrapolation of this empirical estimate to 1990 would yield an estimate of Mexican-born in the United States less than 10 percent higher than that obtained by the constant rates hypothesis.

Return Migration Assumptions

The volume of net migration to the United States is, of course, also determined by return migration to regions 1 and 2. The rate of this migration can be calculated only very approximately. I have utilized an estimate developed by Virgilio Partida for an ongoing evaluation of the 1980 Mexican census.[9] He derives Mexican return migration as a residual of total changes of residence from abroad during 1975-80 as reported in the Mexican census, by age and sex, and aliens who changed residence from abroad to Mexico during the same interval. The age-sex composition of the latter migration flow was assumed to be the same as that obtained from an unpublished tabulation of the same population in 1970. The results appear in table 4.

Table 4. Estimate of Mexican-Born Survivors Who Returned from Region 3 (United States) during Five Years Prior to 1980 Census

	Females		Males	
Returnees to...	Region 1	Region 2	Region 1	Region 2
Total	35,444	15,190	48,969	20,987
Age at 1980				
0-4	0	0	0	0
5-9	4,055	1,737	3,232	1,385
10-14	3,412	1,462	2,720	1,166
15-19	3,693	1,582	3,591	1,539
20-24	5,314	2,277	6,737	2,887
25-29	6,097	2,613	9,753	4,179
30-34	4,673	2,002	7,478	3,204
35-39	2,638	1,130	5,375	2,303
40-44	1,484	636	3,525	1,511
45-49	1,066	457	2,261	969
50-54	1,029	441	1,493	639
55-59	763	327	1,025	439
60-64	462	198	650	278
65-69	305	131	406	174
70-74	189	81	242	103
75-79	105	45	217	93
80-84	83	35	130	55
85+	70	30	128	54

Source: Unpublished estimates of Virgilio Partida, El Colegio de México, Mexico City, 1989. The 70%/30% distribution is an assumption of the author (see text).

Internal Migration Assumptions

A primary obstacle in constructing the final two emigration schedules—the emigration rates from region 1 to region 2 and vice versa—was that the census underestimated the number of persons

---

[9]See note at end of table 4.

who changed residence during their lifetime. The census recorded about 8.98 million persons who stated that they had previously resided out of state. However, an additional 5.07 million—hardly a negligible number—reported that, although they had always resided where censused in 1980, they were born out of state. This category of population is referred to as "undeclared previous residence" in table 5.

Table 5. 1980 Mexican Population that Changed Residence from Out of State

Age	Total Movers	Undeclared Previous Residence	Declared Previous Residence Total	State in Region 1	State in Region 2	Out of Country
Total	14,048,467	5,068,575	8,979,892	2,469,021	5,912,008	598,863
0-4	740,694	367,345	373,349			
5-9	1,113,258	451,075	662,183			
10-14	1,213,706	461,703	752,003			
15-19	1,452,325	485,287	967,038			
20-24	1,633,070	512,554	1,120,516			
25-29	1,490,900	479,568	1,011,332			
30-34	1,280,456	430,596	849,860			
35-39	1,123,788	395,816	727,972			
40-44	911,250	331,809	579,441			
45-49	765,871	284,736	481,135			
50-54	624,567	233,852	390,715			
55-59	501,794	188,088	313,706			
60-64	363,013	135,695	227,318			
65+	833,775	310,451	523,324			

Source: Estimates of persons who declared change of residence derived from 1980 Mexican census of population, *Resumen General*, tables 37 and 39, with nonresponse cases distributed uniformly by author. Estimates of persons who did not declare change of residence derived from unpublished tabulation 1980 census, INEGI, SPP. This category refers to population born out of state who did not declare previous residence out of state.

To correct the census estimate of lifetime movers, the undeclared-residence group was distributed uniformly among all age-sex groups, among all lengths of previous residence (not shown in table 5), and among persons who reported a previous residence out of the country and among all states. This procedure yields a total of lifetime immigrant survivors in 1980 of slightly over 14 million.

The age distribution of migrants between regions 1 and 2 was calculated in several steps. As previously mentioned, movers of undeclared previous residence were distributed uniformly among all immigrant survivors who declared a previous out-of-state residence. Then the group of movers, by sex and state of residence in 1980, whose change of residence occurred during 1975-80 were separated from the total and consolidated in one group. The results of this operation, with states grouped into regions 1 and 2, appear on table 6.

Table 6. Immigrant Survivors from Out of State, 1975-80

Region Moved to by 1980 (all ages)

	Females		Males	
Region of previous residence (1975-80)	Region 1	Region 2	Region 1	Region 2
Total	568,006	2,073,778	648,391	2,040,426
Region 1	171,822	424,331	159,682	408,956
Region 2	311,664	1,550,960	308,689	1,497,867
Foreign country	84,520	98,487	180,020	133,603

	Females		Males	
Age distribution, inter-state immigrant survivors	Region 1	Region 2	Region 1	Region 2
Total	1.0000	1.0000	1.0000	1.0000
Age at 1980				
0-4	0.1255	0.1428	0.1119	0.1473
5-9	0.1362	0.1317	0.1208	0.1351
10-14	0.1040	0.1023	0.0876	0.0937
15-19	0.1303	0.1492	0.1079	0.1136
20-24	0.1454	0.1508	0.1453	0.1413
25-29	0.1046	0.1070	0.1195	0.1161
30-34	0.0707	0.0668	0.0878	0.0833
35-39	0.0488	0.0436	0.0654	0.0564
40-44	0.0325	0.0272	0.0465	0.0358
45-49	0.0245	0.0198	0.0334	0.0247
50-54	0.0199	0.0152	0.0238	0.0167
55-59	0.0157	0.0118	0.0167	0.0122
60-64	0.0125	0.0092	0.0116	0.0080
65-69	0.0103	0.0080	0.0081	0.0060
70-74	0.0083	0.0065	0.0061	0.0046
75-79	0.0056	0.0042	0.0042	0.0030
80-84	0.0032	0.0022	0.0022	0.0014
85+	0.0021	0.0013	0.0013	0.0008

Note: Surviving immigrants who, during previous five years, resided in region 1 or 2 and still reside in same region moved from out of state within region.

Source: Estimates by the author, based on tables 37 and 39, *Resumen General*, Mexican population census of 1980 and unpublished tabulation of INEGI regarding undeclared previous residence of migrants.

The numbers refer to out-of-state movers who changed residence during the five years prior to the 1980 census. For example, 568,006 females residing in region 1 in 1980 had resided out of state during the previous five years; 171,822 had resided in a state within region 1 itself (other than the state of residence at the time of the census); 311,664 had resided in a state in region 2; and 84,520 had moved to region 1 from out of the country. Female intraregional migration represented by out-of-state movers within region 1 is not of interest to this study and is therefore dropped. The same applies to female movers among states within region 2 and males who changed residence from out of state within either region 1 or region 2 (table 6).

The lower portion of table 6 summarizes the proportional distributions, by age and sex, of out-of-state immigrants into regions 1 and 2. There is considerable regularity in the age distribution of out-of-state immigrants. Within regions, the patterns are similar for males and females. The migration proportions of males are generally higher in the older age groups than for females.

To estimate emigrants by age and sex from regions 1 to 2 and vice versa, the age distribution for each sex, by immigrant group, was applied to the region-specific flow of which it is a part. Thus, the 311,664 females who were estimated to have changed residence from region 2 to region 1 in 1975-80 (table 6) are assumed to have the age distribution in that same column, which corresponds to all female immigrants to region 1 over the previous five years. This same procedure was applied for the other three sex-region groups.

The forward emigration rates for regions 1 and 2 utilize the above interregional migrants in the numerator and an estimate of the 1975 population (or births during 1975-80) by age, sex, and region in the denominator. The 1975 population was obtained in the same manner described for calculating forward emigration rates.

Temporary-worker Migration Assumptions

Distinguishing between migration which implies a change of residence, as discussed in all of the examples above, and the migration of temporary workers is essential. Change-of-residence migration of survivors refers to Mexicans who survived during the five-year projection period and resided in a different region at the end than at the beginning of the period. Defining change of residence in this manner fixes on the population's habitual residence at the beginning and at the end of the period; physical presence on those dates is not required in order to be considered usual residents.

Temporary-worker migration, as defined here, refers to the Mexican-born population that was physically present in the United States and employed at some point during the five-year projection interval, with or without documents, and whose usual residence at the end of the interval was in Mexico. Temporary workers could be absent from Mexico at the end of the interval as long as they still considered it their usual residence. The definition also includes persons who changed residence from the United States to Mexico during the interval—as long as they were employed at some point during the five years in the United States. (Including returning migrants in this group does not affect our population estimates by double-counting since temporary workers are not added or subtracted from change-of-residence migration.) The definition excludes persons employed in the United States during the interval whose usual residence at the end of the interval was not in Mexico.

The estimates of temporary-worker migration are based on the results of the national household survey of emigration conducted by CENIET (an agency of the Mexican Department of Labor and Social Welfare) in Mexico during December 1978 and January 1979. This survey, known as ENEFNEU, estimated the number of workers absent from Mexico and present in the United States as reported by relatives left behind, and also the number of workers who had been employed in the United States during the previous five years and were present in Mexico at the time of the survey. The sum of these two numbers is defined as the "total flow of Mexican migratory workers" during the projection interval. This sum in the numerator, and the 1979 Mexican population by age, sex, and region in the denominator were employed to calculate a participation rate. Since the rates are held constant throughout the projection period, the number of future migratory workers is a constant proportion of the Mexican population aged 15 and over, by age and sex, resident in regions 1 and 2 (see table 7).

RESULTS

The Impact of Emigration Flows on Mexico's Population

It may be appropriate at the outset to distinguish the results obtained from what this writer's forecast of future emigration levels would look like, and to do this by first considering the hypothetical

Table 7. Proportion of Mexicans Resident in Mexico Employed as Migratory Workers in the United States (Survivors in 1979)

Age	Females Region 1	Females Region 2	Males Region 1	Males Region 2
15-19	0.018874	0.003952	0.056082	0.011841
20-24	0.036226	0.006765	0.157874	0.032035
25-29	0.019579	0.003560	0.139161	0.026463
30-34	0.023879	0.004881	0.123078	0.022984
35-39	0.010737	0.002113	0.153340	0.030859
40-44	0.018322	0.004040	0.119596	0.025518
45-49	0.021629	0.004212	0.097333	0.019439
50-54	0.006525	0.001199	0.056111	0.010619
55-59	0.015604	0.003294	0.091920	0.018738
60-64	0.007637	0.001799	0.068764	0.014902

Source: Estimates based on Mexico, Secretaría del Trabajo y Previsión Social, Centro Nacional de Información y Estadísticas del Trabajo, *Los trabajadores mexicanos en Estados Unidos; resultados de la Encuesta Nacional de Emigración a la Frontera Norte del País y a los Estados Unidos* (Mexico City: STyPS, 1982), p. 78. Mexico, Secretaría del Trabajo y Previsión Social, Unidad Coordinadora de Políticas, Estudios y Estadísticas del Trabajo, Dirección de Estadísticas del Trabajo, *Encuesta Nacional de Emigración a la Frontera Norte del País y a los Estados Unidos de Norteamérica; Tabulaciones de la Boleta de Selección* (Mexico City: STyPS, 1984), pp. 54-65.

extremes. One extreme would assume that IRCA would stop undocumented immigration without allowing for a significant change in the net legal immigration—presently about 40-50,000 per year. INEGI-CONAPO estimated an average annual net flow of about 110,000 persons, which is at the lower end of the range of sample-based estimates of net migration, documented and undocumented, conducted in the 1980s. The constant rates hypothesis estimates an average annual net migration of varying magnitude which levels off at about 200,000 Mexican-born, which is at the upper end of the range of sample-based estimates. At the other extreme would be the drastic change hypothesis estimates which level off at somewhat under 500,000 Mexican-born per year.

Each of the extremes is unlikely, though for different reasons. The lower extreme is unlikely to occur solely because of IRCA enforcement, though it is conceivable that a severe and prolonged U.S. recession during the 1990s could reduce to about 50,000 the average annual net flow during the decade. The upper range would similarly require extraordinary circumstances: a several-fold increase in U.S. demand for Mexican labor over a few years, significant changes in immigration legislation which would permit much of that labor to enter legally, and substantial changes in both U.S. and Mexican attitudes toward Mexican immigration.

During the 1990s average annual net emigration levels between 50,000 and 100,000 at the low end, and 300,000 and 500,000 at the high end, may seem possible, but they are unlikely. Probable average annual net migration levels lie somewhere between 100,000 and 300,000; the INEGI-CONAPO estimate would be near the lower end of this speculative range and the constant rates hypothesis results would be at the middle. Results derived from the drastic change hypothesis starting in 1995 would lie outside of this range, though perhaps the estimate for the 1990-95 transition period—350,000—just exceeds the upper limit of probable flows.

Students of Mexican demography generally assume that fertility and mortality essentially determine the size and growth of the country's total population and that international migration has a negligible impact. Our regional population projection suggests that this view should be qualified. To be sure, fertility and mortality remain the most important variables determining overall population size and its growth during 1980-2010. However, emigration rates are less fixed than either those of mortality or fertility, and both mortality and fertility rates have declined while emigration rates have risen. Moderate swings in net migration levels can thus produce significantly larger degrees of uncertainty in current estimates of population.

To analyze the effects of different levels of net migration from Mexico to the United States, some of the results from both the constant rates and drastic change hypotheses are summarized and compared to similar estimates from the INEGI-CONAPO alternative hypothesis population projection in table 8. The mortality and fertility assumptions are identical in the three projections. What varies among them are emigration rates to the United States. Uncertainty in future migration levels translates to margins of error in future estimates of population stock and other components of change. Comparing the results of the INEGI-CONAPO projection with those of our constant rates hypothesis yields an approximate measure of this uncertainty.

In 1980 the three projections started with the same base population—almost 70 million. In 1990 there is a small difference of 834,000 persons between the INEGI-CONAPO estimate (86,154,000) and that of the constant rate and drastic change hypotheses. The direct effects of emigration—measured as the net emigration of survivors—and its indirect effects—the change in the number of births and deaths occurring due to emigration—explain the difference. During the 1980s, according to INEGI-CONAPO, there

Table 8. Comparisons of Population Stocks and Components of Change: INEGI-CONAPO Estimates and the Constant Rates and the Drastic Change Hypotheses (in thousands)

Population	1980	1985	1990	1995	2000	2005	2010
INEGI-CONAPO	69,655	77,938	86,154	94,781	103,996	113,570	123,158
Constant rates hypothesis	69,655	77,588	85,320	93,326	101,822	110,619	119,351
Drastic change hypothesis	69,655	77,588	85,320	92,452	99,098	105,969	112,705
Differences							
Constant rates hypothesis	0	-350	-834	-1,455	-2,174	-2,951	-3,807
Drastic change hypothesis	0	-350	-834	-2,329	-4,898	-7,601	-10,453

Births	1980-85	1985-90	1990-95	1995-2000	2000-05	2005-10
INEGI-CONAPO	11,124.6	11,057.5	11,559.1	12,309.9	12,892.8	13,193.3
Constant rates hypothesis	11,095.2	10,952.2	11,366.4	12,031.8	12,541.1	12,777.2
Drastic change hypothesis	11,095.2	10,952.2	11,300.6	11,762.9	12,022.5	12,064.9
Differences						
Constant rates hypothesis	-29.4	-105.3	-192.7	-278.1	-351.7	-416.1
Drastic change hypothesis	-29.4	-105.3	-258.5	-547.0	-870.3	-1,128.4

Deaths						
INEGI-CONAPO	2,316.7	2,316.2	2,406.8	2,568.4	2,792.7	3,078.3
Constant rates hypothesis	2,313.8	2,305.0	2,388.4	2,545.0	2,741.5	3,037.8
Drastic change hypothesis	2,313.8	2,305.0	2,385.2	2,523.8	2,692.7	2,961.8
Differences						
Constant rates hypothesis	-2.9	-11.2	-18.4	-23.4	-51.2	-41.5
Drastic change hypothesis	-2.9	-11.2	-21.6	-44.6	-100	-116.5

Source: Mexico, Instituto Nacional de Estadística, Geografía e Informatica y Consejo Nacional de Población, *Proyecciones de la población de México y de las Entidades Federativas: 1980-2010* (Mexico City: INEGI-CONAPO, 1985).

Table 8. Comparisons of Population Stocks and Components of Change: INEGI-CONAPO Estimates and the Constant Rates and the Drastic Change Hypotheses (in thousands) *(Continued)*

Natural growth					
INEGI-CONAPO	8,807.9	8,741.3	9,152.3	9,741.5	10,100.1	10,115.0
Constant rates hypothesis	8,781.4	8,647.2	8,978.0	9,486.8	9,799.6	9,740.4
Drastic change hypothesis	8,781.4	8,647.2	8,915.4	9,239.1	9,329.8	9,103.1
Differences						
Constant rates hypothesis	-26.5	-94.1	-174.3	-254.7	-300.5	-374.6
Drastic change hypothesis	-26.5	-94.1	-236.9	-502.4	-770.3	-1,011.9
Net Emigration (survivors)					
INEGI-CONAPO	524.8	525.3	525.8	526.1	526.4	526.6
Constant rates hypothesis	846.9	917.9	970.7	992.4	1,000.6	1,007.6
Drastic change hypothesis	846.9	917.9	1,782.2	2,592.5	2,459.4	2,367.1
Differences						
Constant rates hypothesis	322.1	392.6	444.9	466.3	474.2	481.0
Drastic change hypothesis	322.1	392.6	1,256.4	2,066.4	1,933.0	1,840.5
Growth					
INEGI-CONAPO	8,283	8,216	8,627	9,215	9,574	9,588
Constant rates hypothesis	7,933	7,732	8,006	8,496	8,797	8,732
Drastic change hypothesis	7,933	7,732	7,132	6,646	6,871	6,736
Differences						
Constant rates hypothesis	-350	-484	-621	-719	-777	-856
Drastic change hypothesis	-350	-484	-1,495	-2,569	-2,703	-2,852

Source: Mexico, Instituto Nacional de Estadística, Geografía e Informática y Consejo Nacional de Población, *Proyecciones de la población de México y de las Entidades Federativas: 1980-2010* (Mexico City: INEGI-CONAPO, 1985).

were 22,182,110 births, 4,632,900 deaths, and a net emigration of 1,050,100 persons, which imply a net increase in the stock of 16,499,100 persons. (The difference between the stocks actually estimated, 16,499,000, is due to rounding error.)

By contrast, the constant rates hypothesis yielded an estimated 22,047,400 births and 4,618,800 deaths, and net emigration of 1,764,000 persons (implying a growth of 15,663,800 persons—1,200 fewer than the difference between the 1980 and 1990 stocks, again due to rounding error). In sum, the difference between the estimates of net migration—714,700 during the 1980s—accounts for the bulk of the difference in growth (834,000) during the same interval. The direct effects of net emigration thus explain most of the diminished growth; indirect effects—134,700 fewer births, 14,100 fewer deaths—and rounding errors account for the rest.

INEGI-CONAPO's population estimate for 1990 may be inaccurate because net emigration during the 1980s may be underestimated, but comparing the components of change during the 1990s for INEGI-CONAPO and the constant rates hypothesis yields an approximate sense of the different effects of emigration. INEGI and CONAPO estimate, for example, that the population will grow by about 17,842,000 between 1990 and 2000, so that the national population will reach nearly 104 million by the end of the century. The constant rates hypothesis results are lower—the growth is estimated at 16,502,000 and the population at nearly 102 million.

The difference in growth of 1,340,000 persons during the 1990s is due entirely to emigration (including the delayed effects of 1980s migration in the form of smaller stocks). Most of the growth (911,200) is attributable to the higher net migration of survivors under the constant rates hypothesis. However, it also estimates indirect effects—470,800 fewer births and 29,600 fewer deaths than INEGI-CONAPO. Put another way, the difference in population stock reached in the year 2000 between a low emigration hypothesis (INEGI-CONAPO) and a medium-level hypothesis (constant rates) is about 1.3 million persons. Of this difference, about two-thirds is attributable to the direct effects of higher emigration volumes; the remaining third is due to a lower natural growth rate because significant numbers of women of child-bearing age and their husbands have left.

The drastic change hypothesis, as previously mentioned, is an extreme case where net emigration exceeds considerably even the highest likely levels expected for the 1990s. It is useful to note, however, the implied demographic effects of the drastic change hypothesis on the national population between 1990 and 2000. According to table 8 there would be 4.9 million fewer persons in Mexico than estimated by INEGI-CONAPO (although at least 834,000 of that difference is explicitly attributable to an INEGI-CONAPO underestimate of emigration during the 1980s). According to the drastic change hypothesis, Mexico's net growth during the 1990s would be 4,064,000 less than INEGI's, of which 3,322,800 is due to the net migration of survivors. Under these conditions, the national population in 2000 would reach 99 million—a figure lower even than the "planning fertility hypothesis" employed in the INEGI-CONAPO projections (but not presented in table 8). This estimate of net growth—4 million lower than the INEGI figure in the 1990s—is probably an overestimate of the uncertainty that could be expected due to high emigration volumes since the drastic change hypothesis is itself unlikely.

It may be surprising then that obtaining accurate estimates of net emigration during the 1980s and 1990s may be as important to Mexico's makers of population policy as monitoring fertility decline. The uncertainty in estimates of net emigration during the 1990s—perhaps as much as 200,000 annually—could produce an uncertainty in the estimate of the total population in 2000 of nearly three million persons.

Examining the age structure of the population in Mexico clarifies demographic consequences of high levels of emigration, declining fertility and declining mortality. In table 9 the composition of both sexes is presented for broad age groups: children (0-14 years old), young adult working-age (15-44), older adult working age (45-64), and the population 65 and over, which is excluded from our discussion of working-age population. These age groups are useful also because the young adult group includes both women of child-bearing age and persons of both sexes who have the highest rates of emigration to the United States.

During the projection period Mexico will experience continued declining fertility, concurrent with dramatic adult population growth because of high birth rates during past decades. The estimates of stock provided by the constant rates hypothesis best illustrate the effects of these contradictory pressures on the country as a whole. The combination of rapidly declining fertility and the increasing number of potential parents produces a slow and uneven growth in the number of births—from 11.1 million in 1980-85 to nearly 12.8 million in 2005-10 (table 10). The population of children

Table 9. Mexican Population Projection, 1980-2010. The Constant Emigration Rates Hypothesis (both sexes)

Absolute numbers in thousands

	1980	1985	1990	1995	2000	2005	2010
Total	69,655	77,588	85,320	93,326	101,822	110,619	119,351
Age							
0-14	30,809	31,323	30,637	30,837	31,975	33,737	35,335
15-44	29,617	35,398	41,752	46,942	51,131	54,200	56,615
45-64	6,917	8,174	9,672	11,586	13,916	16,952	20,547
65+	2,312	2,693	3,259	3,961	4,800	5,730	6,854

Source: Population projection of the author.

(0-14 age group) grows accordingly—from 30.8 million in 1980 to 35.3 million in 2010 (table 9)—a mere 15 percent in the thirty-year period (table 11). The absolute increases and average annual growth estimated for that age group during the period 1980-2010, however, represent the uneven growth more clearly.

During the 1980s, the child population declined slightly according to these estimates. (A decline of 686,000 in 1985-90 offset the growth of 514,000 in 1980-85, according to table 12). In the first decade of the twenty-first century, it is estimated that this population will grow by more than 1.5 million per five-year period. The average annual growth according to these estimates will fluctuate between -0.4 percent and 1.1 percent (table 13).

Table 10. Mexican Population Projection, 1980-2010. The Constant Rates Hypothesis Summary of Mexico's Components of Change (both sexes)

Births, deaths, and net migration of survivors during five-year interval in thousands

	1980-1985	1985-1990	1990-1995	1995-2000	2000-2005	2005-2010
Net growth	7,934.4	7,729.3	8,007.3	8,494.4	8,799.1	8,732.8
Births	11,095.2	10,952.2	11,366.4	12,031.8	12,541.1	12,777.2
Deaths	2,313.8	2,305.0	2,388.4	2,545.0	2,741.5	3,036.8
Natural growth	8,781.3	8,647.2	8,978.0	9,486.8	9,799.7	9,740.4
Surviving emigrants to the United States	1,012.8	1,132.7	1,234.2	1,301.7	1,348.9	1,388.3
Surviving returnees	165.8	214.9	263.4	309.1	348.3	380.7
Net migration survivors	-846.9	-917.9	-970.7	-992.4	-1,000.6	-1,007.6

Source: Population projection by the author.
Note: Numbers rounded independently.

Table 11. Mexican Population Projection, 1980-2010. The Constant Emigration Rates Hypothesis Summary of Mexico's Population Change (both sexes)

Relative proportions (1980 = 1.00)

	1980	1985	1990	1995	2000	2005	2010
Total	1.00	1.11	1.22	1.34	1.46	1.59	1.71
Age							
0-14	1.00	1.02	0.99	1.00	1.04	1.10	1.15
15-44	1.00	1.20	1.41	1.58	1.73	1.83	1.91
45-64	1.00	1.18	1.40	1.68	2.01	2.45	2.97
65+	1.00	1.16	1.41	1.71	2.08	2.48	2.96

Source: Table 9.

Table 12. Mexican Population Projection, 1980-2010. The Constant Emigration Rates Hypothesis Summary of Mexico's Population Change (both sexes)

Absolute increase during five-year interval in thousands

	1980-1985	1985-1990	1990-1995	1995-2000	2000-2005	2005-2010
Total	7,933	7,732	8,006	8,496	8,797	8,732
Age						
0-14	514	-686	200	1,138	1,762	1,598
15-44	5,781	6,354	5,190	4,189	3,069	2,415
45-64	1,257	1,498	1,914	2,330	3,086	3,595
65+	381	566	702	839	930	1,124

Source: Table 9.
Note: Numbers rounded independently.

Table 13. Mexican Population Projection, 1980-2010. The Constant Emigration Rates Hypothesis Summary of Mexico's Population Change (both sexes)

Percentage of average annual growth during five-year interval

	1980-1985	1985-1990	1990-1995	1995-2000	2000-2005	2005-2010
Average, all ages	2.18	1.92	1.81	1.76	1.67	1.53
Age						
0-14	0.33	-0.44	0.13	0.73	1.08	0.93
15-44	3.63	3.36	2.37	1.72	1.17	0.88
45-64	3.40	3.42	3.68	3.73	4.03	3.92
65+	3.10	3.89	3.98	3.92	3.61	3.65

Source: Table 9.

A similar pattern holds under the scenario of "drastic change," with the recovery of growth in the population of children occurring later and slower (tables 14, 15, 16, and 17). We shall return to this point when we discuss, at the regional level, the effects of high net emigration on the number of births.

Table 14. Mexican Population Projection, 1980-2010. The Drastic Change Hypothesis (both sexes)

Absolute numbers in thousands

	1980	1985	1990	1995	2000	2005	2010
Total	69,655	77,588	85,320	92,452	99,098	105,969	112,705
Age
0-14	30,809	31,323	30,637	30,620	31,260	32,402	33,342
15-44	29,617	35,398	41,752	46,340	49,325	51,316	52,753
45-64	6,917	8,174	9,672	11,540	13,745	16,587	19,875
65+	2,312	2,693	3,259	3,952	4,768	5,664	6,735

Source: Population projection by the author.
Note: Numbers rounded independently.

Table 15. Mexican Population Projection, 1980-2010. The Drastic Change Hypothesis Summary of Mexico's Population Change (both sexes)

Relative proportions (1980 = 1.00)

	1980	1985	1990	1995	2000	2005	2010
Total	1.00	1.11	1.22	1.33	1.42	1.52	1.62
Age
0-14	1.00	1.02	0.99	0.99	1.01	1.05	1.08
15-44	1.00	1.20	1.41	1.56	1.67	1.73	1.78
45-64	1.00	1.18	1.40	1.67	1.99	2.40	2.87
65+	1.00	1.16	1.41	1.71	2.06	2.45	2.91

Source: Table 14.

Table 16. Mexican Population Projection, 1980-2010. The Drastic Change Hypothesis Summary of Mexico's Population Change (both sexes)

Absolute increase during five-year interval in thousands

	1980-1985	1985-1990	1990-1995	1995-2000	2000-2005	2005-2010
Total	7,933	7,732	7,132	6,646	6,871	6,736
Age
0-14	514	-686	-17	640	1,142	940
15-44	5,781	6,354	4,588	2,985	1,991	1,437
45-64	1,257	1,498	1,868	2,205	2,842	3,288
65+	381	566	693	816	896	1,071

Source: Table 14.
Note: Numbers rounded independently.

By contrast to the youngest population, the adult working-age population will grow explosively. Under the constant rates hypothesis, between 1980 and 2010 the 15-44 year-old population will nearly double; that aged 45-64 will almost triple (table 11). Under the drastic change hypothesis—which assumes extremely high levels of net emigration in the late 1990s and early twenty-first century—

Table 17. Mexican Population Projection, 1980-2010. The Drastic Change Hypothesis Summary of Mexico's Population Change (both sexes)

Percentage of average annual growth during five-year interval

	1980-1985	1985-1990	1990-1995	1995-2000	2000-2005	2005-2010
Average, all ages	2.18	1.92	1.81	1.76	1.67	1.53
Age						
0-14	0.33	-0.44	-0.01	0.41	0.72	0.57
15-44	3.63	3.36	2.11	1.26	0.79	0.55
45-64	3.40	3.42	3.59	3.56	3.83	3.68
65+	3.10	3.89	3.93	3.83	3.50	3.52

Source: Table 14.

the 15-44 year-old group grows by 78 percent, and the 45-64 year-old group by 187 percent. Even improbably high net emigration to the United States cannot prevent this group's rapid national growth.

Figure 1, which presents various estimates under the constant rates hypothesis, shows that the national 15-44 year-old population will grow most quickly between 1980 and 1995, as do tables 12, 13, 16, and 16. Under both hypotheses, between 1980 and 1995 this group's growth has been and will continue to be about five million persons every five years; the average annual growth rate is estimated to decline from 3.5 percent in 1980-85 to about 2.1-2.4 percent in 1990-95—still quite high. Thereafter, growth should taper to between 1.4 and 2.4 million persons in 2005-10. At the national level, then, the average annual growth of the 15-44 age group can be expected to slow, mostly due to past declines in fertility, from 3.6 percent in 1980-85 to less than 1 percent in 2005-10.

It may be concluded, then, that the 15-44 age group in Mexico will continue to record moderate but declining rates of growth in the 1990s and first decade of the twenty-first century, provided emigration remains at levels comparable to those of the late 1980s or concentrated in the traditional core sending region or other region of comparable size (constant rates hypothesis). However, if emigration rose to the extreme and dispersed to the degree contemplated under the drastic change hypothesis, the absolute increases in population aged 15-44 after 1995 would plummet to less than half of the increases that occurred fifteen years earlier.

Under the constant rates hypothesis, region 2 will grow considerably more rapidly than region 1, due partly to net migra-

Figure 1. Population of Mexico, 1980-2010 Region 1 and 15-44 age-group eomparisons

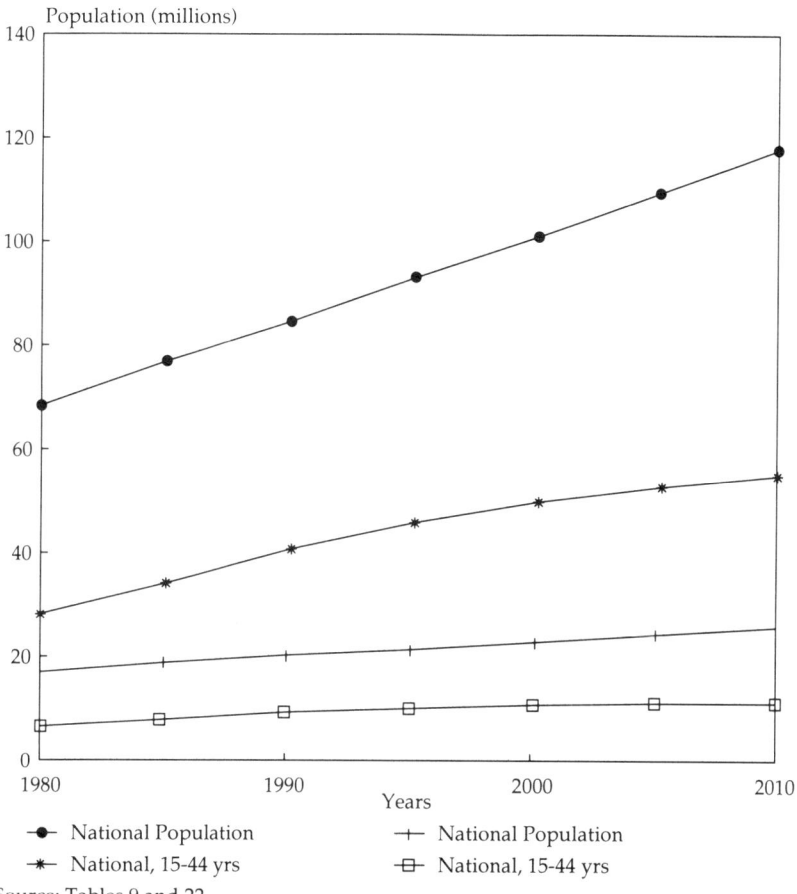

Population (millions)

- ●— National Population
- ✳— National, 15-44 yrs
- ╋— National Population
- ⊟— National, 15-44 yrs

Source: Tables 9 and 22.

tion between region 2 and region 1, but mostly to differences in natural growth and net emigration to the United States. Natural growth in region 1 in absolute terms is expected to decrease unevenly, from 2.4 million to 2.3 million, between 1980-85 and 2005-10 (table 20), contributing to the slow population growth trend observable in figure 1. The natural growth of region 2, by contrast, will probably rise—from 6.4 million persons in the first projection interval to 7.5 million in the last (table 19). The growth of the stock, which considers the net migration of survivors, shows similar regional differences (tables 18 and 19). This is also observable in figure 1, which shows that the population in region 1 grows hardly at all as opposed to a marked rise for the country as a whole.

Consequently, the share of the national population in region 1 declines from 26.1 percent in 1980 to 24.9 percent in 1990 and 23.7 percent in 2000.

Table 18. Mexican Population Projection, 1980-2010. The Constant Rates Hypothesis Summary of Region 1 Components of Change (both sexes)

Births, deaths, and net migration of survivors during five-year interval in thousands

	1980-1985	1985-1990	1990-1995	1995-2000	2000-2005	2005-2010
Net growth	1,615.2	1,434.2	1,412.1	1,476.8	1,508.8	1,512.7
Births	3,027.3	2,877.8	2,870.6	2,942.1	3,000.4	3,001.0
Deaths	600.3	597.3	604.2	634.5	700.0	740.0
Natural growth	2,427.0	2,280.6	2,266.3	2,307.5	2,300.4	2,261.1
Surviving stayers	18,917.5	20,224.2	21,507.7	22,864.2	24,264.6	25,679.2
Surviving emigrants	1,664.0	1,826.0	1,962.3	2,059.3	2,128.5	2,183.3
Surviving immigrants	852.1	979.6	1,108.1	1,228.4	1,336.9	1,435.0
Net migration survivors	-811.9	-846.4	-854.2	-830.9	-791.6	-748.3

Source: Population projection of the author.

Note: Numbers rounded independently.

Note: Region 1 comprises the States of Baja California, Chihuahua, Durango, Guanajuato, Jalisco, Michoacán, San Luis Potosí, and Zacatecas.

Table 19. Mexican Population Projection, 1980-2010. The Constant Emigration Rates Hypothesis Summary of Components of Change (both sexes) Region 2

Births, deaths and net migration of survivors during five-year interval in thousands

	1980-1985	1985-1990	1990-1995	1995-2000	2000-2005	2005-2010
Net growth	6,319.3	6,295.2	6,595.1	7,017.6	7,290.1	7,220.0
Births	8,067.8	8,074.3	8,495.8	9,089.7	9,540.7	9,776.1
Deaths	1,713.6	1,707.7	1,784.3	1,910.4	2,041.5	2,296.8
growth	6,354.4	6,366.6	6,711.6	7,179.3	7,499.3	7,479.3
Surviving stayers	56,810.0	63,005.9	69,512.1	76,456.2	83,688.8	90,861.6
Surviving emigrants	1,045.0	1,180.5	1,314.6	1,433.2	1,538.2	1,635.8
Surviving immigrants	1,009.9	1,109.1	1,198.0	1,271.6	1,329.2	1,376.5
Net migration survivors	-35.1	-71.4	-116.5	-161.7	-209.2	-259.3

Source: Population projection of the author.

Note: Numbers rounded independently. Region 2 comprises the twenty-four states of Mexico not in Region 1.

The Mexican-born Population in the United States

Perhaps the most direct measure of supply of emigrants is the stock of Mexican immigrants residing in the United States at various points in time. Both the constant rates and drastic change hypotheses estimate the stock of Mexicans resident in the United States—documented and undocumented combined—at 2.5 million in 1980 and 4.1 million in 1990. After 1990, however, the two hypotheses diverge. The constant rates hypothesis results in 5.8 million Mexican-born U.S. residents in the year 2000 and nearly 7.5 million in 2010 (table 20). The drastic change hypothesis produces higher numbers—8.2 million Mexican-born residents in the United States in 2000 and 12.6 million in 2010 (table 21). In this extreme case, the United Sates would have almost as many Mexican-born residents in 2010 as it had foreign-born of all nationalities in 1980.

The supply of Mexican emigrants to the United States estimated for the 1990s and early twenty-first century seems high compared

Table 20. Mexican Population Projection, 1980-2010. The Constant Emigration Rates Hypothesis Summary of Population Change, Mexican-born in the U.S. (both sexes)

Absolute numbers in thousands

	1980	1985	1990	1995	2000	2005	2010
Total	2,531	3,287	4,103	4,959	5,819	6,658	7,470
Age							
0-14	377	424	424	423	425	439	457
15-44	1,616	2,204	2,839	3,420	3,894	4,215	4,410
45-64	355	476	624	865	1,187	1,604	2,084
65+	183	183	216	251	314	400	520

Source: Population projection of the author.

Table 21. Mexican Population Projection, 1980-2010. The Drastic Change Hypothesis Summary of Population Change, Mexican-born in the U.S. (both sexes)

Absolute numbers in thousands

	1980	1985	1990	1995	2000	2005	2010
Total	2,531	3,287	4,103	5,771	8,223	10,492	12,613
Age							
0-14	377	424	424	578	820	957	1,007
15-44	1,616	2,204	2,839	4,023	5,699	7,099	8,211
45-64	355	476	624	911	1,357	1,969	2,756
65+	183	183	216	259	346	467	639

Note: The above population estimate corresponds to the total Mexican-born population resident in the United States regardless of immigration status.

to the size of the Mexican-born population as recently as 1980. Even the more probable scenario of the constant rates hypothesis yields rather high estimates of the supply of Mexican immigrants. The increase of total stock during the 1990s—from 4.1 to 5.8 million—is about two-thirds of the entire stock of Mexican-born residents in 1980.

Though these numbers seem large by current standards, the drastic change hypothesis leads to a much larger estimate of the supply of Mexican immigrants: the Mexican-born population would grow by 1.7 million during 1990-95 and an additional 2.5 million in 1995-2000. Under conditions of the constant rates hypothesis, 5.4 percent of the Mexican population would be resident in the United States in the year 2000—a proportion approaching the historical maximum estimated for 1930.[10] Under conditions of the drastic change hypothesis, nearly 7.7 percent of Mexico's population would reside in the United States in 2000—a proportion well above the historical maximum.

These estimates of the supply of 5.8 to 8.2 million Mexican-born emigrants in the year 2000 cannot be taken as a forecast of probable stocks in the United States without considering some of the conditions necessary for such stocks to actually emerge.

First, in order for the constant rates hypothesis to hold, demand for Mexican labor would have to remain about the same and future enforcement of immigration laws would have to accommodate net flows of the magnitude observed in the late 1980s. This could either occur as a result of legalizing an increasing proportion of new migrants or of tolerating net flows of about 200,000 mostly undocumented Mexicans. For the drastic change hypothesis to hold, demand would have to grow sharply throughout the 1990s—from 200,000 to about 500,000 per year. The obstacles and conditions of the constant rates hypothesis also apply here, though they would of course be more difficult to meet.

Second, even if the U.S. economy actually demanded comparable numbers of Mexican workers, and even if government regulation of the border and of the labor market could accommodate

---

[10]The 1930 Mexican population census recorded 16,553,000 persons in Mexican national territory. The U.S. census of the same year recorded 641,000 Mexican-born, though some analysts suggest that, due to nativity reporting errors in that census, the correct number should be about one million. This implies a total Mexican population of about 17,553,000 in 1930, not taking into account underenumeration in the Mexican census.

flows of these magnitudes, it is still questionable that U.S. society would accept this influx of Mexicans without demanding additional measures to restrict the flow. Concerns that surfaced during the debate leading to the adoption of IRCA persist—about the use of languages other than English and the growth of the foreign-born population. And there is the perennial association of immigration in the mind of the U.S. public with crime, loss of jobs, lower wages, rising welfare costs, and other social ills. Even if labor demand increases sharply, estimates of 8.2 million Mexican-born in the United States in 2000 and 12.6 million in 2010, as suggested by the drastic change hypothesis, are not realistic in the face of general and active public hostility to the growth of the Mexican-born population in the United States. Similarly, it is doubtful that Mexican polity and society would complacently accept a massive outflow of emigrants.

Third, in both the constant rates and the drastic change hypotheses the estimates of net flow are too large to be accommodated by existing U.S. legislation. If those numbers are a guide to the actual magnitude of future flows, the United States would either have to tolerate large flows of undocumented workers or change immigration laws substantially to allow for a drastic increase in legal flows of residents. Otherwise net migration flows would have to fall substantially below the numbers arrived at under the constant rates hypothesis. In that event, because of declining demand induced either by the economy or by IRCA enforcement, emigration rates to the United States would have to decline from levels observed during the 1980s.

Finally, the initial point is worth reiterating: the supply of emigrants to the United States can grow substantially during the remainder of this century, even without going as far as the drastic change hypothesis. Indeed, emigration could grow beyond the capacity of the political system of either the United States or Mexico to accept it.

The extraordinary conditions in the United States and Mexico necessary to produce flows approaching the levels of the drastic change hypothesis suggest how far off the mark the recent U.S. debate on the number of undocumented Mexican immigrants has been. Even under extraordinary and unlikely assumptions, a stock of 8 million or so Mexican-born persons, including legal immigrants, is out of reach until the end of the century. But in policy circles during the late 1970s, and in the popular press still in the late 1980s, it was not unusual to assert that average annual net undocumented Mexican immigration approached 500,000 and that the bulk of supposedly 4 to 12 million undocumented aliens was composed of Mexicans residing in the United States. Indeed, one study contracted and paid for in 1975 by the U.S. government estimated that there were 8 million undocumented Mexican in the country at that time.

Potential Limits on the Supply of Emigrants

Another way to analyze the supply of emigrants is to examine its growth via net migration flows. To this end we focus on the size of the population groups most likely to emigrate: young adults in the 15-44 age group.

Earlier we discussed the positive, though decelerating growth of the 15-44 age group for the country as a whole (figure 1, above). However, since 70 percent of the emigration is estimated to originate in region 1, it is the trend of that region for the most part, rather than of the country as a whole, which will probably influence the supply of emigrants. As figure 1 shows, the growth of the 15-44 age group in region 1 is practically nonexistent when compared to that of the same age group in the national population. This group grows by 70 percent during 1980-2010 in region 1, as opposed to 91 percent for the country as a whole. Average annual growth rates start at a lower level in 1980-85—3.3 percent in region 1 as opposed to 3.6 percent for the country as a whole—and drop to lower levels by 2005-10—0.5 percent as opposed to 0.9 percent. These data can be found in tables 11, 13, 22, and 23. Hence a clear trend: though each new age cohort that enters the group of young adults is still larger than the previous groups, the increment is progressively smaller.

The relative weight of past fertility decline and present emigration is a key issue in determining this trend. Fertility decline could either result from high levels of net emigration, thereby cutting substantially into the natural growth of cohorts, or alternatively produce weak growth in the size of successive cohorts and translate into diminishing increases in the supply of emigrants.

Examining how net migration between region 1 and the rest of the country and the United States affects increases in the stock of persons aged 15-44 could answer this. The absolute increase of this age group in region 1 for each five-year interval is presented in table 24; these increments decline from 1,288,000 persons in 1980-85 to 294,000 in 2005-10. But net emigration from region 1 to region 2 also declines, from 125,900 in 1980-85 to 75,800 in 2005-10. So obviously net internal migration is not contributing to the slowing down of population growth of this age group in region 1.

By contrast, the net migration of persons in the same age group to the United States does increase slowly from 405,500 in 1980-85 to 476,500 in 2005-10, but this increase is miniscule; it does not explain the slowing down of the growth of the 15-44 age group in region 1. Indeed, one might note that the slow-growing net emigration to the United States from region 1 is partially offset by decreasing net emigration to region 2.

The slowing growth of the 15-44 age group in region 1, then, is attributable mostly to a declining number of births two decades earlier. This deceleration is large and meaningful. The differences in the demographic dynamics between the traditional core spending region and the rest of the country during 1990-2010 could restrict the growth of the supply of emigrants to the United States below expectations based on national demographic trends.

Figure 2 illustrates the impact of this growth in the stock of 15-44 year olds in region 1 (see the constant rates hypothesis: emigration to the United States). The number of emigrants begins to level off during 1990-95, at nearly 250,000. The number is estimated to continue to increase—to nearly 280,000 in 2005-10, but the post-1995 growth is hardly spectacular. Since emigration rates are held constant, this pattern of declining growth is entirely attributable to a slowing down in the growth of the young adult population, especially in region 1, during the 1990s and first decade of the twenty-first century, as described in figure 1.

The feeble but positive growth of emigration leads to a leveling of net migration to the United States: as the emigrant population grows in the United States, from about 2.5 million in 1980 to 4.1 million in 1990, and subsequently to 5.8 million in 2000 and 7.5 million in 2010 (table 20), return migration to Mexico grows at approximately the same rate (return migration rates are held constant) and return migration eventually offsets much of the growth of emigration from Mexico to the United States (see figure 2). Return migration grows from 33,500 in 1980-85 to 76,800 in 2005-10. Consequently, average annual net migration to the United States

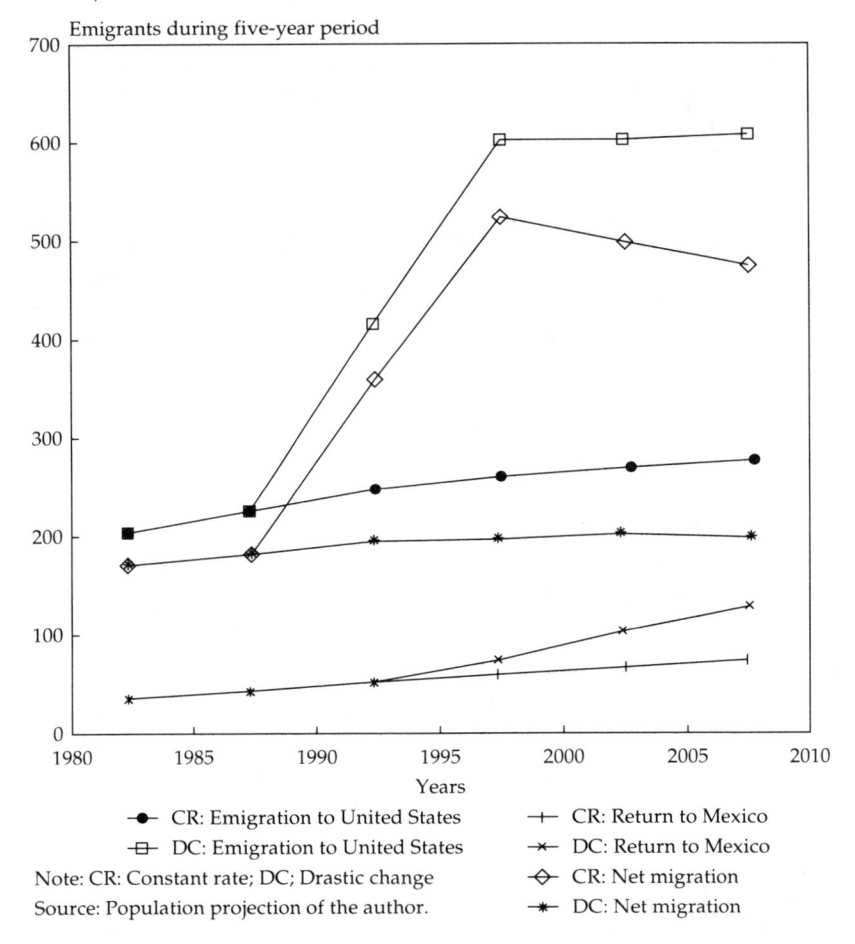

Figure 2. Average Annual Emigration between Mexico and the United States, 1980-2010

Emigrants during five-year period

- ●— CR: Emigration to United States
- ◻— DC: Emigration to United States
- ╋— CR: Return to Mexico
- ✶— DC: Return to Mexico
- ◇— CR: Net migration
- ✱— DC: Net migration

Note: CR: Constant rate; DC; Drastic change
Source: Population projection of the author.

approaches 195,300 in 1990 and continues to grow at a snail's pace over the next fifteen years to 202,400.

For all practical purposes, holding 1975-80 emigration rates constant limits growth of the supply of emigrants, in terms of annual net migration, to about 200,000, only slightly more than estimations of about 185,000 for 1985-90. Put another way, though the total Mexican working-age population (15-64 years old) will grow rapidly well into the twenty-first century, the population likely to emigrate to the United States will probably not grow much after 1995. If the conditions of the constant rates hypothesis hold, the specific regional dynamics of the 15-44 age group and foreseeable increases in return migration to Mexico can produce a ceiling on the growth of the supply of emigrants at a level only slightly higher than that experienced in the late 1980s.

This analysis, of course, rests upon the two key assumptions of the constant rates hypothesis: constant emigration rates and a geographical concentration of emigration in the eight traditional sending states that comprise region 1. The proportion of emigration from region 1 would fall gradually if the constant rates hypothesis proved correct, from 69.4 percent in 1980-85 to 66.3 percent in 2005-2010. This would occur, as discussed above, because the proportion of the population in region 1 also declines.

The drastic change hypothesis was developed to see the effects of drastically altered assumptions. Figure 2, above, shows the effects if emigration rates to the United States between 1985-90 and 1995-2000 doubled for region 1 and tripled for region 2. Average annual emigration, of course, rises over 160 percent, from slightly over 225,000 in 1985-90 to about 600,000 in 1995-2000. Average annual net migration to the United States rises almost as quickly, peaks at 521,500 during 1995-2000, and declines slowly thereafter to about 475,000. This decline in the twenty-first century is entirely attributable to the sharply rising flow of return migration to Mexico due to the application of constant return migration rates to a rapidly increasing population of Mexican-born in the United States. Return flow grows from 53,400 in 1985-90 to 131,200 in 2005-10 (figure 2). Under the drastic change hypothesis, then, the growth of supply would appear to have the rather high ceiling of about 500,000 "net emigrants" annually.

The results associated with the drastic change show, in a manner that those of the constant rates hypothesis could not, that the annual net migration "ceiling" of 200,000 previously mentioned is somewhat arbitrary. However, as we have seen, an accelerated growth of supply will not result automatically from a fast-growing working-age population in the nation because the population in the specific ages and region exposed to high risks of emigrating will grow quite slowly. If the growth in the supply of emigrants rises substantially above 200,000 net migrants annually, it will be driven by rising emigration rates. The ceiling may be arbitrary, but large, sustained increases in emigration rates are not easily attained, nor can they be expected to occur without limit.

The net flows between region 1 and the United States and region 2 and the United States are summarized in figure 3. It shows that during the 1980s, net migration from region 1 to region 3 constitutes the bulk of net migration from Mexico to the United States (e.g., 127,100 out of 184,900 average annual net migration during 1985-1990). Due to the assumptions adopted under the drastic change hypothesis (region 2 emigration to the United States triples while region 1 doubles), to the different age structures of the two regions, and to the assumption that the bulk of the return migration continues to flow to region 1, the share of net emigration in region 2 rises dramatically. In 1995-2000, when estimated net migration is 521,500 annually, the contribution in region 1 (291,800) is large, but region 2's relative weight has increased substantially (figure 3). By the early twenty-first century, region 1 would contribute only slightly over 50 percent of the net migration to the United States.

Figure 3. Net Migration, Regions 1 and 2 to the United States (Drastic change hypothesis estimates)

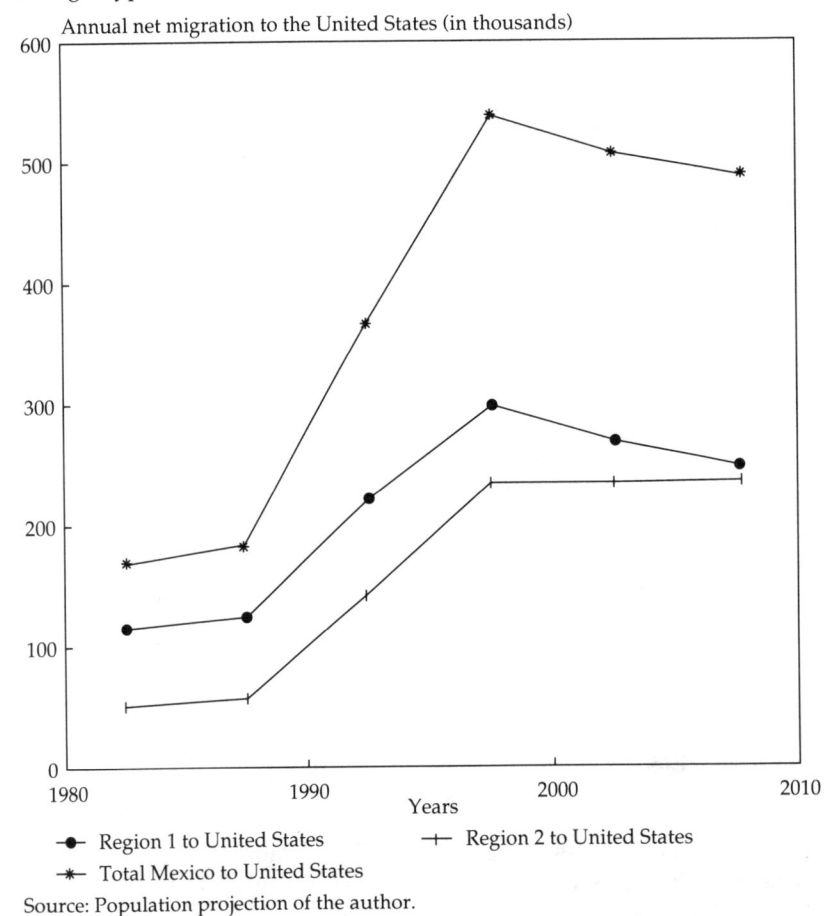

Annual net migration to the United States (in thousands)

─●─ Region 1 to United States ─+─ Region 2 to United States
─*─ Total Mexico to United States

Source: Population projection of the author.

Previously we considered the effects of a growing working-age population on the growth of the supply of emigrants. The drastic change hypothesis allows examination of the reverse—how high levels of emigration can absorb the natural growth of the young adult population, especially in region 1. The effects of actually doubling emigration rates between 1985-1990 and 1995-2000 can be seen by comparing the 15-44 age group in tables 22 and 26. Under the constant rates hypothesis, this group is expected to continue to grow though slowly, after 1995—from 11 million to nearly 12.6 million in 2010. Under the drastic change hypothesis, however, this age group reaches 10.7 million in 1995 and never reaches 11 million, because large-scale net emigration siphons practically all of the growth that would have occurred. Though the growth of the group was expected to decelerate anyway, it was not expected to halt—the case if emigration rates rose to levels assumed under the drastic change hypothesis.

Table 22. Mexican Population Projection, 1980-2010. The Constant Emigration Rates Hypothesis Summary of Region 1 Population Change (both sexes)

Absolute numbers in thousands

	1980	1985	1990	1995	2000	2005	2010
Total	18,154	19,769	21,203	22,615	24,094	25,600	27,113
Age							
0-14	8,292	8,237	7,872	7,736	7,747	7,931	8,124
15-44	7,395	8,683	10,030	11,004	11,807	12,295	12,589
45-64	1,809	2,097	2,414	2,816	3,285	3,907	4,686
65+	658	752	887	1,059	1,255	1,467	1,714

Source: Population projection of the author.
Note: Numbers rounded independently. Region 1 is defined on table 18.

Table 23. Mexican Population Projection, 1980-2010. The Constant Emigration Rates Hypothesis Summary of Region 1 Population Change (both sexes)

Relative proportions (1980 = 1.00)

	1980	1985	1990	1995	2000	2005	2010
Total	1.00	1.09	1.17	1.25	1.33	1.41	1.49
Age							
0-14	1.00	0.99	0.95	0.93	0.93	0.96	0.98
15-44	1.00	1.17	1.36	1.49	1.60	1.66	1.70
45-64	1.00	1.16	1.33	1.56	1.82	2.16	2.59
65+	1.00	1.14	1.35	1.61	1.91	2.23	2.60

Source: Table 22.

Table 24. Mexican Population Projection, 1980-2010. The Constant Emigration Rates Hypothesis Summary of Region 1 Population Change (both sexes)

Percentage of average annual growth during five-year interval

	1980-1985	1985-1990	1990-1995	1995-2000	2000-2005	2005-2010
Average, all ages	1.72	1.41	1.30	1.28	1.22	1.16
Age						
0-14	-0.13	-0.90	-0.35	0.03	0.47	0.48
15-44	3.26	2.93	1.87	1.42	0.81	0.47
45-64	3.00	2.86	3.13	3.13	3.53	3.70
65+	2.71	3.36	3.61	3.45	3.17	3.16

Source: Table 22.

Table 25. Mexican Population Projection, 1980-2010. The Constant Emigration Rates Hypothesis Summary of Region 1 Population Change (both sexes)

Absolute increase during five-year interval in thousands

	1980-1985	1985-1990	1990-1995	1995-2000	2000-2005	2005-2010
Total	1,615	1,434	1,412	1,479	1,506	1,513
Age						
0-14	-55	-365	-136	11	184	193
15-44	1,288	1,347	974	803	488	294
45-64	288	317	402	469	622	779
65+	94	135	172	196	212	247

Source: Table 22.
Note: Numbers rounded independently.

Table 26. Mexican Population Projection, 1980-2010. The Drastic Change Hypothesis Summary of Region 1 Population Change (both sexes)

Absolute Numbers in thousands

	1980	1985	1990	1995	2000	2005	2010
Total	18,154	19,769	21,203	22,162	22,747	23,437	24,183
Age							
0-14	8,292	8,237	7,872	7,625	7,395	7,306	7,230
15-44	7,395	8,683	10,030	10,690	10,914	10,961	10,916
45-64	1,809	2,097	2,414	2,793	3,200	3,735	4,380
65+	658	752	887	1,054	1,238	1,435	1,657

Source: Population projection of the author.
Note: Numbers rounded independently.

The missing increments of growth from region 1 that would occur after 1995 appear as large increments of net emigrant survivors in the United States. The net emigration of survivors aged

15-44 from region 1 during 1985-90 was estimated at 455,600 persons; drastic change hypothesis conditions produce a jump to 1,075,000 during 1995-2000. (Constant rate hypothesis conditions, by contrast, would have this number hovering between 476,000 and 492,000 between 1995 and 2010.) Net emigration of survivors during subsequent five-year periods declines steadily to 850,800 during 2005-10. Obviously, another type of ceiling has been reached here: were emigration rates to rise even higher than the levels contemplated by the drastic change hypothesis, the stock of persons aged 15-44 in region 1 would begin to decline in absolute terms.

Indeed, the combination of a young adult population that hardly grows at all in region 1 and a continually declining fertility would produce an unusual situation in the region: a steady decline, in absolute terms, in the number of births after 1990 (table 27). This, combined with the outmigration of children accompanying their young parents, would lead to a steady decline in the population under fifteen years of age. The population aged 0-14 in region 1, estimated at 7,872,000 in 1990, would decline to 7,395,000 by 2000 and to 7,230,000 in 2010.

Table 27. Mexican Population Projection, 1980-2010. The Drastic Change Hypothesis Summary of Components of Change (both sexes) Region 1

Births, deaths, and net migration of survivors during five-year interval in thousands

	1980-1985	1985-1990	1990-1995	1995-2000	2000-2005	2005-2010
Net growth	1,615.2	1,434.2	958.9	585.3	687.0	747.6
Births	3,027.3	2,877.8	2,835.0	2,803.2	2,745.6	2,669.7
Deaths	600.3	597.3	602.5	623.8	675.1	704.7
Natural growth	2,427.0	2,280.6	2,232.5	2,179.4	2,070.5	1,965.0
Surviving stayers	18,917.5	20,224.2	21,054.8	21,481.3	21,992.6	22,595.5
Surviving emigrants	1,664.0	1,826.0	2,381.4	2,860.8	2,825.7	2,804.3
Surviving immigrants	852.1	979.6	1,107.8	1,266.6	1,442.2	1,587.0
Net migration survivors	-811.9	-846.4	-1,273.6	-1,594.1	-1,383.5	-1,217.4

Source: Population projection of the author.
Note: Region 2 is defined on table 19.

All of these associated patterns in region 1 suggest that the effects in Mexico of a doubling of emigration rates from that region would be extraordinary. By contrast, even a tripling of the emigration rates from region 2 has little noticeable effect on its demography because emigration is so small relative to its size. If such growth in emigration rates in region 2 is improbable, it is because these assumptions seem extraordinary—both in terms of the magnitude of the increase and the geographical deconcentration of emigration source regions. Even though changes in the geography of emigration are not unprecedented in Mexico, a very high proportion of emigration still comes from a relatively small proportion of the country's population, and this pattern will probably be expected to change slowly in the future.

The Virtually Unlimited Supply of Temporary Workers

In these regional projections, the number of surviving migratory workers employed in the United States during each five-year projection period and surviving at the end as residents in Mexico is calculated after the emigrants have been subtracted from Mexico's population. The complement of migratory workers—Mexican stay-at-homes—are working-age persons residing in Mexico at the end of the five-year projection interval and not working in the United States during that interval.

Holding the participation rate of migratory workers constant increases the number of migratory workers obtained for 2005-10 by about 68 percent—1.9 million—relative to 1.1 million in 1980-85. This is about 3 percent of the total working-age population. The 15-64 age group is expected to grow dramatically—from about 42.4 million in 1985 to 75.3 million in 2010, an average of 1.3 million per year during that period, though growth from 1985-90 is expected to be more than 1.5 million per year. The labor force aged 15-64 during this period is likely to be at least 60 percent of the total population in that same broad age group—it could be higher if the labor force participation rate of women grows as expected. In any event, from the standpoint of the total national labor force, the proportion of migratory workers, about 4 percent, is not substantial—certainly not so as to present an issue of supply.

A sharp increase in emigration, e.g., the high migration projection, slightly decreases the number of migratory workers available in the long term—from 1.9 million to 1.7 million in 2010. The drop of 200,000, however, is not significant. Even a drastic increase in change-of-residence migration over the long term does not appreciably cut into the number of temporary workers if constant participation rates are assumed. Whatever plausible ceiling might be placed on the migratory worker participation rates, then, is more likely to determine the limits on the supply of migratory workers than are the effects of the voluminous emigration of persons who give up the possibility to migrate temporarily and establish their usual residence in the United States. This appears true regardless of whether emigration remains concentrated in the traditional core sending states or disperses geographically.

From a demographic standpoint, then, there are no clearly discernible limits on the supply of migratory workers. An analysis focusing on the economic activities in region 1 and on the likely impact of increased numbers of migratory workers could find noticeable limits—or at least could suggest what kinds of distortions in the occupational and sectoral distribution of the labor force these increases might cause. That type of analysis, though similar to that presented here, would identify economic rather than demographic limits on the supply of temporary workers.

CONCLUSIONS

This paper began with the argument that both migration pressures in Mexico and demand for Mexican labor in the United States are expected to intensify in the 1990s. Generally, the regional population projections developed for this paper support what might be expected intuitively: the supply of emigrants will grow during this decade and can accommodate significant increases in the stock of Mexican-born persons in the United States. In the constant rates hypothesis estimate, the Mexican immigrant population (documented and undocumented combined) grew from about 4.1 million in 1990 to 5.8 million in the year 2000—an average annual net migration of 190,000 per year. However, although the growth of the supply can be estimated to be of these dimensions or more, migration levels can be lower (INEGI-CONAPO's projections assume an average annual net migration of 110,000) or higher (300,000 is considered an upper bound for the range of probable flows). Any instance between these extremes assumes that significant levels of undocumented migration will continue.

The most extreme possibility considered—the drastic change hypothesis—increases the emigration rates to the United States above those of the constant rates hypothesis sharply and quickly, simulates an average annual net emigration to the United States which peaks at 521,500 in 1995-2000, and produces a stock of 8.2 million Mexican-born residents in the United States in the year 2000. This projection shows that such high levels of migration would produce demographic distortions and anomalies in Mexico, such as an absolute decline in the number of children in region 1.

Theoretically, emigration rates from region 2 can grow substantially. Indeed, if net emigration volumes rise substantially above 200,000 per year, much of that growth is likely to come from region 2, signifying a break with a six-decade pattern of high geographic and demographic concentration of emigration.

Though the supply of emigrants will grow, the demography of the principal sending region—region 1—will begin to restrict this growth during the 1990s. This finding is a most satisfactory result after having employed a methodology which pays attention to the peculiarities of regional demography. Though the national working-age (15-64 years) population will grow by more than 3 percent per year during the 1990s, the young adult population (15-44 years) in region 1—thus far the main contributor of emigration to the United States—will grow only moderately (less than 2 percent per year). This growth is expected to decline steadily between 1990 and 2010. A growing working-age population in Mexico under the circumstances of the 1990s cannot automatically produce an increase in the supply of emigrants. Largely because of this, and because return migration to Mexico can be expected to grow proportionately to the growth of the Mexican emigrant population in the United States, net emigration trends will correspond roughly to those of emigration rates. A constant level in one is likely to be accompanied by a roughly constant level in the other. If emigration rates during the 1990s remain at levels estimated for 1975-80, and which correspond to the upper end of estimates for the 1980s, then net emigration to the United States during the 1990s can be expected to peak at about 200,000 per year.

Temporary-worker migration, as defined here, has no demographically discernible limits on supply. Indeed, if demand for Mexican labor grew substantially during the 1990s, both governments would probably respond by promoting temporary migration to hold net migration of Mexicans within tolerable limits, socially and politically. Estimating those limits, as in the case of the limits which demography imposes on emigration volume and characteristics, is not easy. However, demographic limits to the growth of the supply of emigrants, though somewhat larger, probably exceed the political and social limits to net immigration of Mexicans to the United States.

Since IRCA's implementation is so recent, there are as yet few indicators on which to base any prognoses of its impact on both the size and features of the supply of Mexican emigrants to the United States. Given the substantial numbers of Mexicans who availed themselves of IRCA's provisions to legalize their presence in the United States, the considerable number of their family members who may seek immigrant visas throughout the 1990s, the lack of vigor thus far in enforcing employer sanctions, and the probability that many Mexicans will be recruited legally after 1990, we should expect the emigration rates of the past to hold steady or even to increase between 1990 and 1995, before they eventually begin to drop. However, the increase in the flow of legal migrants cannot go beyond certain limits unless the United States alters its immigration legislation. Thus, for much of this decade, the supply of Mexican emigrants may be determined more by economic conditions in both countries and regional demographics in Mexico than by the possible consequences of IRCA's implementation.

4

Measuring the Flow of Undocumented Immigrants

Jorge A. Bustamante

This essay reports the most recent findings from an ongoing research project based at El Colegio de la Frontera Norte, known as the Zapata Canyon Project (ZCP).[1] The main objective of the project is to provide an alternative source of data on the flow of undocumented migration from Mexico to the United States, beyond the statistics on apprehensions of clandestine entrants routinely compiled by the U.S. Immigration and Naturalization Service (INS).

Alternative methodologies are needed to create a data base adequate for evaluating the impact of the U.S. Immigration Reform and Control Act of 1986 (IRCA). More than two years have passed since President Ronald Reagan signed this legislation, and the two main innovations in the law (legalization programs for undocumented immigrants, and sanctions upon employers who "knowingly" hire *indocumentados*) have either been fully implemented or are now fully enforceable. Thus 1989 will be the first year in which it could become clear whether one of IRCA's principal objectives—i.e., to stem the flow of undocumented immigration—is being attained.

---

[1] Reports of earlier findings from the project can be found in Jorge A. Bustamante, "La migración de los indocumentados," *El Cotidiano* (UAM-Azcapotzalco), Número Especial 1 (1987): 13-29; and Bustamante, "Undocumented Immigration: Research Findings and Policy Options," in *Mexico and the United States: Managing the Relationship*, edited by Riordan Roett (Boulder, Colo.: Westview, 1988).

This paper begins with a discussion of some of the main features of the social, political, and economic context in which IRCA emerged. The second section addresses the paradox created by legislative reform that adds important new restrictions on immigration, precisely at a time when the U.S. capability for replenishing an increasingly older domestic labor force is declining. The third section describes the main methodological features of the ZCP and presents some of its most recent findings. The concluding section discusses the implications of the trends revealed by the ZCP data for an assessment of the effects of IRCA.

The Context of IRCA

The assertion that the United States had "lost control" of its borders summarized for the American public the main justification for the 1986 immigration law. This rhetoric was first heard in 1980, at a time when U.S. television viewers were confronted with dramatic scenes of thousands of Cuban exiles pouring onto the shores of Florida, in what was quickly dubbed the "Mariel Invasion." By the time the "invasion" ended, the U.S. government had to deal with almost a quarter of a million unexpected immigrants from Cuba. Meanwhile, "boat people" from Haiti were attempting to follow in the footsteps of the "Marielitos," and an electoral campaign was underway in which Republicans were blaming President Jimmy Carter for a perceived decline of the United States' position of leadership in the eyes of the world. Meanwhile, Alan K. Simpson, a rising star in the Republican ranks of the U.S. Senate, had already gained bipartisan recognition as an intelligent, hardworking member of the Senate Subcommittee on Immigration. This led to his appointment by President Carter as a member of the U.S. Select Commission on Immigration and Refugee Policy, chaired by the Rev. Theodore Hesburgh, and to his subsequent leadership role in pushing immigration reform through the U.S. Congress. This was the political context in which the Simpson-Mazzoli bill[2]—the first of a series of "immigration reform" proposals that preceded IRCA—emerged.

The economic context included the highest unemployment rate in the United States since the years preceding World War II.

---

[2]The same legislative project was registered in the U.S. Senate as S-2222 and in the House of Representatives as HR-5872. Both versions were officially introduced on March 17, 1982. The official title of the bill was "Immigration Reform and Control Act of 1982."

Undocumented immigration was cited as a principal cause for the high rate of unemployment. New restrictions on immigration were justified as a necessary tool in the effort to curb unemployment. Interestingly, no attention was drawn to the spurious correlation between undocumented immigration and unemployment, as the U.S. unemployment rate declined from 10.8 percent when the first Simpson-Mazzoli bill was introduced in 1982, to 6.3 percent when IRCA was finally enacted in 1986.

By the end of 1986, unemployment had been replaced by another social calamity for which undocumented immigrants were also blamed: drug traffic.[3] But the predominant U.S. perception of undocumented immigration from Mexico as a serious problem was being contradicted by some of the country's leading economists, who pointed out the net macroeconomic benefits deriving from the presence of immigrants, legal as well as undocumented.[4]

Such contrasts illustrate the continuing tension between *economic* interests in the United States—concerned with perpetuating their access to a source of cheap labor—and the *political* interests shaped by nationalistic values, of which nativism and xenophobia are the extreme manifestations. One force is pushing toward a relative opening of the border to foreign workers, while the other is pushing toward virtual closure. The history of Mexican migration to the United States[5] shows that the predominance of one force over the other tends to be determined by the state of the U.S. economy. In periods of economic expansion, economic interests maintain a de facto opening of the border to undocumented immigrants. In periods of economic recession, political interests prevail over economic interests, provoking immigration restrictions and mass deportations.[6]

---

[3]A few weeks before the final vote in the House of Representatives, where the Simpson-Rodino bill passed by a slim margin of seven votes, U.S. Attorney General Edwin Meese and INS Commissioner Alan Nelson stated in a press conference that a direct relationship had been found between drug traffic and illegal aliens.
[4]See, for example, U.S. Council of Economic Advisors, *Economic Report of the President* (Washington, D.C., 1986), p. 233; and Thomas Muller and Thomas J. Espenshade, *The Fourth Wave: California's Newest Immigrants* (Washington, D.C.: Urban Institute Press, 1985).
[5]See Jorge A. Bustamante, "La política de inmigración de Estados Unidos: un análisis de sus contradicciones," in *Migración en el Occidente de México*, edited by Gustavo López Castro and Sergio Pardo Galván (Zamora, Mich.: El Colegio de Michoacán, 1988).
[6]See Mercedes Carreras de Velasco, *Los mexicanos que devolvió la crisis* (México, D.F.: Secretaría de Relaciones Exteriores, 1975); and Abraham Hoffman, *Unwanted Mexican Americans in the Great Depression* (Tucson: University of Arizona Press, 1974).

This analysis becomes relevant when one examines more closely the changes in U.S. immigration policy brought by IRCA. It could be argued that both political and economic interests profited from these changes. Political interests gained in the sense that most of the penalizing aspects—especially sanctions on employers—are rooted in values of sovereignty or national interest. On the other hand, most of the provisions related to legalization of undocumented workers and issuance of temporary work permits for foreign workers were introduced or supported by legislators whose political careers have been dependent on agribusiness.

Furthermore, it could be argued that the health of the U.S. economy will largely determine whether IRCA's employer sanctions provisions will eventually be fully enforced or will fade into oblivion. If the economy of the United States or, even more specifically, the state of California[7] falls into recession, all of the penalizing aspects of IRCA will probably be enforced to their maximum. On the other hand, if both the national and California economies continue to expand, enforcement of sanctions will be held to a minimum, and IRCA provisions for legalization—particularly the Special Agricultural Workers (SAW) program—are likely to be extended.

A PARADOX

If we can assume that the presence in the United States of undocumented immigrants from Mexico is partially due to a U.S. demand for foreign-born labor, it is paradoxical that restrictive immigration legislation was enacted in the same year in which a long period of U.S. labor shortages began. Economists in the U.S. Department of Labor have reported that 1986 represented a turning point toward deficits of new entrants into the U.S. labor force. They foresee a 6 percent shortage of male job seekers between 16 and 24 years of age by the year 2000, and an even larger deficit of 15 percent within the 24-to-34 age cohort. In 1972, 23 percent of the U.S. labor market was occupied by male workers of the youngest cohorts. By 1986, when IRCA was enacted, this proportion had fallen to 20 percent, and it is estimated that by the year 2000, the

---

[7]At any given time, close to 60 percent of the total of undocumented Mexican immigrants in the United States can be found in the state of California, where employer demand for Mexican undocumented immigrants is higher and more diversified than in any other state, according to survey data of ZCP.

proportion will descend to 16 percent. In contrast, the proportion of workers in the age cohorts of 35 and older will rise from 51 percent in 1986 to 61 percent in 2000.[8]

Short of a new generation of robots that could, at competitive costs, do the work of the absent young workers, the U.S. economy could face serious difficulties in achieving reasonable rates of growth.[9] This problem seems to be all the more acute in light of projections indicating that the fastest-growing demand for labor from 1986 to the year 2000 will be in such occupations as kitchen helper, domestic service, bartender, janitor, department store clerk, fast-food restaurant helper, and security guard for industry. In other words, some of the lowest-paid occupations in the service sector are among the fastest growing in terms of the demand for workers.[10] And these are precisely the occupations where the demand for *foreign* workers, undocumented or otherwise, is the fastest growing in the state of California, according to findings of the Zapata Canyon Project.

MEASURING THE TRANSBORDER LABOR FLOW

The Zapata Canyon Project departs from the assumption that the effects of IRCA would be reflected in the volume of the flow and the socioeconomic characteristics of undocumented immigrants crossing northbound through the U.S.-Mexico border. Previous research had shown that the border crossing of undocumented immigrants is not evenly distributed. The ETIDEU study[11] found that more than 50 percent of the total flow of undocumented immigrants into the United States passes through the city of Tijuana. Thus, a special emphasis was placed on Tijuana in the research design.

---

[8]Howard N. Fullerton, Jr., "Labor Force Projections: 1986 to 2000," *Monthly Labor Review* 110 (1987): 19-21.
[9]This point was made more than ten years ago by Clark Reynolds in his pioneering analysis of economic interdependence between Mexico and the United States. See Reynolds, "Labor Market Projections for the United States and Mexico and Their Relevance to Current Migration Controversies," *Food Research Institute Studies* (Stanford University) 17:2 (1979).
[10]George T. Silvestri and John M. Lukasiewics, "A Look at Occupational Employment Trends to the Year 2000," *Monthly Labor Review* 110 (1987): 46-63.
[11]Consejo Nacional de Población, *Encuesta en la frontera norte a trabajadores indocumentados devueltos por las autoridades de Estados Unidos de América, diciembre de 1984* (México, D.F.: CONAPO, 1986).

Two basic data collection methods have been used. The first, based on photographic techniques, systematically examines the habitual gatherings of people once they have crossed the U.S.-Mexico border "without inspection" by U.S. immigration authorities. The second method consists of survey interviewing using a standardized questionnaire.

Photographic slides of the two principal gathering places for undocumented immigrants crossing through Tijuana are systematically taken each day. One site is an esplanade located in the western foothills of Otay Mesa, near the Tijuana airport. This area, already in U.S. territory, is known as the "soccer field" in the United States and as the Zapata Canyon in Mexico. The terrain allows a perfect view of the entire area from a convenient distance, in the hills of the northernmost section of Tijuana. Since the gathering of people takes place in U.S. territory, all the people focused on by the camera are technically undocumented. A daily photographic register of the flow of undocumented immigrants in the Zapata Canyon has been kept by the ZCP since August 1986. An initial photograph is taken two hours and ten minutes before sunset, the second one hour later, and the third ten minutes before sunset. The number of people appearing in each picture is entered into a computerized data base.[12]

The flow of undocumented immigrants is a dynamic phenomenon. Not only does it change in volume according to time of day, day of the week, week of the month, and month of the year, but in the proportion of people using the habitual crossing points. This is why the ZCP extended the photographic register to include another area of Tijuana known as *"el bordo"* (the river bank), located to the west of the San Ysidro international port of entry. The gathering here of undocumented immigrants before advancing farther into the San Ysidro area is a more ephemeral event. Therefore only two pictures per day, with an hourly interval, have been taken at this site since October 1988.

In addition to the photographic records, the ZCP conducts personal interviews with randomly selected undocumented immigrants. Interviews are conducted three days per week—usually weekends—at habitual crossing points of undocumented immigrants in the border cities where El Colegio de la Frontera Norte has permanent offices (Tijuana, Mexicali, Nogales, Ciudad Juárez,

---

[12]The collection of daily photographic slides and computer records of the ZCP are available for examination by appointment.

Nuevo Laredo, and Matamoros). This ongoing survey began in April 1987. It employs a short, standardized questionnaire—one specifically designed not to take too much time (2-3 minutes) from someone who is in the process of entering a foreign country illegally. The main objective of the survey interviewing is to detect changes in the socioeconomic profile of the undocumented immigrants.

Research Findings

Figure 1 derives from the photographic documentation of the immigrant flow at the Zapata Canyon in Tijuana, where the research project began. It depicts the monthly averages of the highest number of undocumented immigrants found, after a comparison is made of the three photographs taken daily. Considering the pattern of decline toward the month of December (which has occurred cyclically for several decades), as well as the normal increase in the month of January as migrants who have been visiting their home towns head north again, it can be concluded that the flow of undocumented immigrants through the Zapata Canyon continued without significant changes, at least through April 1988—seventeen months after the approval of IRCA.

Figure 1. Emigration from Mexico: Average Daily Counts in Zapata Canyon, August 1986-April 1988

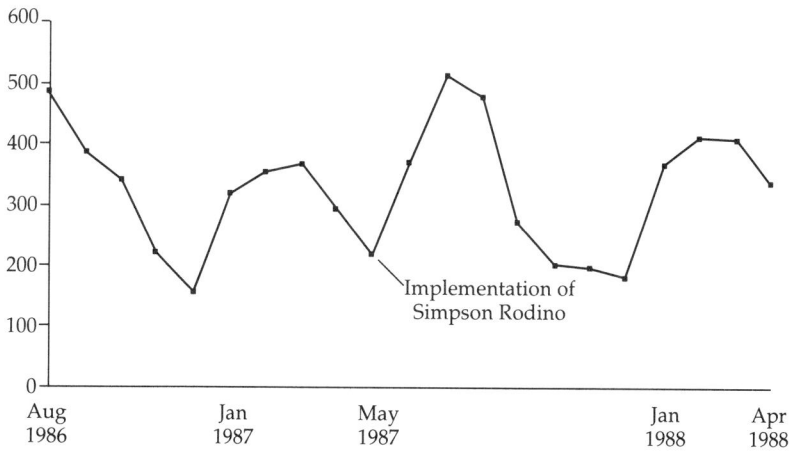

Source: Zapata Canyon Project, El Colegio de la Frontera Norte; adapted from Bilateral Commission on the Future of United States-Mexican Relations, *The Challenge of Interdependence: Mexico and The United States* (Lauham, Md: University Press of America, 1988), p. 106

The remaining graphs are based on the ZCP's survey data. In figure 2, a distinction is made between "first-timers" and "experienced" immigrants. The former category includes undocumented immigrants who said at the time of the interview that it was the first time they were trying to enter the United States in search of a job. Our data, like that of previous researchers, show that "first-timers" are the clear majority of those Mexicans who try to enter the United States without proper documents.[13] This suggests a high degree of turnover in the migratory flow; those experienced in clandestine border crossing tend to have a short career. They drop out of the flow, by settling permanently in the United States, by staying in a Mexican border city, or by returning to their place of origin on a permanent basis. Our data indicate that the proportion of "first-timers" in the migratory flow is higher than previously reported. Moreover, the proportion of undocumented immigrants in this category is growing. This could mean that the "career" of the undocumented immigrant is shortening, notwithstanding a stable or even increasing total volume of immigrants. The data on migratory experience have been cross-tabulated by the migrant's

Figure 2. Undocumented Immigrants: Monthly Percentages of First-timers, by Region of Origin through Tijuana

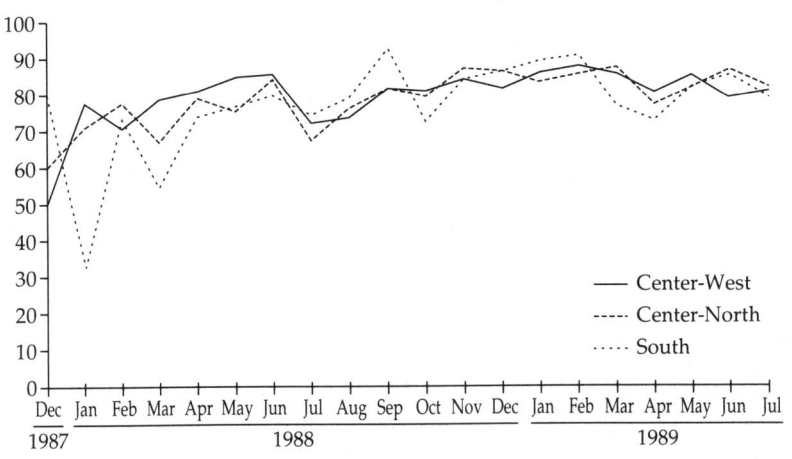

Source: Zapata Canyon Project, El Colegio de la Frontera Norte.

---

[13]The same pattern was reported in Julian Samora, *Los Mojados: The Wetback Story* (Notre Dame, Ind.: University of Notre Dame Press, 1971). It was also found in the ETIDEU survey cited above.

region of origin.[14] The regions represented in figure 2 are those with the highest volume of outmigrants who cross the U.S. border at Tijuana (i.e., those supplying at least thirty migrants per month).

Figure 3 depicts responses to the survey question, "Have you had a job in the United States before?" regardless of the duration of their stay. It appears that this type of "labor market-experienced" migrant was on the decline until May 1988. The figure suggests that there was a turning point, when those with previous U.S. employment experience ceased to decline as a proportion of undocumented border-crossers, and resumed their previous practice of going back and forth in a more or less stable pattern. This turning point coincides with the end of the application period (May 4, 1988) for those who wanted to legalize their status under the so-called general amnesty provision of IRCA. This provision was intended for those who could demonstrate continuous residence in the United States since January 1, 1982. It therefore appears that the labor market-experienced undocumented migrants represented in this figure slowed down their "shuttle" migration to and

Figure 3. Undocumented Immigrants with Working Experience in the United States, by Region of Origin

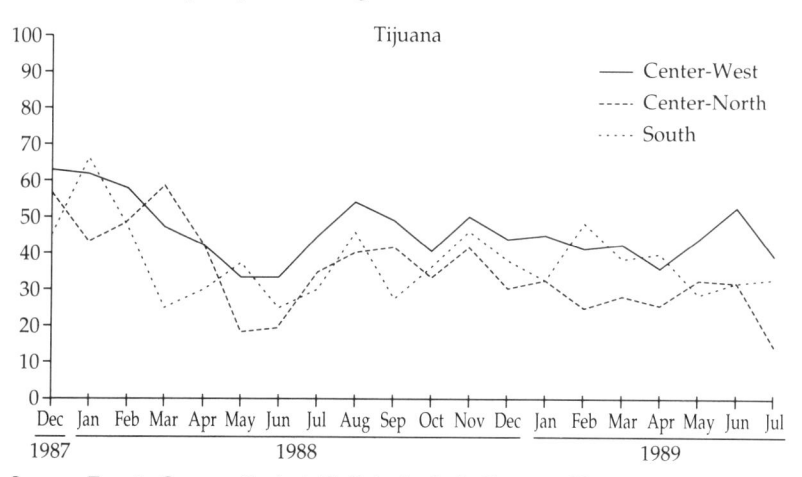

Source: Zapata Canyon Project, El Colegio de la Frontera Norte.

---

[14]The "Center-West" region is defined as including the states of Jalisco, Michoacán, Guanajuato, Guerrero, Colima, and Nayarit. The "Center-North" area includes the Federal District, Estado de México, Querétaro, Aguascalientes, San Luis Potosí, Zacatecas, and Durango. The "South" includes Puebla, Oaxaca, Chiapas, and Quintana Roo.

from Mexico, or stayed in the United States for longer periods of time, in hopes of legalizing themselves. Once the amnesty application period ended, those who did not qualify resumed their "normal" practice of temporary visits to Mexico followed by return trips to the United States without documents—undeterred by IRCA's employer sanctions.

We hypothesize that "cost of migration" is the most important factor determining changes in the socioeconomic profile of undocumented immigrants.[15] The ZCP data show significant differences in the cost of migration to the United States among those crossing at the six cities included in our survey. Monthly data on inflation rates in each city were compiled from Banco de México sources. The sharpest contrast is between cities where total expenses are below the local rate of inflation (Tijuana and Nuevo Laredo-Matamoros) and those where total expenses are above the inflation rate (Mexicali), or where only one type of migrants' expenses appears above the inflation line (Ciudad Juárez). The relevant data for undocumented immigrants crossing through Tijuana are presented in figure 4.

Figure 4. Uncodumented Immigrants: total Expenses (Monthly averages in pesos)

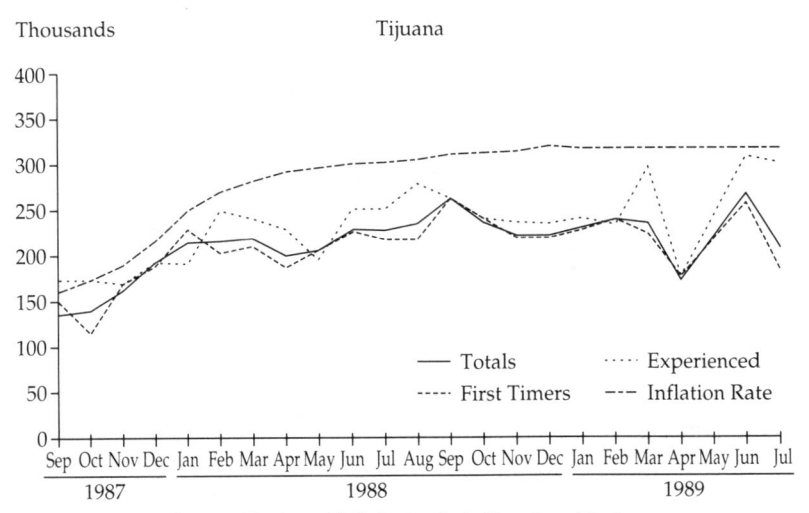

Source: Zapata Canyon Project, El Colegio de la Frontera Norte.

---

[15]In our analysis, "cost of migration" encompasses all expenses incurred by a migrant in getting to the United States, from the moment he or she leaves home. These expenses include transportation, shelter, food, "*coyote*" (smuggler) services, costs resulting from failed illegal entries (i.e., apprehension and expulsion by the U.S. Border Patrol), Mexican police extortions, and so forth.

A more detailed analysis of the profile of migrants crossing at each city reveals the following:

- Migrants entering the United States through Mexicali and Ciudad Juárez tend to originate locally in greater proportions than those crossing at Tijuana and Nuevo Laredo-Matamoros, cities which serve as transit points for higher proportions of long-distance migrants.

- Because of their proximity to the United States and the associated lower cost of migration, the cities of Nuevo Laredo and Matamoros tend to be favored as border crossing points by the poorest, least educated, most rural-origin undocumented immigrants.

- Migrants who come from distant places tend to finance their expenses with U.S. dollars in greater proportion than "locals."

- Contrary to what one would expect, "experienced" migrants crossing at Tijuana, Mexicali, and Nuevo Laredo-Matamoros showed a stronger tendency to use the services of smugglers ("*coyotes*" or "*polleros*") than "first-timers" interviewed in these cities. This was not the case in Ciudad Juárez, however.

- The use of dollars obtained from personal savings or from relatives or friends in the United States appeared to be the most powerful factor in determining whether migrants' total expenses were above or below the rate of inflation in each city.

A pattern seems to be emerging in the sense that the higher the cost of migration, the higher the socioeconomic level of the migrant who reaches the United States. It is reasonable to assume that the higher the socioeconomic status of the person who decides to go to the United States in search of a job, the greater will be Mexico's loss of human capital, and the higher the cost in productivity for Mexico through emigration. If this assumption proves correct, the characterization of undocumented migration as an "escape valve"—which has been so prevalent in Mexico—should be replaced by a new notion of loss of human capital.

Conclusions

The Zapata Canyon Project data provide no evidence to support the contention of U.S. immigration officials that IRCA has been successful in achieving its primary objective—reducing the flow of undocumented immigrants from Mexico.[16] The law's future as an effective regulatory tool will depend heavily upon the state of the U.S. economy, and especially the economy of California. The brighter the economic prospects for the United States, the more "flexible" or obsolete IRCA will become. The darker the United States' economic future, the wider and more intense the enforcement of IRCA will be. Under conditions of sustained economic growth, U.S. employers will tend to pay more attention to the laws of labor supply and demand than to immigration laws.

The aging of the U.S. labor force, in combination with a healthy economy, could open new conditions for negotiation of a bilateral agreement between Mexico and the United States on immigration. In the long term, however, Mexico should develop a migratory policy based on full recognition of its human capital losses through outmigration. No nation can base its future economic development on the exportation of its own labor force.

If it is valid to think that in the long run labor outmigration is contrary to Mexico's national interests, this should not obscure current realities. In the foreseeable future, it would be very difficult if not impossible for Mexico to stop the large-scale emigration of its workers. Thus the most appropriate policy at this juncture would be to seek a bilateral accord, whose main objective would be managing the migratory flow in a manner more consistent with the interests of Mexico and the migrant workers themselves.

---

[16] A recent, highly detailed analysis of INS apprehension statistics for the last three years suggests that increases and decreases in apprehensions by the Border Patrol before and after the approval of IRCA are not necessarily due to changes in the actual volume of undocumented immigration. Apprehension levels were found to correlate highly with changes in Border Patrol "linewatch hours." See Michael J. White, Frank D. Bean, and Thomas J. Espenshade, "The U.S. Immigration Reform and Control Act and Undocumented Immigration to the United States," paper presented at the conference on "Illegal Immigration Before and After IRCA," the Urban Institute, Washington, D.C., July 21, 1989.

SECTION II

Consequences

5

Looking to the 1990s: Mexican Immigration in Sociological Perspective

Marta Tienda

After forty years of steady development, Mexico-United States migration is now so institutionalized, so widespread, so much a part of family strategies, individual expectations, and community structures, in short, so embedded in social and economic institutions, that the idea of controlling it is probably unrealistic.[1] Migration is inherently a social process—one coterminous with social change when two cultures, two national identities, and two standards of living are engaged. Thus defined, the movement of people across the Rio Grande since the turn of the century, and especially since 1940, has transformed hundreds of Mexican and U.S. communities involved in the exchange of people, goods, and capital. Exactly how migration affects the receiving and sending areas depends on several factors, including the timing and volume of the flow; its social and demographic composition; the migrants' settlement, consumption, and expenditure patterns; and the "auspices of migration"—the complex set of social and economic

---

I acknowledge institutional support from the Institute for Research on Poverty under a grant from the Department of Health and Human Services, and from the College of Agricultural and Life Sciences, University of Wisconsin, Madison, under the auspices of a Hatch grant. I am grateful for technical assistance from Sarah Rudolph and Gary Heisserer. A preliminary and abbreviated version of this paper was published in *Ethnic Studies* 2 (Summer 1988).
[1] See Douglas S. Massey, "Understanding Mexican Migration to the United States," *American Journal of Sociology* 92 (1987):1399.

arrangements which organize international migration streams.[2] This essay postulates that the nature and scope of the social impacts associated with decades of heavy immigration have as much or more to do with settlement patterns and the auspices of migration as they do with sheer numbers.

Technically, migrant streams represent a succession of demographic events based on individual (family) decision-making. Migration behavior responds to perceived opportunities elsewhere, but the factors which initiate flows often differ from those which perpetuate them.[3] Economic factors, such as lack of access to property and capital in sending communities and labor recruitment strategies in host communities, generally activate wage-labor migrant streams. However, economic imperatives yield to social forces within a generation or less, and migration flows become self-perpetuating.[4] The social consequences of international migrant streams are less well understood than economic consequences, in part because the burgeoning literature has been preoccupied with narrowly economic issues, and in part because individual, or micro-level, perspectives have prevailed over structural, macro-level ones.[5]

This essay identifies issues for bilateral negotiation and binational research strategies based on a selective but critical review of studies about the social consequences of Mexican immigration. This task is complicated by the diffuseness of the concept of "social effects" and the paucity of studies dealing with social impacts.

Delimiting the charge further, the paper discusses themes that illustrate the social content of migration decision-making and the social significance of Mexican origin in the U.S. stratification regime. That is, the discussion of integration processes emphasizes

---

[2]Charles Tilly and C. Harold Brown, "On Uprooting, Kinship and the Auspices of Migration," *International Journal of Comparative Sociology* 8 (1967): 139-164; Harvey M. Choldin, "Kinship Networks in the Migration Process," *International Migration Review* 7:2 (1973): 163-176; Marta Tienda, "Familism and Structural Assimilation of Mexican Immigrants in the United States," *International Migration Review* 14:3 (1980): 383-408.

[3]Alejandro Portes and Robert L. Bach, *Latin Journey: Cuban and Mexican Immigrants to the United States* (Berkeley: University of California Press, 1985), chap. 1; Douglas S. Massey, Rafael Alarcón, Jorge Durand, and Humberto González, *Return to Aztlan: The Social Process of International Migration from Western Mexico* (Berkeley: University of California Press, 1987); Everett S. Lee, "A Theory of Migration," *Demography* 3:1 (1966).

[4]Massey, "Understanding Mexican Migration"; Lee, "A Theory of Migration."

[5]See Robert W. Gardner, "Macrolevel Influences on the Migration Decision Process," in *Migration Decision Making: Multidisciplinary Approaches to Macrolevel Studies in Developed and Developing Countries*, edited by Gordon F. De Jong and Robert W. Gardner (New York: Pergamon Press, 1981).

the perpetuation of structured inequities between Mexican immigrants and other social groups, particularly Mexican natives and native whites. From a sociological standpoint, the persisting correspondence between socioeconomic disadvantage and Mexican origin raises challenging questions about the relative weight of continued immigration from Mexico versus institutionalized discrimination in maintaining the minority status of the Chicano/Mexican-American population.[6] In specifying social consequences of migration, there is a tendency to confuse *migrants* and *communities* as objects of study.[7] Social-impact assessment generally focuses on how places change as a result of migration, while studies of social integration (assimilation) focus on the migrants themselves. This distinction is important; policy implications differ substantially, depending on whether the focus is individual migrants or social aggregates such as institutions, organizations, and communities.

DEFINING THE ISSUES

Three questions have dominated American attitudes and hence academic and policy discussions regarding the effects of Mexican immigration on the United States:

- Do unskilled immigrants compete with and displace native-born workers by undercutting their wages?

- Does immigrants' use of entitlement programs drain public coffers?

- Are Mexican immigrants more difficult to integrate culturally and socially because they speak Spanish and huddle in ethnic niches where Mexican cultural patterns flourish?[8]

---

[6]This conception of minority status defined by the coincidence of cultural/racial distinctiveness and socioeconomic disadvantage is narrow, but it distinguishes ethnic groups for whom cultural diversity is totally a matter of choice from minority groups for whom it is not. See Marta Tienda and Leif I. Jensen, "Poverty and Minorities: A Quarter Century Profile of Color and Socioeconomic Disadvantage," IRP Conference Paper (Madison, Wis., 1987); Candace Nelson and Marta Tienda, "The Structuring of Hispanic Ethnicity: Historical and Contemporary Perspectives," *Ethnic and Racial Studies* 8:1 (1985): 49-74.
[7]This problem appears to be less serious in the economic literature, which casts the economic consequences in terms of taxes, employment, and social expenditures on the one hand, and the economic assimilation of migrants on the other.
[8]Kevin F. McCarthy and R. Burciaga Valdez, *Current and Future Effects of Mexican Immigration in California* (Santa Monica, Calif: Rand Corporation, 1986); George Borjas and Marta Tienda, "The Economic Consequences of Immigration," *Science* 235 (1987): 645-651.

Despite the scope of these concerns, the literature on the impact of Mexican immigration has emphasized economic issues, particularly those revolving around labor-market outcomes,[9] to the relative neglect of broader social issues such as the reification of ethnic inequality and the persistence of language diversity.

Much of the recent sociological literature, following the traditions of economists concerned with earnings "assimilation,"[10] emphasizes the socioeconomic integration of immigrants. Some authors, however, examine occupational placement[11] and language shifts,[12] the social and economic significance of spatial concentration,[13] the proliferation of immigrant enterprises,[14] the organization of ethnic enclaves,[15] and patterns of language retention among ethnic groups.[16]

---

[9] For a more comprehensive review of the economic perspective, see Michael J. Greenwood and John M. McDowell, "The Factor Market Consequences of U.S. Immigration," *Journal of Economic Literature* 24 (December 1986): 1738-1772. A more selective overview appears in Borjas and Tienda, "The Economic Consequences of Immigration."

[10] See Barry R. Chiswick, "An Analysis of Earnings among Mexican Origin Men," in *Proceedings of the American Statistical Association*, Business and Statistics Section, 1977; Barry R. Chiswick, "The Effect of Americanization on the Earnings of Foreign-Born Men," *Journal of Political Economy* 86:5 (1987): 897-921; and George Borjas, "The Earnings of Male Hispanic Immigrants in the United States," *Industrial and Labor Relations Review*, April 1982, pp. 343-353.

[11] Matthew C. Snipp and Marta Tienda, "Chicano Career Mobility," *Studies in Social Stratification and Mobility* 4 (1985): 177-194; Marta Tienda and Patricia Guhleman, "The Occupational Position of Employed Hispanic Women," in *Hispanics in the U.S. Economy*, edited by George Borjas and Marta Tienda (Orlando, Fla.: Academic Press, 1985).

[12] J.A. Fishman, "Language and Ethnicity," in *Language, Ethnicity and Intergroup Relations*, edited by Giles Howard (London: Academic Press, 1977); Reynaldo Flores Macías, "Mexicano/Chicano Socio-linguistic Behavior and Language Policy in the United States" (Ph.D. dissertation, Georgetown University, 1979); Calvin Veltman, "Language Planning in the United States: The Politics of Ignorance," paper presented at the Annual Meeting of the American Sociological Association, Quebec, 1981.

[13] Marta Tienda and Ding-Tzann Lii, "Minority Concentration and Earnings Inequality: Blacks, Hispanics and Asians Compared," *American Journal of Sociology* 93:1 (1987): 141-163; Douglas Massey, "Ethnic Residential Segregation: A Theoretical Synthesis and Empirical Review," *Sociology and Social Research* 69 (1985): 315-350; Douglas S. Massey and Nancy A. Denton, "Spatial Assimilation as a Socioeconomic Outcome," *American Sociological Review* 50 (1985): 94-105.

[14] Alejandro Portes and Robert D. Manning, "The Immigrant Enclave: Theory and Empirical Examples," in *Competitive Ethnic Relations*, edited by J. Nagel and S. Olzak (New York: Academic Press, 1986); Roger Waldinger, "Immigration and Industrial Change in the New York City Apparel Industry," in *Hispanics in the U.S. Economy*, edited by George Borjas and Marta Tienda (Orlando, Fla.: Academic Press, 1985).

[15] Kenneth L. Wilson and Alejandro Portes, "Immigrant Enclaves: An Analysis of the Labor Market Experiences of Cubans in Miami," *American Journal of Sociology* 86:2 (1980): 295-319; Portes and Bach, *Latin Journey*.

[16] Nelson and Tienda, "The Structuring of Hispanic Ethnicity"; R.L. Skrabanek, "Language Maintenance among Mexican Americans," *International Journal of Comparative Sociology* 11 (1970): 272-282; Fishman, "Language and Ethnicity."

Hindsight indicates that the emphasis on economic processes responded to a pressing need; it ajudicated competing claims about the migrants' impacts on native-born workers[17] and on the availability of fiscal resources for public services.[18] However, public concern with economic consequences may have deflected attention from broader social issues, such as the cultural diversification of several major cities in the Southwest[19] and ethnic tensions in areas of high immigrant concentration.[20]

Empirical support for allegations that Mexican immigrants are more difficult to integrate into U.S. society than were European arrivals is mostly indirect, reflected in differential income growth according to national origin[21] or descriptions of gross social and economic differences between native- and foreign-born, between legal and illegal immigrants. Fears about the cultural diversity produced by the "new immigration" often surface in debates on the merits of bilingual education versus the perils of linguistic pluralism.[22] Researchers also identify other social problems, such as low educational achievement and limited socioeconomic mobility of Chicanos[23] and low levels of political participation and

---

[17]George Borjas, "The Substitutability of Black, Hispanic and White Labor," *Economic Inquiry*, January 1983, pp. 93-106, and "The Sensitivity of Labor Demand Functions to Choice of Dependent Variable," *Review of Economics and Statistics*, February 1986, pp. 58-66; Frank D. Bean, B. Lindsay Lowell, and Lowell J. Taylor, "Undocumented Mexican Immigrants and the Earnings of Other Workers in the United States," *Demography*, 1987; McCarthy and Valdez, "Current and Future Effects of Mexican Immigration."
[18]Marta Tienda and Leif I. Jensen, "Immigration and Public Assistance: Dispelling the Myth of Dependency," *Social Science Research* 15:4 (1986): 372-400; Francine D. Blau, "The Use of Transfer Payments by Immigrants," *Industrial and Labor Relations Review* 37:2 (1984): 222-239; Julian L. Simon, "Immigrants, Taxes, and Welfare in the United States," *Population and Development Review* 10:1 (1984): 55-69; Borjas and Tienda, "The Economic Consequences of Immigration."
[19]John D. Kasarda, "Hispanics and City Change," *American Demographics*, November 1984, pp. 25-29.
[20]Suzanne Nagel and Susan Olzak, *Competitive Ethnic Relations* (New York: Academic Press, 1986).
[21]Barry R. Chiswick, "The Economic Progress of Immigrants: Some Apparently Universal Patterns" (Washington, D.C.: American Enterprise Institute for Public Policy Research, 1979); Cordelia W. Reimers, "A Comparative Analysis of the Wages of Hispanics, Blacks, and Non-Hispanic Whites," in *Hispanics in the U.S. Economy*, edited by George Borjas and Marta Tienda (Orlando, Fla.: Academic Press, 1985); George Borjas, "The Economic Status of Male Hispanic Migrants and Natives in the U.S.," *Research in Labor Economics*, October 1984, and "Assimilation, Changes in Cohort Quality and the Earnings of Immigrants, *Journal of Labor Economics*, October 1985; Marta Tienda, "Nationality and Income Attainment of Native and Immigrant Hispanic Men in the United States," *Sociological Quarterly* 24:2 (1983): 253-272.
[22]Debates about whether English should be made the official language of the United States and about the financial responsibility for maintaining bilingual/bicultural instructions programs starkly illustrate these fears.
[23]Snipp and Tienda, "Chicano Career Mobility."

naturalization[24] as evidence of immigrants' limited integration prospects. When images of ethnic diversity are popularized by the media and misunderstood by the general public, the prospects for assimilation seem remote.

Following sections of this essay will discuss features of Mexican migration which have altered over time, with important social implications; the migrants' integration, especially in terms of structured social inequities along national-origin lines;[25] and research and policy implications, as well as bilateral negotiation priorities. The final section distinguishes aspects of the flow which are amenable to intervention from those which are not, and highlights the "unintended" or "latent" effects of immigration reform over the past quarter century.

SOCIAL CONTEXT OF MEXICAN IMMIGRATION: HISTORICAL AND CONTEMPORARY PERSPECTIVES

Two of the most distinctive features of Mexican immigration in the post-World War II era are its increasing volume and its heterogeneity.[26] Both of these features have important implications for the social impacts on U.S. society, as well as for the integration prospects of the migrants who eventually settle permanently. Table 1 reports the absolute numbers of legal Mexican immigrants admitted each decade since the turn of the century and expresses these as a share of the total number of immigrants admitted from all countries. In the aftermath of World War II and the Korean conflict, immigrants from war-torn countries flooded U.S. shores. But as of 1961, Mexico replaced Germany as the largest single source of immigrants, and it continues to hold that distinction to this day.[27]

---

[24]Alejandro Portes and Cynthia Truelove, "Making Sense of Diversity: Recent Research on Hispanic Minorities in the United States," *Annual Review of Sociology* 13 (1987): 359-416; Alejandro Portes and John Curtis, "Determinants of Naturalization among Recent Mexican Immigrants, Re-Analysis of a Six Year Follow-Up" (Baltimore, Md.: Johns Hopkins University, 1985).

[25]The massiveness of the research and writing on Mexican immigration mandate selectivity in reviewing the studies. My intention is not to be exhaustive but to cite only studies pertinent to the subject matter, without misrepresenting the state of the art on the topics considered.

[26]The growth and diversity of the illegal component of Mexican immigration add to the heterogeneity of Mexican immigration. However, this segment of the population has received so much attention in recent years that the legal flow has often faded into the background in policy debates. Therefore, my discussion focuses on the legal flow.

[27]During the 1950s, Mexico sent approximately 300,000 immigrants to the United States, second only to Germany, with 478,000. See U.S. Department of Justice,

Table 1. Legal Mexican Immigration by Year, 1900 to 1985

Year	Numbers	Percent of Total Admitted
1901-10	49,642	0.6
1911-20	219,004	3.8
1921-30	459,287	11.2
1931-40	22,319	4.2
1941-50	60,589	5.9
1951-60	299,811	11.9
1961-70	453,937	13.7
1971-80	640,294	14.2
1981-85	335,563	11.7

Source: U.S. Department of Justice, *1985 Statistical Yearbook of the Immigration and Naturalization Service*, (Washington, D.C.: U.S. Government Printing Office, 1985): table 1.2.

The volume of legal Mexican immigrants during the post-war period is impressive. However, its demographic impact has not yet fully unfolded, owing to the relatively short duration of Mexico's primacy among immigrant source countries.

Despite popular stereotypes to the contrary, the Mexican immigrant pool has become more heterogeneous since the mid-1960s, partly because of increasing restrictions on legal admission,[28] the expansion of migrant networks,[29] and the institutionalization of the "acceptability of migration."[30] These forces converged and interacted with increased flow to stratify the migrant streams. First, the termination of the Bracero Program shifted the movement of seasonal workers from a predominantly legal to a predominantly illegal flow, thereby reinforcing legal status as a social category.[31]

Statistical Yearbook of the Immigration and Naturalization Service (Washington, D.C.: Immigration and Naturalization Service, 1986): table 1.2.
[28]McCarthy and Valdez, *Current and Future Effects of Mexican Immigration.*
[29]Massey et al., *Return to Aztlan.*
[30]Massey and García España observe that in its early phases, Mexican migration to the United States was confined to a small segment of the population—usually young, single men. But as the social networks sponsoring migration expand, migration becomes more generalized. This interpretation is consistent with other studies which point to a shift from a predominantly male seasonal migration to a year-round flow involving both sexes and a greater age span. See Douglas S. Massey and Felipe García España, "The Social Process of International Migration" (Philadelphia: Population Studies Center, 1987); R. Burciaga Valdez, Kevin McCarthy, and Connie Malcolm Moreno, "An Annotated Bibliography of Sources on Mexican Migration" (Santa Monica, Calif: Rand Corporation, 1987); Gardner, "Macrolevel Influences on the Migration Decision Process."
[31]Given the limit on annual legal entries from Mexico and the large backlog of visa requests, the end of the Bracero Program indirectly encouraged even those who might have a legal claim to entry to bypass the system and enter illegally.

Second, the 1965 shift in U.S. immigration policy—which placed greater emphasis on family reunification and less emphasis on labor certification—made it virtually impossible for unskilled Mexican migrants to cross the U.S. border legally unless they had relatives who were citizens or legal resident aliens.[32] These policy changes differentiated the Mexican wage-labor flow on the demand side, while expanding migration networks had a similar effect on the supply side.

In response to the increasing dominance of Mexicans among legal immigrants admitted, Congress passed the Western Hemisphere Act in 1987, which extended the ceiling of 20,000 persons per country to countries of the Western Hemisphere.[33] This act decreased the number of quota visas available to Mexicans and reduced the flow of legal immigrants somewhat over the short term.[34] However, over the medium term, the net change on the absolute numbers admitted appears to be minimal. In fact, between 1982 and 1985, the number of legal Mexican immigrants admitted fluctuated between 56,000 and 61,000. If current immigration rates continue (exclusive of the numbers of Mexicans who may adjust their legal status under provisions of the 1986 Immigration Reform and Control Act), the number of Mexicans legally admitted during the decade of the 1980s will probably match, if not exceed, the number admitted during the 1970s.[35] Legal Mexican migration will continue to rise, thanks in large degree to the growing importance of family ties as a basis for gaining legal admission (see table 2).

One facet of the social impact of Mexican immigration is strictly demographic. Greater numbers of immigrants increase the visibility of the foreign-born population, an outcome accentuated by the fact that Mexican immigrants are highly concentrated geographically.[36] As public awareness of Mexican immigration rises, it becomes more controversial—both because of the emphasis on illegal immigration and because of misunderstandings about the

---

[32]McCarthy and Valdez, *Current and Future Effects of Mexican Immigration.*
[33]Leif I. Jensen, "The New Immigration: Implications for Poverty and Public Assistance Utilization" (Ph.D. dissertation, University of Wisconsin-Madison, 1987).
[34]Prior to 1976, Mexico contributed 50-60 percent of all Western Hemisphere immigrants. Consequently the extension of the 20,000 annual country limit to the Western Hemisphere tolled especially hard on Mexico. However, the total volume of nonquota admissions increased, party offsetting the effects of the 1976 act.
[35]If an additional 335,000 legal Mexican immigrants are admitted between 1986 and 1990, the absolute number during the 1980s will be larger than that for the 1970s, exclusive of the individuals who might eventually legalize their status. It is unclear how the INS will report this.
[36]Frank D. Bean and Marta Tienda, *The Hispanic Population of the United States* (New York: Russell Sage, 1987): chap. 3.

Table 2. Legal Mexican Immigrants Admitted by Type of Admission: Selected Years 1947-85

	Quota Number	Quota Percent	Non-Quota Number	Non-Quota Percent
1947	286	3.8	7,272	96.2
1950	174	2.6	6,570	97.4
1955	88	0.2	43,614	99.8
1960	150	0.5	32,558	99.5
1965	168	0.4	40,518	99.6
1970	27,267	60.8	17,554	39.2
1975	42,218	67.5	20,334	32.5
1980	24,831	43.8	31,849	56.2
1985	20,633	33.8	40,444	66.2

Source: U.S. Department of Justice, Annual Reports of the Immigration and Naturalization Service for years ending June 30, 1947, 1950, 1955, 1960, 1965, 1970, 1975, in Table 6A "Immigrant Aliens Admitted by Classes under the Immigration Laws and Country of Last Permanent Residence"; U.S. Department of Justice, *1980 Statistical Yearbook of the Immigration and Naturalization Service,* table 7, and *1985 Statistical Yearbook of the Immigration and Naturalization Service,* table 2.1

contribution of immigration to the growth of the Mexican-origin population. These misunderstandings precipitate fears about the "Hispanicization of the American Southwest" and reinforce beliefs about the difficulty of integrating Spanish-speaking immigrants into U.S. society.

Despite claims that immigration is the major component of growth of the Mexican-origin population, this growth is actually due to the group's youthfulness and fertility.[37] If fact, even in the absence of immigration, the Mexican-origin population will probably increase more rapidly than the Anglo population, at least for the next decade.

Second, the impacts of Mexican immigration also depend on the age-sex configuration of the new arrivals. As shown in figure 1, the increasing diversification of the Mexican flow is evident in the higher shares of women and children among post-1970, as compared to pre-1970, Mexican immigrants. For example, over the short term, the higher presence of children among the Mexican immigrant pool means greater social outlays for education. Over the long term, the prospects for successful integration of the Mexican-born youth who are educated in the United States probably are greater[38] since these immigrants conceivably will benefit from more exposure to U.S. institutions.

---

[37] Bean and Tienda calculate that between 1970 and 1980, net immigration accounted for less than half, and legal immigration substantially less than half, of that growth. Ibid.
[38] Borjas, "The Earnings of Male Hispanic Immigrants."

Figure 1. 1980 Age-Sex Composition of Persons of Mexican Origin by Nativity

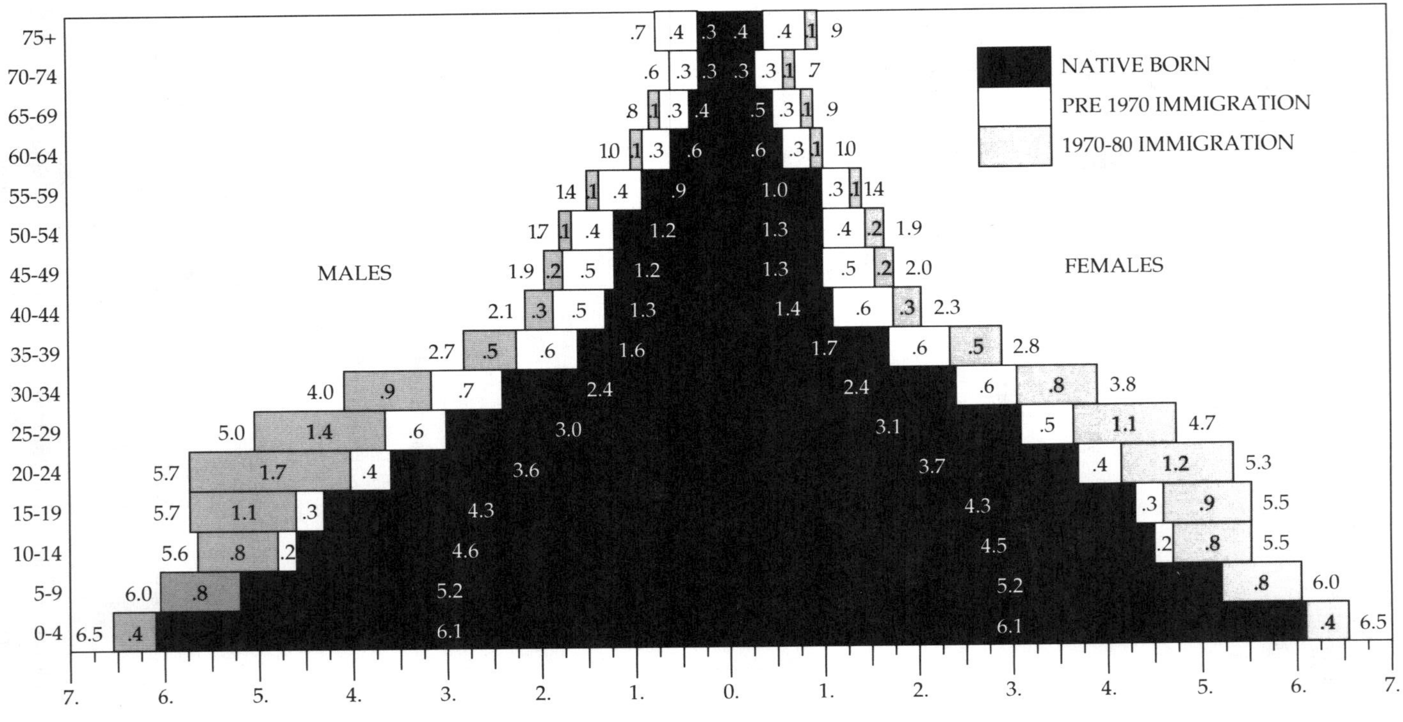

Source: 1980 PUMS, A Sample

Changes in U.S. immigration policy since 1964 have sought to curtail the supply of legal Mexican immigrants by changing the ground rules for entry, but they have not altered the demand for Mexican immigrant workers. Moreover, by the time the changes were implemented, migrant social networks were already fully mature and able to facilitate the continued flow.[39] Because the social ties between former Mexican immigrants and prospective migrants spanned the border, the changed admission guidelines were less effective in stemming the flow than they might have been.

In the aggregate, the social auspices of the Mexican migrant stream manifest themselves in the distribution of visas by admission category,[40] reported in table 3. As greater restrictions on visas subject to numerical limitation were implemented, the share of Mexican immigrants admitted in categories exempt from numerical limitation doubled, rising from about one-third of those admitted in 1975, prior to the lowered annual ceiling, to approximately two-thirds of 1985 entrants. In 1985, the most recent year for which published INS data are available, 87 percent of Mexicans who entered with numerically restricted visas did so under the family reunification provisions, while only 13 percent of non-exempt visas were granted on the basis of occupational preference.[41] Moreover, of the 2,602 visas granted to Mexicans for occupational specialization, only 924, roughly one-third, were granted for principals, while the remainder were granted for accompanying family members.

The wide acceptance by the mid-1960s of the "idea" of U.S.-bound migration increased the pool of individuals who eventually would migrate. It also contributed to the heterogeneity of the streams in terms of social background and duration of stay. Distinguishing between legal and illegal migrants—and within these broad categories, among short-term, cyclical, and permanent migrants—explains the relationship between the stream's diversity and shifts in immigration policy, and how various segments of the increasingly heterogeneous pool of immigrants, particularly legal and undocumented, are themselves interrelated.[42]

The increased heterogeneity of the migrant stream is important because it similarly diversifies the social impacts of migration in receiving communities. The distinction between sojourners, or

---

[39] Massey et al., *Return to Aztlan*.
[40] Ibid.
[41] The distribution of visa categories was: first preference, 12 percent; second preference, 36 percent; fourth preference, 15 percent; and fifth preference, 24 percent.
[42] McCarthy and Valdez, *Current and Future Effects of Mexican Immigration in California*.

Table 3. Sectoral Allocation of Mexican-origin and Non-Hispanic White Workers by Nativity and Gender: 1960-80

	Women Aged 16-64				Men Aged 16-64			
	Mexican		Anglo		Mexican		Anglo	
	Native	Foreign	Native	Foreign	Native	Foreign	Native	Foreign
Extractive	7.7	11.6	2.1	1.2	17.9	36.0	10.4	4.0
Transformative	22.1	29.9	25.6	34.8	38.4	31.3	42.9	48.9
Distributive services	23.9	17.1	24.9	20.1	21.8	17.4	23.2	20.7
Producer services	5.6	3.0	9.6	8.3	2.4	1.9	5.7	5.9
Social services	14.2	7.9	23.3	16.0	10.6	3.8	11.3	8.6
Personal services	26.6	30.4	14.6	19.6	9.1	9.6	6.4	11.9
Total[a]	100.1	99.9	100.1	100.0	100.2	100.0	99.9	100.0
1960 Dissimilarity Index,[b] Native-Foreign	23.3		18.8		23.0		17.0	
Extractive	5.3	11.0	1.5	1.4	11.6	19.3	7.0	3.4
Transformative	20.8	32.6	21.9	26.4	38.3	43.0	41.8	43.7
Distributive services	20.7	17.5	22.8	22.9	22.7	18.2	23.2	20.8
Producer services	7.0	4.3	10.4	11.4	3.7	2.5	6.7	8.8
Social services	24.9	13.1	29.1	22.3	14.6	6.1	14.4	11.4
Personal services	21.2	21.4	14.2	15.6	8.9	10.9	6.9	11.8
Total	99.9	99.9	99.9	100.0	99.8	100.0	100.0	99.9
1970 Dissimilarity Index,[b] Native-Foreign	25.0		12.0		19.0		15.6	
Extractive	4.0	10.0	1.8	0.9	9.1	17.0	6.3	2.6
Transformative	20.6	39.5	18.2	22.8	38.9	46.5	39.5	40.8
Distributive services	19.3	12.7	20.4	21.0	22.0	14.5	22.9	19.4
Producer services	9.2	5.6	12.9	14.1	4.9	3.1	8.2	10.0
Social services	31.0	15.4	32.7	27.6	15.6	5.3	15.0	15.3
Personal services	15.7	16.7	14.0	13.6	9.6	13.4	8.1	12.0
Total	99.8	99.9	100.0	100.0	100.1	99.8	100.0	100.1
198 Dissimilarity Index,[b] Native-Foreign	30.2		10.0		24.2		12.0	

Source: 1960, 1970 and 1980 PUMS files.
[a] Numbers may not equal 100 percent because of rounding error.
[b] Compares industry distributions of native- versus foreign-born.

temporary migrants (both short term and cyclical), and settlers, or permanent migrants, is especially critical for deciphering social impacts and may be more important than legal status for two reasons. First, temporary migrants usually reside in areas of high immigrant concentration, where they can activate a dense network of social ties to secure employment and basic social amenities. Permanent migrants (both legal and illegal) are more apt to venture far from the border, where the social distinctions between native-born and foreign-born can blur. Second, distinguishing between permanent and temporary migrants refines explanations about which "pull" factors are responsible for luring different types of prospective migrants.[43] Temporary migrants probably are driven by cyclical fluctuations in U.S. industries (especially agriculture, but also many service and light manufacturing industries), while permanent settlers' integration prospects are less closely associated with fluctuations in aggregate demand. They are determined, rather, by the consolidation of social relationships and obligations.

Further insight into the diversification of the Mexican immigrant pool is afforded by the interconnections among various types of migrants. That many temporary migrants become permanent settlers illustrates how "different types of immigrants are related through an underlying settlement process."[44] In fact, greater U.S. experience is a necessary ingredient for eventual settlement, irrespective of legal status.[45] In lowering the costs of migration and facilitating the process of integration, friendship and kinship networks are strengthened and strong networks increase the likelihood that temporary immigrants will eventually settle. This applies to both legal and illegal migrants, thereby calling into question the social significance of legal status per se. While not minimizing the scale and consequences of temporary Mexican flows, it is probably safe to assume that the social effects of migration are greatest when permanent settlement results.[46]

The concept of "auspices of migration," which refers to the social context in which decisions are made, is not new.[47] Recently,

---

[43]Ibid.
[44]Ibid., p. 16.
[45]Massey, "Understanding Mexican Migration to the United States."
[46]The work of Massey and associates (Massey et al., *Return to Aztlan*) has been most instructive about the nature of social processes responsible for changing the character and social foundations of the Mexican flow. Their work is particularly instructive about the social mechanisms that transform temporary migrants into permanent settlers.
[47]See, for example, Tienda, "Familism and Structural Assimilation of Mexican Immigrants in the United States"; Choldin, "Kinship Networks in the Migration Process"; Tilly and Brown, "On Uprooting, Kinship and the Auspices of Migration."

however, it has been revitalized and eloquently documented for Mexican migration by Massey and his associates.[48] Two of Massey's basic premises concerning the social nature of Mexican immigration have direct implications for its effects on U.S. society. First, even though migrant streams may emerge for narrow economic reasons (through deliberate labor recruitment, or to join the bracero work force, for example), once begun they develop a "social infrastructure" which in turn facilitates mass movement. Second, the settlement process with its momentum is so powerful that it leads to formation of "daughter communities," which subsequently provide landing grounds for newer arrivals and stepping stones for established permanent settlers to move elsewhere in search of better opportunities. Massey and his associates showed that the process by which networks expand and semi-institutionalize the notion of migration involves several stages following the original departures: repeat migration, settlement, and eventually, but not in all instances, return migration. This sequence does not apply to all individuals who migrate. Instead, these broad features outline the general process.[49]

Portes and Bach have arrived at a similar conclusion about the importance of social ties in sustaining immigrant flows, but their conceptualization distinguishes between processes that originate the flows (determinants of original departures in Massey's framework) and determinants that stabilize the flows (subsumed under the rubric of social networks in Massey's scheme).[50]

The deeply rooted social foundations of Mexican immigration suggest that the volume of Mexicans legally admitted to the United States is not likely to diminish. To alter the flow we must first understand the social process of settlement and then differentiate between aspects of the flow which can and cannot be modified through intervention.

IMMIGRATION AND STRATIFICATION: ON THE SOCIOECONOMIC SIGNIFICANCE OF MEXICAN ORIGIN

Evaluating migration's social and cultural impacts on U.S. society in general, and on communities receiving large numbers of immigrants in particular, raises the thorny issue of assimilation,

---

[48]Massey et al., *Return to Aztlan.*
[49]Massey, "Understanding Mexican Migration to the United States"; Massey and García España, "The Social Process of International Migration."
[50]Portes and Bach, *Latin Journey.*

the process by which two cultural groups mingle and fuse, adopting each other's culture and social institutions.[51]

Immigrant assimilation is a politically charged issue because of divided opinion on what form it should assume: "Anglo conformity" or "cultural pluralism."[52] At one extreme stands the Anglo conformity model which dominates public opinion about the new immigration.[53] This perspective expects a "complete renunciation of an immigrant's ancestral culture in favor of the behavior and values of the Anglo-Saxon core group" as a condition for socioeconomic integration.[54] Proponents of this perspective argue that because the decision to migrate is taken voluntarily, immigrants should be prepared to adopt U.S. customs and values on a wholesale basis. At the opposite pole, the cultural pluralism model expects minimal cultural concessions, provided that civic functioning and responsibility are not impaired. More to the point, cultural diversity should not be the basis for the uneven distribution of social and economic rewards.

Cultural pluralism draws support as a force promoting social justice; it demands equity while maintaining ethnic distinctiveness. Yet, with few exceptions (Jews, Cubans, and some Asian nationalities), history shows that it is within the context of assimilation that social justice and socioeconomic success are attained.[55] The salient research and policy question is, in what form can and must U.S. society accommodate cultural diversity to satisfy the legal mandate of providing equal social and economic opportunities without jeopardizing the civic functioning and collective goals of the nation?

---

[51]Milton Gordon characterizes this process as consisting of several stages, bginning with cultural assimilation and proceeding with structural, marital, and identification assimilation. See Gordon, "The Nature of Assimilation," in *Assimilation and American Life: The Role of Race, Religion, and National Origins*, edited by M. M. Gordon (New York: Oxford University Press, 1964); Franklin Goza, "Adjustment and Adaptation among Southeast Asian Refugees in the United States (Ph.D. dissertation, University of Wisconsin-Madison, 1987).

[52]Intermediate between these extremes is the melting pot, which refers to the unique national culture resulting from the comingling and amalgamation of various distinct groups. The melting pot model represents an ideal type which Milton Gordon believes never existed in the United States. See Gordon, "The Nature of Assimilation."

[53]Jensen, "The New Immigration."

[54]Gordon, "The Nature of Assimilation," p. 85.

[55]The distinction between symbolic ethnicity and minority status best illustrates the differing outcomes of the conformity and pluralist models of immigrant integration. See Nelson and Tienda, "The Structuring of Hispanic Ethnicity."

Outrage at pervasive social and economic inequities between Anglos and people of Mexican origin explains the emphasis on cultural pluralism—the reaffirmation of ethnicity and national origin as a source of pride and solidarity—that emerged from the Civil Rights movement and the rejection of the Anglo conformity model in a quest for cultural pluralism and self-determination. Many Hispanic leaders feel that assimilation threatens their cultural identity, but what concrete benefits a culturally plural society can offer the Hispanic community remains unclear.

Assimilation and cultural pluralism remain at the core of a decades-old debate about the social consequences of immigration, particularly when culturally distinct immigrant minorities are involved. Thus, the level at which society can tolerate cultural diversity affects how Mexican immigration will alter or influence U.S. society, in terms of both the significance of Mexican origin in the stratification regime and the imprint of cultural pluralism in spatial and organizational social forms. As such, the tolerable limits of inequality and of cultural diversity are intricately interwoven.

To be sure, the social integration of the Mexican-origin population goes well beyond the experiences of immigrants; it includes the social and economic progress of U.S.-born Chicanos. Over time there has been a steady improvement in the social position of the native-born Mexican-origin population, though less than in some other ethnic groups. Yet, even though the socioeconomic status of the Chicano population has improved appreciably over the past quarter century, most of the intra- and intergenerational occupational mobility resulted from structural rather than circulation mobility. In other words, the improvements in social position were due mostly to the elimination of low status positions rather than to substantial gains in social standing relative to Anglos.

Integration and Residential Concentration

Such findings raise questions about the role of immigrant composition in maintaining inter-period differentials in the socioeconomic status of the Mexican-origin population vis-à-vis Anglos.[56] Unfortunately, cross-sectional data have limited ability to indicate whether the integration prospects of Mexican immigrants are restricted permanently, or whether advances appear

---

[56]See Tienda and Jensen, "Poverty and Minorities," for a twenty-five year overview.

to be slow because of the continuing influx of Mexican immigrants in selected areas of the Southwest.

This section addresses the pluralism-versus-assimilation debate by evaluating Mexican immigrant integration in terms of residential concentration, labor-market segmentation, and ethnic cultural markers, of which Spanish-language maintenance is the most prominent. It first considers integration as an immigrant settlement process, addressing how and why public perception of residential concentration sustains the belief that recent immigrants are disinclined to join the social mainstream. It then discusses the persistence of Mexican origin as an allocative mechanism based on evidence from employment and migration patterns. Finally, it briefly considers two other ethnic markers which shape the social effects of Mexican immigration—naturalization and language diversity.[57]

Social and cultural impacts of Mexican immigration depend on the demographic features of the flow: how many come, who comes, how they enter, how long they stay, and especially how the social context of migration structures the settlement process and residential configurations of immigrant populations. Allegations that Mexican immigrants are less easily assimilated than earlier arrivals draw their support from two broad empirical generalizations. One—the "declining cohort quality" argument—focuses on the socioeconomic backgrounds of the new arrivals and claims that their low skill levels will hinder their economic assimilation.[58] A major advocate of this interpretation argues that because immigrants who arrived prior to 1965 are fundamentally different from subsequent arrivals, the positive association between earnings and length of U.S. residence observed in the past will not materialize during the socioeconomic life cycle of today's "average" immigrant.[59]

A second, more structural generalization relies more on impressionistic evidence than empirical facts. Residential concentrations of recent immigrants stimulate images of a proliferating Mexican culture and limited integration prospects. Although research on

---

[57] A chapter on residential segregation which appears in Bean and Tienda, *The Hispanic Population of the United States* was prepared in collaboration with Douglas Massey. This discussion relies heavily on Massey's contributions to this chapter.
[58] Barry R. Chiswick, "A Troubling Drop in Immigrant Quality," *New York Times*, 21 December 1986; Borjas, "Assimilation, Changes in Cohort Quality and the Earnings of Immigrants."
[59] Borjas, "Assimilation, Changes in Cohort Quality and the Earnings of Immigrants."

Hispanic residential segregation shows that immigration drives the process of residential segregation, this is not evidence that recent immigrants are more difficult to integrate than earlier arrivals.[60] Such interpretations emerge from popular writings which implicitly or explicitly arouse fears that Mexican immigrants and their offspring will become a permanent underclass, a Spanish-speaking majority in segregated areas.[61] Also, population projections about the ethnic composition of the United States or selected southwest states for the next thirty to fifty years often activate nativist sentiments about the potential dilution of Anglo "culture."[62]

Spatial integration is an important indicator of social position. Because economic and social resources are unevenly distributed in space, residential configurations determine groups' and individuals' access to jobs, housing, schooling, health care, and other social amenities. Spatial arrangements also influence the expression of cultural diversity via the maintenance of native languages and the viability of ethnic enterprises and social institutions. Thus, perceptions that Mexican immigrants are less inclined to intermingle with Anglo society are nurtured by the visible growth of Mexican immigrant neighborhoods.

Although the Mexican-origin population has historically concentrated in the Southwest, during the 1970s the foreign-born segment tended to increase residential concentration in a handful of states, while the native-born segment increased its residential dispersion.[63] In 1980, 58 percent of the foreign-born Mexican-origin population and approximately half of all illegal aliens from Mexico lived in California.[64] Moreover, within states—predominantly Texas and California—disproportionately large numbers of Mexican immigrants locate in large metropolitan areas, particularly those near the U.S.-Mexican border.[65]

---

[60]Massey and Denton, "Spatial Assimilation as a Socioeconomic Outcome"; Bean and Tienda, *The Hispanic Population of the United States*, chap. 5.
[61]See Valdez et al., "An Annotated Bibliography of Sources on Mexican Immigration," for supporting references.
[62]Ray Marshall, former secretary of labor, predicted that Anglos, who have been the dominant ethnic group in Texas since independence from Mexico, will lose their majority status within thirty years. Marshall predicted that immigration and lower Anglo fertility will dramatically shift the ethnic compositon of Texas, which in turn will strain the educational system as the school-age population becomes increasingly Spanish-speaking.
[63]Bean and Tienda, *The Hispanic Population of the United States*.
[64]Leon F. Bouvier and Robert W. Gardner, *Immigration to the U.S.: The Unfinished Story* (Washington, D.C.: Population Reference Bureau,. 1986).
[65]Bouvier and Gardner, ibid., report that Mexican immigrants, both legal and illegal, have always concentrated along the southern border of the United States, where travel costs can be kept to a minimum, and where the culture and climate most

Residential segregation may be imposed by the dominant group, or self-imposed by a minority group. If residential segregation is voluntary, then it is conceivable that Mexican immigrants choose areas of high Mexican concentration to preserve linguistic and other ethnic traits, or to avail themselves of the social supports provided by ethnic social networks. Alternately, residential segregation may reflect exclusion of a subordinated group by the dominant majority, as in white-black segregation patterns.

Massey's work on Hispanic residential segregation provides important insights about the social forces which have produced increasing residential concentration of Mexican immigrants.[66] As a driving force in residential succession (the process by which persons of Mexican origin replace Anglo residents), immigration increases Mexican immigrants' residential concentration as it reflects the Mexican-origin population's socioeconomic differentiation vis-à-vis Anglos, and as it seeks a means to facilitate the integration process of newly arriving migrants.[67]

But the influence of economic growth in promoting spatial assimilation, and institutionalized discrimination's role in precipitating ethnic resilience, also increased residential concentration of Mexican immigrants during the 1970s.[68] Regarding the former, Massey's work shows that Hispanic spatial assimilation was more pervasive than residential succession during the relatively prosperous 1960s. Consequently, Hispanic residential segregation and social isolation decreased between 1960 and 1970. However, the economic stagnation characterizing the 1970s reversed this trend because slow growth meant fewer opportunities for spatial assimilation.[69] When combined with an increase in immigration, predominantly of persons with limited skills whose social distance from the Anglo majority vitually demanded physical distance, residential succession—and hence higher levels of spatial segregation—resulted.

---

closely approximate Mexico's. However, McCarthy and Valdez (*Current and Future Effects of Mexican Immigration in California*) would argue that this generalization applies more to temporary and cyclical than to permanent settlers.
[66]Massey and Denton, "Spatial Assimilation as a Socioeconomic Outcome"; Bean and Tienda, *The Hispanic Population of the United States*, chap.5.
[67]Massey, "Understanding Mexican Migration to the United States"; Massey et al., *Return to Aztlan*.
[68]Portes and Bach, *Latin Journey*, chaps. 8 and 9.
[69]Spatial assimilation is the integration of Mexican-Americans with Anglos of similar socioeconomic backgrounds. For spatial assimilation to occur, Mexican-Americans as a group would need to experience social mobility as a condition of gaining access to the residential areas occupied by the Anglo middle classes.

The increase in residential segregation during the 1970s also reflects a voluntary preference for residence in ethnic neighborhoods. In explaining the seemingly counter-intuitive increase in the strength of ethnic ties as Mexican migrants became more familiar with U.S. society, Portes and Bach argue that concentration in ethnic neighborhoods and the accentuation of ethnicity as a basis for social organization were responses to rejection by the dominant society.[70] As Mexican immigrants sought refuge among persons of similar cultural backgrounds, symbols of Mexican culture became an enduring rather than a transitional aspect of social relationships and a defining feature of Mexican integration. This finding runs counter to the predictions of assimilation theory, which requires acculturation as a condition for structural integration, and it calls into question allegations that Mexican immigrants and barrio residents are unable to adapt to U.S. society.

For Mexican immigrants, ethnic relationships were organized by place of residence rather than place of employment. Thus, Mexican immigrants residing in ethnic neighborhoods were more likely to restrict their friendship ties to other Mexicans, both native- and foreign-born. Relying on ethnic ties as a base of support does not mean that Mexicans could not adapt; it reflects rather a realistic assessment of their tentative acceptance by the dominant society. Mexican immigrants' ethnic resilience is "not a force leading to collective withdrawal, but rather a moral resource, an integral part of the process of establishing and defining a place in a new society."[71]

In summary, allegations that Mexican immigrants are disinclined or difficult to integrate into U.S. society appear to be rooted in public perceptions about the increasing residential concentration of the Mexican-origin population. Just as cross-sectional analyses of immigration and its consequences fail to capture the dynamism in settlement patterns, popular accounts of residential concentration patterns based on occasional snapshots can argue that the growth and vitality of Mexican barrios reflects a disinclination to integrate into U.S. society.

However, such allegations of limited integration prospects do not square with the facts about the social underpinnings of Mexican immigration—in particular, the virtual inevitability of settlement as migrants acquire experience in the United States—and about the

---

[70] Portes and Bach, *Latin Journey*.
[71] Ibid, p. 333.

role of ethnic ties in promoting social integration. Massey's findings that legal status loses strength as a predictor of settlement, and that greater U.S. experience increases migrants' economic success and their likelihood to settle, show that integration is highly feasible.[72] If it is difficult to integrate Mexicans socially and economically, how can we explain the number of legal and illegal migrants who have settled permanently in the United States over the past forty years?

It is clear that the appropriate question is not whether Mexican migrants can be integrated, but how much the growing Mexican presence—especially along the U.S.-Mexico border—strains U.S. tolerance for cultural diversity.

In summary, persisting residential segregation between Mexican immigrants and Anglos raises structural questions about the long-run implications of restricted access to spatially distributed social and economic resources. Evidence of lower socioeconomic achievements among Chicanos compared to Anglos may itself result from spatial restrictions in access to jobs, schooling, and health services—and not from immigration's retarding impact on the socioeconomic assimilation of the Mexican-origin population as a whole. Finally, the influence of the general state of the economy, and especially business-cycle variation, in promoting or discouraging spatial integration also raises serious questions about the role of immigration versus institutionalized discrimination in structuring economic inequality between Anglos and persons of Mexican origin.

National Origin, Migrant Status, and Structured Inequities

The importance of national origin and nativity in stratifying the Hispanic population in general, and the Mexican-origin population in particular, is well documented.[73] Nevertheless, persisting socioeconomic differences between Anglos and persons of Mexican origin raise questions about the relative weight of ascriptive versus meritocratic forces in the assignment of status positions. That

---

[72]Douglas S. Massey, "Do Undocumented Mexican Migrants Earn Lower Wages?" *International Migration Review*, forthcoming.
[73]See Borjas and Tienda, "The Economic Consequences of Immigration"; Bean and Tienda, *The Hispanic Population of the United States*, chaps. 9 and 10; Marta Tienda, "The Mexican American Population," in *Nonmetropolitan America in Transition*, edited by Amos Hawley and Sara Mills Mazie (Chapel Hill: University of North Carolina Press, 1981).

ascribed characteristics, like Mexican ancestry and birth, are key stratifying variables is less debated than how they influence individual life chances and the relative positioning of groups in a status hierarchy. There exist various schools of thought on this question.

The most common interpretation of how national origin and nativity stratify population subgroups focuses on individual differences in social background and human capital investments.[74] From this perspective, socioeconomic differences between native- and foreign-born Mexicans, and between both groups and Anglos, will disappear once their social origins and human capital endowments are equal. Thus, Mexican origin and nativity carry no social or economic content per se, except perhaps cultural differences which presumably are inconsequential for status differentiation. A naive corollary of this interpretation is that an end to or substantial slowdown in Mexican immigration should improve the relative standing of the Mexican-origin population by drastically reducing the replenishment of individuals with low stocks of human capital. However, this simplistic solution begs the question as to why differences in social investments persist between Anglos and native-born Chicanos and why rewards to schooling differ according to nativity and national origin.[75]

An alternative interpretation, derived from ethnic stratification literature in sociology, recognizes that ascribed characteristics, such as nativity and national origin, determine not only the allocation of social rewards, but also the ability of dominant groups to protect their interests.[76] From this perspective, social inequities between the Mexican-origin and Anglo populations arise from several social processes, including

- discrimination, which both restricts access to valued social resources that determine subsequent achievements (notably

---

[74]David Featherman and Robert Hauser, *Opportunity and Change* (New York: Academic Press, 1978).
[75]Critics of the status-attainment and human capital approaches to socioeconomic differentiation among national-origin and nativity groups have argued that these perspectives underrate structural factors as determinants of social opportunities, particulary the importance of ethnic affiliation in determining social position.
[76]Charles Hirschman, "Theories and Models of Ethnic Inequality," in *Research in Race and Ethnic Relations*, vol. 2, edited by C. Marrett (Greenwich, Conn.: JAI Press, 1980); Donald J. Noel, "A Theory of the Origin of Ethnic Stratification," *Social Problems* 16 (1968): 157-172; Teresa A. Sullivan, "Racial and Ethnic Differences in Labor Force Participation: An Ethnic Stratification Perspective," in *The Demography of Racial and Ethnic Groups*, edited by F.D. Bean and W. Parker Frisbie (New York: Academic Press, 1978).

education and training) and perpetuates unequal reward structures according to ascribed criteria;

- residential segregation, which restricts access to spatially distributed resources and maintains social distances between groups; and

- the resurgence of ethnicity as a basis for ordering social relationships.

The idea that ethnicity is used to assign status positions challenges classical achievement models which tend to understate the power of ascription in ranking the Mexican-origin population. The social differentiation of the Latino work force may be better understood by investigating how national origin is used both to structure job queues and to match individuals to jobs.[77] Simply put, "Mexican jobs" were those in which Mexicans were overrepresented relative to Anglos, while the reverse describes "Anglo jobs."[78] Based on Hechter's notion of the cultural division of labor and Leiberson's notion of ethnic queues,[79] national origin acquires a structural property in defining the stratification regime, and a primary rather than a secondary role as an individual allocative mechanism.

While not denying the micro-social exchange value of Mexican origin, how Mexican origin is used to define and maintain job queues has implications for the ethnic composition of labor demand and the role of national origin and/or immigrant status in matching Mexican-origin workers to specific jobs. Thus, the idea that jobs are "ethnically typed" explicitly acknowledges that vacancy competition is not a random process. It is systematically ordered by national origin. Moreover, structural arrangements maintain the demand for Mexican labor even during periods of slow economic

---

[77] See Tienda and Lii, "Minority Concentration and Earnings Inequality"; Marta Tienda and Elaine Fielding, "Migration, Preferential Worker Status, and Employment: Divergent Paths of Hispanic Market Insertion in the United States," IRP Discussion Paper (Madison: University of Wisconsin, 1987).

[78] A typology of jobs in which Mexican-origin workers are overrepresented relative to Anglos can be devised using accounting techniques based on simple distributions, such as indexes of dissimilarity or, more analytically, using log-linear statistical procedures. In either case, designating boundaries separating jobs in which Mexicans are over- or underrepresented relative to Anglos is somewhat arbitrary. These decisions, while posing a technical research problem, represent a more fundamental social policy concern, namely, the tolerable limits of cultural pluralism and ethnic inequality.

[79] Michael Hechter, "Group Formation and the Cultural Division of Labor," *American Journal of Sociology* 84:2 (1978): 293-317; Stanley Lieberson, *A Piece of the Pie* (Berkeley: University of California Press, 1980).

growth. The fact that Mexican workers are preferred for designated jobs provides a more structural perspective to the social underpinnings of the Mexican migrant stream. Figure 2 provides one version of the ethnic job queue for Mexican-origin and Anglo workers.

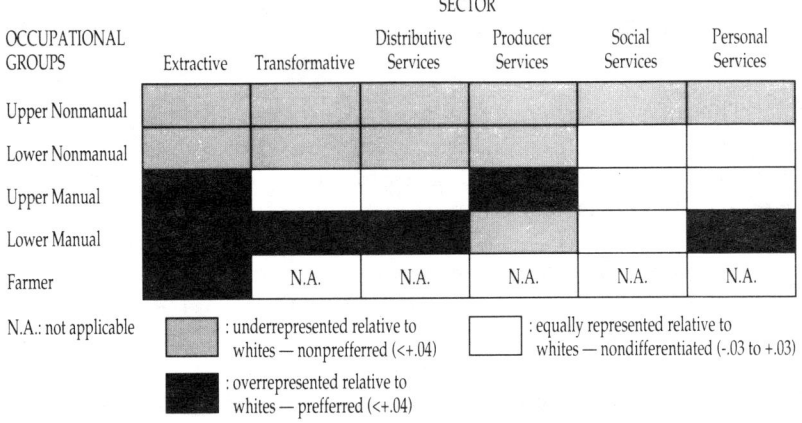

Figure 2. Preferential Status and Mexican Origin

SECTOR

OCCUPATIONAL GROUPS	Extractive	Transformative	Distributive Services	Producer Services	Social Services	Personal Services
Upper Nonmanual						
Lower Nonmanual						
Upper Manual						
Lower Manual						
Farmer		N.A.	N.A.	N.A.	N.A.	N.A.

N.A.: not applicable

▨ : underrepresented relative to whites — nonprefferred (<+.04)

☐ : equally represented relative to whites — nondifferentiated (-.03 to +.03)

■ : overrepresented relative to whites — prefferred (<+.04)

Viewing job queues as structured along ethnic lines provides an explanation of persisting social inequality between Anglo and Mexican-origin workers, irrespective of their nativity. If Mexican workers are preferred for some jobs, as indexed by their disproportionate concentration relative to Anglos, then unemployment probabilities should be lower for these workers. In fact, Tienda and Fielding showed that Mexican-origin workers destined for "Mexican-typed" jobs experienced lower unemployment probabilities compared to their (statistical) counterparts destined for jobs where Anglos were dominant or both groups were uniformly represented.[80] This provides preliminary support to the claim that some jobs may be "reserved" for Mexican (immigrant) labor because of the way national origin is used to array employment hierarchies.

The role of national origin and nativity in matching persons to jobs can be both positive and negative from a socioeconomic standpoint. For example, Mexican workers have been preferred in agricultural jobs at least since the mid-1800s.[81] While the incomes

---

[80] Tienda and Fielding, "Migration, Preferential Worker Status, and Employment."
[81] Preference for Mexican immigrant labor in seasonal crops was made explicit in the Bracero labor agreement and has remained on an implicit basis through the heavy reliance on illegal workers in agriculture since that time.

of agricultural workers are low by comparison to other low-skill jobs, particularly in construction and small manufacturing industries, they are much higher than in Mexico.

Thus, the preferential recruitment of Mexican workers for "Mexican" jobs may be positive because ethnic job queues "reserve" jobs for them. But this is offset by significantly lower earnings than those of their counterparts holding jobs where the ethnic mix is neutral or favors Anglos.[82] In other words, the economic protections associated with preferential worker status do not carry over into earnings. Rather, the disproportionate representation of Mexican-origin workers in low status jobs practically ensures that the association between Mexican origin and low socioeconomic status will persist for some time to come.

The critical question is whether Mexican immigration helps maintain the cultural division of labor. To the extent that demand for Mexican workers is nativity specific, the admission of low-skill workers may retard the socioeconomic assimilation of prior immigrants and their native-born offspring. Evidence that job configurations of native- and foreign-born Mexicans have converged would allow for alternative interpretations and, in particular, draw attention to the force of history and the role of institutionalized discrimination in defining the relative social position of the Mexican-origin population.

Tables 3 and Table 4 provide some perspective on the influence of nativity on stratification between 1960 and 1980. Those who most felt the decline of agricultural employment—as the economy shifted from goods to service production—were Mexican-origin men. Although the share of all Mexican-origin men engaged in extractive pursuits fell 10 percentage points during the 1970s, these workers' movement out of agriculture slowed, thanks to the persistence of Mexican immigrants in this industry. Similarly, the increasing

---

[82]Tienda and Lii ("Minority Concentration and Earnings Inequality") show that recent Mexican immigrants who were employed in jobs where Mexicans were disproportionately represented earned roughly 20 percent less than recent immigrants employed in jobs where the work force was more ethnically diverse. These results, however, apply to recent immigrants residing in states where Hispanics were not numerically dominant. For earlier immigrants and native-born Chicanos, the income penalty associated with incumbency in "Mexican" jobs was slightly less—roughly 15 percent relative to Chicanos and prior immigrants who were employed in ethnically diverse or Anglo-typed jobs. That this effect applied both to high and low Hispanic concentration states indicates that nativity is less critical than national origin in defining and maintaining ethnic job queues.

Table 4. Occupational Distribution by Mexican-origin and Non-Hispanic White Workers by Nativity and Gender: 1960-80

	Women Aged 16-64			
	Mexican		Anglo	
	Native	Foreign	Native	Foreign
Professional	3.9	2.1	10.9	6.9
Semiprofessional	0.7	0.4	1.4	1.4
Farmers	0.1	0.1	0.3	0.4
Managers	1.4	2.4	3.4	4.6
Clerical	22.1	9.5	37.8	24.0
Sales	9.9	7.0	11.0	8.7
Crafts	1.1	0.9	1.1	1.7
Operatives	27.0	36.2	16.6	30.1
Service workers	25.7	29.3	15.7	21.1
Laborers	1.2	1.1	0.5	0.6
Farm laborers	6.9	11.1	1.3	0.6
Total[a]	100.0	100.1	100.0	100.1
1960 Dissimilarity Index,[b] Native-Foreign	18.0		20.0	
Professional	5.9	3.7	13.4	12.1
Semiprofessional	0.8	0.3	1.6	1.2
Farmers	0.1	0.1	0.2	0.0
Managers	2.0	1.7	3.3	3.4
Clerical	29.3	16.3	37.2	30.5
Sales	7.0	3.8	8.6	9.8
Crafts	2.0	2.4	1.7	2.0
Operatives	20.9	37.0	14.1	20.4
Service workers	26.2	23.5	18.4	19.3
Laborers	1.4	1.7	1.0	0.9
Farm laborers	4.4	9.6	0.7	0.3
Total[a]	100.0	100.1	100.2	99.9
1970 Dissimilarity Index,[b] Native-Foreign	22.0		9.0	
Professional	8.0	3.5	15.4	13.8
Semiprofessional	1.9	0.9	2.6	3.4
Farmers	0.1	0.1	0.3	0.1
Managers	3.8	2.0	6.4	7.0
Clerical	33.7	15.7	35.0	31.1
Sales	5.5	3.2	7.9	8.1
Crafts	2.3	2.8	1.9	2.6
Operatives	16.6	37.2	10.5	15.5
Service workers	22.9	22.2	17.9	17.3
Laborers	2.1	3.4	1.6	1.0
Farm laborers	2.9	8.8	0.5	0.2
Total[b]	99.8	99.8	100.0	100.1
1980 Dissimilarity Index, Native-Foreign	28.3		7.2	

Source: Adapted from Bean and Tienda, *The Hispanic Poulation of the United States*, tables 9-8 and 9-9.
[a] Numbers may not equal 100 percent because of rounding error.
[b] Compares occupation distributions of native- versus foreign-born.

Table 4. Occupational Distribution by Mexican-origin and Non-Hispanic White Workers by Nativity and Gender: 1960-80 *(Continued)*

	Men Aged 16-64			
	Mexican		Anglo	
	Native	Foreign	Native	Foreign
Professional	3.3	2.1	9.3	8.1
Semiprofessional	1.3	0.4	2.0	1.8
Farmers	1.9	1.7	5.3	1.7
Managers	4.1	2.8	11.2	12.8
Clerical	5.2	2.4	7.9	7.0
Sales	3.4	2.1	7.6	5.2
Crafts	16.4	12.6	21.3	26.1
Operatives	26.8	19.0	21.1	21.6
Service workers	8.0	7.5	5.0	8.8
Laborers	17.6	18.0	6.7	6.0
Farm laborers	12.1	31.4	2.6	0.9
Total[a]	100.1	100.0	100.0	100.0
1960 Dissimilarity Index,[b] Native-Foreign	19.8		10.6	
Professional	5.1	3.4	12.0	14.8
Semiprofessional	1.7	0.6	2.5	2.2
Farmers	0.7	0.6	2.8	1.1
Managers	4.9	2.9	11.5	10.2
Clerical	6.7	3.5	7.6	7.2
Sales	3.9	2.6	7.2	7.3
Crafts	20.2	18.8	21.1	22.9
Operatives	26.2	28.2	19.0	16.6
Service workers	11.0	9.9	7.4	12.3
Laborers	13.0	14.3	7.2	5.1
Farm laborers	6.7	15.2	1.8	0.4
Total[a]	100.1	100.0	100.1	100.1
1970 Dissimilarity Index,[b] Native-Foreign	11.8		9.6	
Professional	5.7	2.5	12.1	17.0
Semiprofessional	2.1	0.8	2.7	3.2
Farmers	0.5	0.5	2.1	0.5
Managers	6.9	3.6	13.6	16.5
Clerical	7.9	3.7	6.9	5.5
Sales	3.7	1.7	7.0	5.2
Crafts	20.7	17.7	20.7	22.1
Operatives	24.0	30.0	17.4	14.6
Service workers	11.8	13.0	8.6	9.8
Laborers	12.6	14.3	7.5	5.1
Farm laborers	4.1	12.2	1.3	0.4
Total[b]	100.0	100.0	100.0	99.9
1980 Dissimilarity Index, Native-Foreign	17.0		10.9	

Source: Adapted from Bean and Tienda, *The Hispanic Poulation of the United States*, tables 9-8 and 9-9.
[a]Numbers may not equal 100 percent because of rounding error.
[b]Compares occupation distributions of native- versus foreign-born.

share of Mexican-origin workers in the transformative sector during the 1960s and 1970s reflected almost exclusively the increased participation of immigrants in manufacturing industries. For the country as a whole, employment in personal services dropped between 1960 and 1980.[83] This was not the case for Mexican-origin men. In fact, the share of Mexican men engaged in personal service industries increased, owing to the growing presence of foreign-born workers in these industries.

That nativity differentials in the industrial employment structures of Hispanic workers persist does not preclude increased similarity in their industry and sectoral distributions over time. The index of dissimilarity, which summarizes the share of workers who would have to change industry categories for two compared distributions to be identical, provides a useful way to assess whether the industry profiles of native- and foreign-born men converged or diverged over time. Calculations based on thirty-seven detailed industries show that the industry employment structures widened during the 1980s for Mexican-origin men, after narrowing during the 1970s.[84] Nativity distribution for Anglo men, on the other hand, converged gradually over time. However, the greater dissimilarity between the industry distributions of native and immigrant Mexican-origin men may be an artifact of the increased presence of undocumented immigrants in the 1980 census, the large undercount of native-born men in the 1970 census, and the persisting job segregation among Chicanos, *mexicanos*, and *indocumentados*.

Compared to men, the average share of Mexican-origin women engaged in agricultural pursuits was lower. Yet when compared to their Anglo counterparts, Mexican-origin women were disproportionately represented in extractive industries throughout the period. That Mexican immigrant men would continue to enter extractive jobs at a faster rate than the growth of the total labor force,[85] despite shrinking extractive opportunities nationally, contributes to the image of agricultural jobs as "Mexican work." Also, unlike other Latino women, those of Mexican origin increased their

---

[83]Joachim Singleman and Marta Tienda, "The Process of Occupational Change in a Service Society: The Case of the United States, 1960-1980," in *New Approaches to Economic Restructuring, Unemployment and the Social Division of Labor*, edited by Bryan Roberts, Ruth Finnegan, and Duncan Gallie (Manchester, England: University of Manchester Press, 1985).
[84]Bean and Tienda, *The Hispanic Population of the United States*, chap. 9.
[85]Marta Tienda, Leif I. Jensen, and Robert L. Bach, "Immigration, Gender and the Process of Ocupational Change," *International Migration Review* 18:4 (1984): 1021-1044.

participation in manufacturing industries over the twenty-year period while decreasing their presence in personal services—a pattern consistent with the national trend.

Nativity differentials in the industry distributions of Mexican women increased throughout the twenty-year period, a pattern which distinguishes them from other Latino-origin women.[86] The ID (index of dissimilarity) values comparing the industry distributions of native and immigrant Mexican-origin women rose slightly during the 1960s and even more during the 1970s, indicating growing disparities over time. By contrast, the nativity differences in the industry distributions of Anglo women gradually narrowed. In large measure, the increased nativity differentials in the industrial allocation of Mexican women resulted from the opposed tendencies of native and immigrant women to enter manufacturing jobs.

Table 4 further illustrates the importance of birthplace in stratifying the work force. The ID measure comparing the occupational structures of native- and foreign-born Mexican-origin men converged during the prosperous 1960s, when the volume of immigration was lower and opportunities for social mobility relatively more fluid. But it diverged thereafter, when high levels of immigration confronted economic stagnation. Part of the growing disparity reflects the changing legal status and demographic composition of Mexican immigrants, as well as the undercount of Mexican-origin workers in the 1970 census. Paralleling the results based on the industry classification, nativity differentials in the occupational allocation of Mexican-origin women increased between 1960 and 1980, owing to growing disparities in the placement of these women in clerical, operative, and farm labor jobs.

Thus, while there is evidence that immigration has played an increasing role in stratifying the Mexican work force during the last decade, the persistent ascriptive importance of national origin and changes in macroeconomic conditions also played important parts in preserving the profile of Mexican workers as a low-status, blue-collar work force. This is not to argue that occupational upgrading and social mobility have totally bypassed the Chicano population.[87] Rather, because the Anglo population also has experienced social mobility, the improvements in the relative standing

---

[86]Bean and Tienda, *The Hispanic Population of the United States*, chap. 9.
[87]Snipp and Tienda, "Chicano Career Mobility."

of Mexican-origin workers are less pronounced. To be sure, group disparities in education and labor market skills account for a large share of the unequal social position of Mexicans vis-à-vis majority Anglos, but to explain one set of social inequities with another begs the question about how these arise in the first place. How they are perpetuated over time is less of a mystery.

Pluralism versus Inequality: Language and Political Power

Language—

The issue of integration lies at the core of a philosophical debate about cultural pluralism versus Anglo conformity assimilation. Language is a focal point of assimilationist efforts because Spanish retention has been blamed for the disadvantaged socioeconomic status of the Mexican-origin population. Since language is the key cultural vehicle through which the values, ideals, and behaviors of the dominant culture are imparted, Spanish-dominant individuals cannot achieve equal access to that culture, its behavior patterns, or its economic benefits.[88]

The pluralism-versus-conformity debate with respect to immigration and language is pointedly illustrated by the extreme positions expressed by former Colorado governor Dick Lamm, who argues for forced assimilation, and Cruz Reynoso, the first Mexican-American appointee to the California Supreme Court.

- Lamm: "America can accept additional immigrants, but we must be sure they become American.... We should be color blind, but not linguistically deaf.... We can teach English via bilingual education, but we should take care not to become a bilingual society."

- Cruz: "America is a political union—not a cultural, linguistic, religious or racial union.... But we should no more demand English-language skills for citizenship than we should demand uniformity of religion."

Despite controversy over bilingualism's socioeconomic consequences, most research shows that Spanish retention (bilingualism) does not hinder the socioeconomic achievements of Hispanic-origin

---

[88]Candace Nelson, "Hispanic Educational Attainment: An Ethnic Issue?" (M.S. thesis, University of Wisconsin-Madison, 1984).

groups, provided that they acquire a reasonable level of proficiency in English. One possible exception to this generalization are Mexican immigrants, for whom Spanish bilingualism and monolingualism appear to lower occupational status.[89] The effect of English proficiency on labor-market position depends on the outcome of interest (i.e., educational attainment, labor force participation, earnings, or occupational status) as well as gender.[90]

Since English proficiency represents human capital necessary to function effectively in U.S. society, a substantial correlation with socioeconomic achievement is not surprising. That recent Mexican immigrants generally are less proficient in English than the Mexican-origin population as a whole largely reflects their more limited exposure to the language. But English fluency does increase over time. Fully 90 percent of the Mexican-origin population enumerated in 1980 reported speaking English well, although only about 30 percent use English exclusively.[91] Moreover, Spanish retention is not confined to the foreign born. Hence, concern over linguistic diversity is not uniquely an immigration problem. Research showing that the language environment of the home exerts little impact on educational outcomes contradicts the inference that cultural pluralism, reflected in Spanish retention, is a source of low educational attainment among Mexican-origin youth. Indeed, the most powerful predictor of Mexican-origin youths' socioeconomic achievements proved to be the class backgrounds of their parents.[92]

Because the transition from Spanish to English begins among the foreign born and proceeds rapidly among successive generations,[93] the long-term socioeconomic implications of Spanish retention should be less serious than opponents of bilingual education claim. Since formal schooling is the key to subsequent employment opportunities and long-term life chances, the importance of acquiring proficiency in English cannot be overstated. But Spanish retention by itself does not hinder integration.

---

[89]Marta Tienda and Lisa J. Neidert, "Language, Education and the Socioeconomic Achievement of Hispanic Origin Men," *Social Science Quarterly* 65:2 (1984): 519-536.
[90]Bean and Tienda, *The Hispanic Population of the United States*, chaps. 8-10.
[91]Ibid.
[92]Nelson, "Hispanic Educational Attainment."
[93]Portes and Bach, *Latin Journey*; Nelson and Tienda, "The Structuring of Hispanic Ethnicity."

Political Power—

If symbolic expressions of cultural diversity, such as deliberate Spanish retention, do not hinder Mexican immigrants' socioeconomic integration—as the preponderance of empirical research suggests—then the critical question becomes, what does limit integration? The answer may well be the low levels of political participation among the foreign-born Mexican-origin population and their low rates of naturalization. Mexican immigrants who arrived during the 1970s have the lowest naturalization rates among all nationality groups and a longer average waiting period before naturalization among those who eventually become citizens.[94]

Unable to determine conclusively which elements influence naturalization rates for recent Mexican immigrants, Portes and Curtis identified three factors which limit the political participation and influence of Mexican immigrants. First, permanent settlement, indicated by home ownership and family responsibilities, positively influenced the propensity to naturalize. Second, residential segregation patterns could either encourage or discourage naturalization: positive contacts with Anglos increase naturalization rates, while discrimination decreases them. Finally, variations in social capital, reflected in English proficiency levels, influenced the likelihood of naturalization but not in an unequivocal way. While knowledge of English broadens the range of possible experiences with U.S. society, it also increases immigrants' exposure to prejudice and discrimination, thereby activating ethnic resilience and ultimately deterring naturalization.[95]

While the determinants of naturalization remain somewhat hazy, naturalization's social implications are clear. As long as much of the foreign-born Mexican-origin population fails to seek citizenship, the political potential of a large population base will remain unrealized. Action in this issue area depends largely on the political participation of the native-born Mexican-origin population, even though the citizenship issue does not affect them directly. This fact dramatically shifts the base of the social dilemma of integration and political participation. No longer is it a question of cultural pluralism and ascriptive characteristics, but an issue deeply rooted in the class location of the Chicano population. This aspect of social

---

[94]Portes and Curtis, "Determinants of Naturalization among Recent Mexican Immigrants."
[95]Ibid.

inequality, with its long historical antecedents, cannot be corrected through immigration reform, or by blaming immigrants for Chicanos' unequal social, economic, and political position vis-à-vis Anglos.

Summary

Immigration's role in stratifying the Mexican-origin population fits two scenarios. One is that socioeconomic gains among the Mexican-origin population are limited by the "weight" of new cohorts of Mexican immigrants who are largely unskilled and destined for low status jobs in the United States. This "composition effect" is consistent with the historical experience of European immigrants, who entered at the bottom of the stratification hierarchy and moved up over generations.[96] In this scenario, Mexican immigrants follow historical patterns to the extent that immigrants' social mobility occurs mainly through generational transitions.[97] However, the experience of recent Mexican immigrants differs from that of previous immigrants. The difference we can attribute to the state of the economy and the relative consolidation of Mexican origin as an axis of the stratification regime.

An alternative scenario suggests that the Mexican-origin population has limited social mobility partly because of the public's failure to differentiate between native- and foreign-born segments of the population, and partly because of institutionalized discrimination against persons of Mexican origin irrespective of birthplace. This interpretation accords greater weight to Mexican origin per se, and emphasizes negative stereotyping and the consolidation of Mexican origin in the cultural division of labor.

These alternative interpretations hold important implications for future policy-making. But these are not immediately apparent because the same evidence can be used to support restrictive or permissive immigration policies. For example, the first scenario appeals to advocates of restrictive immigration policy, who emphasize the need for socioeconomic advancement and cultural integration among the resident Mexican-origin population. Proponents of a liberal immigration policy, on the other hand, cite evidence of intergenerational socioeconomic progress to substantiate claims

---

[96]Lieberson, *A Piece of the Pie*; Featherman and Hauser, *Opportunity and Change*.
[97]McCarthy and Valdez, *Current and Future Effects of Mexican Immigration in California*.

that incoming cohorts of Mexican immigrants do not retard the social mobility of earlier arrivals and their native-born offspring. There is an obvious need to compare the immigration experiences of Mexicans and other recent arrivals and to defer judgment on the social impacts of Mexican immigration until intergenerational consequences have had time to unfold. In either case, the need to shift from cross-sectional to longitudinal research designs is clear.

CONCLUDING REMARKS: RESEARCH AND POLICY IMPLICATIONS

The unintended social consequences of policies motivated by narrow economic, political, or demographic considerations may be far greater than the perceived "problems" these policies seek to correct. Herein lies the dilemma of Mexican immigration in the 1990s. A U.S. immigration policy which strives to balance political, economic, social, humanitarian, and ideological considerations is certain to fail because these diverse goals themselves pose the irreconcilable dilemma.

> [I]f we emphasize the economic role of immigration and admit more and more skilled workers, we sacrifice the goal of reuniting families; if we stress (as is now the case) the admission of relatives, we lose control of the effect of immigration on our labor markets. If we admit highly skilled immigrants, we may be hurting their home countries and our own less privileged citizens; if we fail to admit the highly skilled applicants, we deprive our country of their badly needed talents.[98]

Whether Mexican immigration represents a major social problem remains unclear, but the level of concern over the social and economic impacts of immigration—especially Mexican immigration—is unwarranted.[99] The growing empirical literature falls squarely on the side of net gains for the host society. Moreover, this net advantage should continue unless growth slows to the point that the economy can no longer absorb immigrants. This scenario is not totally implausible. A severe recession could prompt the virtual elimination of immigration for an indefinite period in an

---

[98] Elliot Abrams and Franklin S. Abrams, "Immigration Policy—Who Gets In and Why?" *Public Interest* 30 (Winter 1975): 28.
[99] Borjas and Tienda, "The Economic Consequences of Immigration."

effort to protect the social and economic interests of the resident population. The social consequences of such a measure would be profound, and the humanitarian effects could be disastrous.

Such drastic reform in U.S. immigration policy is unlikely in the foreseeable future. Nevertheless, this scenario highlights the importance of macrostructural economic conditions in shaping public perceptions of immigration as a problem, and it underscores two additional elements which reinforce this negative perception. The first is the focus on the illegal contingent within the migratory stream. This social issue becomes a political issue because it challenges the United States' ability, if not the right, to control its borders. Second, because Mexican immigration is predominantly a wage-labor flow,[100] any increase in U.S. unemployment invites scapegoating.[101] Although allegations about the adverse effects of immigration are no longer blatantly racist,[102] new immigrants—particularly those with limited labor-market skills and distinct national cultures—are still an "easy target for anxieties over high unemployment rates, public spending and taxation, and the quality of schools."[103] Among the general public and lay politicians, fears of cultural pluralism are fed by the regional and metropolitan concentration of Mexican immigrants, slowed residential succession, heightened awareness of Spanish retention, and the resurgence of ethnicity as a basis for social functioning.

Popular portrayals of Mexican immigration tend to misinterpret indicators of cultural pluralism as signs of the immigrants' unwillingness to become socially integrated. Not only does this assessment omit reception factors, but its static pictures of socioeconomic and cultural differentiation fail to capture the dynamism inherent in the settlement and assimilation/integration processes, as well as the increasing heterogeneity of the stream in terms of demographic composition, duration of U.S. visits, and modes of entry. These changed circumstances have direct implications—as yet poorly understood—for the nature of social impacts on U.S. society.

A serious misunderstanding concerns where Mexican migration's costs and benefits fall. Do the net gains accrue to Mexico

---

[100]Portes and Bach, *Latin Journey*.
[101]Alejandro Portes and A. Douglas Kincaid ("Alternative Outcomes of Reform," *Society* 22:4 [1985]) note that casting recent immigrants to the United States as scapegoats in times of social and economic distress has been a recurring phenomenon in Mexican history, most recently during the late 1970s and early 1980s.
[102]See Jensen, "The New Immigration," for a recent review.
[103]Portes and Kincaid, "Alternative Outcomes of Reform."

or the United States? To the sending communities or the receiving communities? To the migrants themselves or the institutional settings in which they interact? Unfortunately, these questions do not admit any clear and specific responses because of the difficulty of reconciling aggregate costs and benefits with their micro-level sources. Although the aggregation-disaggregation issue cuts across methodological and substantive issues, most social analysts have avoided the challenging task of resolving the fallacy of displaced scope. In the words of Helmut Wagner:

> Modern sociology ... is hardly closer to solving it [now] than it was in the first decade of our century. Consequently, it would be premature to predict the eventual elimination of the problem with progressing methodological sophistication on the one hand, and theoretical refinements or new departures on the other. By the same token, we are not prepared to take the opposite stand and to declare the given dualism of micro and macro-sociological orientations and operations an inherent and irrevocable feature of sociology as a whole. But, whether unavoidable or not, the differentiation of scope poses serious problems of theoretical consistency as well as of general coherence of the discipline. Indeed, the problems of consistency and coherence extend to all social sciences and to the policy process.[104]

Wagner's concern with the fallacy of displaced scope is particularly pertinent to the analysis of Mexican immigration as a social problem and its resolution through policy intervention. That the errors of misspecified reference points continue in practical research ensures their perpetuation in the policy solutions they engender. Hence, as the evolution of Mexican immigration testifies, a "problem" and its proposed "solutions" rarely engage.

Misunderstanding the social effects of Mexican immigration also results when we fail to recognize that Mexican immigration has evolved and its evolution carries significant implications. Once driven by narrowly economic considerations, the migratory flow is now sustained by broader social processes: family reunification, the expansion of social networks within migrant communities in

---

[104]Helmut R. Wagner, "Displacment of Scope: A Problem of the Relationship between Small-scale and Large-scale Sociological Theories," *American Jounral of Sociology* 69 (May 1964): 571-584.

both countries, and the rising financial and social commitments of Mexican migrants in the United States.

A central question is whether it is even possible to devise a policy to regulate social processes. Since this question is rarely asked, little wonder that the restrictions governing Mexican immigration have failed in their goals. Immigration reforms address a narrowly conceived "economic" problem, but they totally bypass the critical importance of social organization, the key to understanding how the stream is perpetuated and how migrants secure a niche in U.S. society.

This discussion has deliberately played down the special problems of *illegal* immigration, which have dominated policy and research discussions of Mexican migration in recent years. This is not to minimize the importance of undocumented migration, nor to imply that it should be ignored in bilateral negotiation. Rather, this essay sought to balance the research and policy discussions of Mexican immigration while emphasizing that its social impacts are as diverse as the migration streams themselves, and that legal status is but one facet of the underlying diversity. The diversity of Mexican migration, more than any other single factor, deserves the attention of researchers and politicians who wish to understand migration's social impacts and to identify intervention strategies which are ethically acceptable, administratively feasible, and politically viable on a bilateral basis.

Research Needs

The bilateral research agenda includes the following priorities:

- Aligning social consequences with their social origins. There is a pressing need for analyses which differentiate social impacts by immigrant category—temporary vs. permanent immigrants, legal vs. illegal migrants, and immigrants by visa admission catgories.

- Sorting cause and effect. A second research priority is to document whether the social impacts of Mexican immigration have changed over time, and how and why. Much misunderstanding about the causes and consequences of Mexican immigration stems from a confusion of cause and effect.

- Identifying the social consequences of amnesty. The recently enacted Immigration Reform and Control Act offers a unique opportunity for a vision into the future. Political rather than humanitarian forces are responsible for IRCA's amnesty provisions. Yet the success of the amnesty program can teach us much about the social foundations of Mexican migration, the nature of the integration process, the relationships between legal and illegal migrant streams, and the prospects of curtailing future illegal immigration through selected policy reforms. However, because of the limitations of cross-sectional designs in the study of inherently dynamic processes, we should pursue a longitudinal study of legalization and social integration. Cost considerations have hitherto prevented longitudinal surveys of legal immigrants, but as we look toward the 1990s, we must give them priority if we hope to understand immigrant adaptation and social integration.

- Determining the form of integration. Social issues which reflect the nature of the integration process deserve further research attention. Moving away from the distortions produced by static snapshots is crucial to resolving misunderstandings about the Mexicanization of the Southwest. Although philosophical debates about Anglo conformity versus cultural pluralism integration models will continue, we must not hold Mexican immigration accountable for national resistance to cultural diversity. That the Chicano population remains distinct from the Anglo majority challenges the viability of the Anglo conformity model for groups whose entry to mainstream society has been obstructed.

As such, the Chicano/*mexicano* interface may hold clues to the nature of the integration process among recent Mexican immigrants. Careful scrutiny of this topic may well show some recent Mexican immigrants to be more prosperous than native-born Chicanos whose families have been in the United States for decades. Evidence of this kind would deflect attention from the immigrants as a social problem and direct it to the structural arrangements which assign social position on the basis of national origin or ancestry.

Bilateral Negotiation

To confront the "problem" of Mexican immigration, we must first put the cards of history and political interests on the table. The historical cards will show that the migration flow is self-perpetuating—often as a by-product of changes in the admission rules—and very likely not able to be curtailed within current admission guidelines which stress family reunification. The political interest cards will indicate that not all segments of society share in the benefits of Mexican immigration, although migration's social consequences are discussed as national issues. The first order of business is to clarify for whom in Mexico and the United States immigration is a problem and why. Second, discrepancies about the source of the problem and its perceived consequences must be resolved. Third, the contemporary definition of the problem must be placed in proper historical perspective in order to differentiate between the intended and unintended consequences of deliberate policy reforms. This discussion should distinguish between conjunctural and institutional factors which have virtually ensured the continuation of the flow.

In devising a strategy for bilateral negotiation of future reforms, the United States must admit to an active role in institutionalizing and diversifying the contemporary streams and to its qualified acceptance of Mexican migrants throughout the post-war period. Also to be addressed when devising a coherent bilateral framework for regulated migration streams are the contradictions of a social philosophy which extols the virtues of cultural pluralism while tolerating pervasive inequality.

SECTION

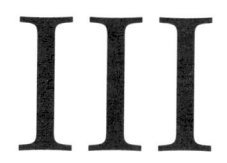

III

Policy Options

6

The Immigration Policy Debate: Critical Analysis and Future Options

Kitty Calavita

For over a decade, policymakers have sought solutions to the "immigration problem." A series of interagency task forces, committees, and special commissions have grappled with the issue, their conclusions almost always characterized by lack of consensus, and frequently by serious disagreement and dissension. The Immigration Reform and Control Act of 1986 (IRCA) overcame enormous political obstacles in achieving congressional support, but its actual ability to affect immigration flows is far from clear.

The immigration issue represents a particularly complex policy area, and this complexity is responsible, in part, for the dilemmas that have frustrated immigration policymakers over the last decade. The failure to arrive at a workable solution to the immigration problem is due to a lack of common understanding or definition of what the immigration problem *is*. This lack of agreement is not merely a reflection of the variety of conflicting interests involved in the immigration debate. Rather, it is the product of the conflation of a series of myths—about immigration and immigration policy—with reality.

One myth in particular permeates and obfuscates the immigration policy-making debate. This "myth of unilateral benefits" is based on the notion that immigration to the United States has exclusively benefited the immigrants themselves. The corollary is that U.S. immigration policy, in permitting the immigration of large numbers of legal and illegal immigrants, has been shortsighted and self-sacrificing. Thus, the premise of the reform efforts that led to the passage of IRCA in 1986 is that the United States must "regain control of its borders" and in so doing assert its "national interest."

This essay first examines this myth, using historical data to uncover its origins and evaluate its validity. Next, based on this discussion, it assesses the merits of a variety of immigration policy proposals, ranging from militarizing the border to maintaining the status quo. The paper concludes by sketching the rudimentary outlines of a viable alternative.

REALITY AND RHETORIC: IMMIGRATION POLICY REEXAMINED

The Ideology of Immigration Reform

As Senator Alan Simpson exhorted his colleagues on the Select Commission on Immigration and Refugee Policy (SCIRP) to support measures to restrict immigration, he warned them that Americans were experiencing "compassion fatigue."[1] He later elaborated that, despite humanitarian concern for the poor of other countries, "somewhere along the line we're going to have to say 'no'."[2] Citing statistics that show the United States receiving more immigrants and refugees than the rest of the world combined, much of the recent discussion surrounding immigration reform implicitly or explicitly assumes that U.S. immigration policies have heretofore been motivated by altruism, and that this is a luxury we can no longer afford.

In this context, we are simultaneously asked rhetorically if the United States must keep its borders open to solve the economic problems of its neighbors[3] and warned in a similar vein that "the immigration policy of the United States has been allowed to function without regard to its economic consequences [for the United

---

[1] U.S. Select Commission on Immigration and Refugee Policy, *U.S. Immigration Policy and the National Interest: The Final Report and Recommendations of the Select Commission on Immigration and Refugee Policy to the Congress and the President of the United States* (Washington, D.C.: U.S. Government Printing Office, 1981), p. 409.
[2] Quoted in John Crewdon, *The Tarnished Door: The New Immigrants and the Transformation of America* (New York: Times Books, 1983), pp. 308-309.
[3] Leon Bouvier and David Simcox, "Many Hands, Few Jobs: Population, Unemployment and Emigration in Mexico and the Caribbean," Center for Immigration Studies, paper 2 (Washington, D.C., November 1986).

States]."[4] Virtually every immigration task force and commission in the recent period echoes this view. The Interagency Task Force on Immigration Policy in 1979, for example, concluded that, "Unlike other major immigrant-receiving nations, we have not shaped immigration policy to assist in the attainment of national or demographic goals."[5]

This view parallels the notion that immigration—particularly undocumented immigration—is spontaneous and out of control. The dominant push-pull migration theory focuses on impersonal economic forces that simultaneously propel immigrants from poor countries and attract them to opportunities in the industrialized world. The only deliberate ingredient in this depiction is the individual migrant's rational decision. From this perspective, heavy immigration to the United States is merely an unintentional side effect of the magnetic force of the U.S. economy. "The national community—government officials and ordinary citizens alike—views the 'undocumented Mexican problem' as the product of social, economic, and geographical circumstances beyond its control."[6]

This view of immigration to the United States as out of control and of U.S. immigration policy as altruistic to a fault is so ingrained that it constitutes one of the sole sources of agreement among immigration policymakers and has become the basis for immigration reform discussions in the 1980s.

The following section refutes this view by drawing upon the historical record. Documented and undocumented immigration to the United States are historically the predictable consequence of de facto and de jure immigration policies. These policies coincide with the perceived need for an immigrant work force.

Immigration as the Movement of a Work Force

In 1791, Alexander Hamilton warned Congress that if the U.S. economy were to develop and compete with Europe's, immigration must be encouraged so as to mitigate the "scarcity of

---

[4] Vernon Briggs, *Immigration Policy and the American Labor Force* (Baltimore, Md.: Johns Hopkins University Press, 1984), p. viii.
[5] Interagency Task Force on Immigration Policy, *Final Report, Departments of Justice, Labor, and State* (Washington, D.C.: U.S. Government Printing Office, 1979), p. 3.
[6] Gerald López, "Undocumented Mexican Migrants: In Search of a Just Immigration Law and Policy," *UCLA Law Review* 28 (1981): 707.

hands."[7] Recruitment efforts by the federal government, the states, and private employers in the following century saturated Europe with promotional campaigns to stimulate emigration to the United States. Andrew Carnegie appreciatively called the immigration "a golden stream which flows into the country each year."[8]

The economic downturns of the nineteenth century triggered occasional anti-immigrant backlashes among policymakers and employers,[9] but they were not institutionalized at the policy level. Nor did the ongoing protests of domestic labor against competition with the "pauper labor of Europe"[10] deter immigration policymakers from their pursuit of increased immigration.

By the end of the nineteenth century, Congress had enacted a series of apparently restrictive measures, including the exclusion of convicts, the diseased, anyone "likely to become a public charge," and those with pre-arranged work contracts. In practice, however, these combined measures excluded only about 1 percent of the annual flow.[11] The creators of these selective devices designed them, according to one observer in Congress, "along conservative lines [so as to] avoid measures so drastic as to cripple American industry."[12] One immigration inspector of the period explained that it was "better to run the risk of the occasional admission of an alien inadmissible under the law than to slow up the process."[13]

Of course, these essentially open-door policies occasionally served political and symbolic purposes, as in the case of the Statue of Liberty inscription addressing the "huddled masses." In general, however, economics motivated immigration policymakers in the nineteenth and early twentieth centuries. The 42-volume Dillingham Commission report of 1911—typifying the economic pragmatism dominant in immigration policy debates—opened with the declaration that immigration policy should be considered "an economic problem."[14]

---

[7]Alexander Hamilton, "Report on Manufacturing," *American State Papers, Finance* (1791): 123.
[8]Andrew Carnegie, *Triumphant Democracy, or Fifty Years' March of the Republic* (New York: Charles Scribners' Sons, 1886), p. 35.
[9]John Higham, *Strangers in the Land: Patterns of American Nativism, 1860-1925* (New York: Atheneum, 1977), pp. 51-52.
[10]*Philadelphia Times*, 18 June 1882.
[11]J.W. Jenks, *The Immigration Problem* (New York: Funk and Wagnalls, 1913).
[12]*Congressional Record*, 57th Congress, 1st Session (1902), pp. 5763-5764.
[13]W.C. Van Vleck, *The Administrative Control of Aliens: A Study in Administrative Law and Procedure* (New York: Commonwealth Fund, 1932), p. 28.
[14]U.S. Congress, Senate Immigration Commission, *Immigration Commission Report*, 61st Congress, 3d Session, Senate Document no. 747 (1911), p. 25.

The quota laws of 1921 and 1924 represent a turning point in immigration history. The political rhetoric of immigration policy-making shifted decisively with their passage. They also constitute the first apparent attempt to reduce the numbers of immigrants to the United States. In summarizing the reasons for the quotas, Albert Johnson, chair of the House Committee on Immigration and Naturalization at the time of the restrictions, reinterpreted the economic pragmatism of the previous decades of immigration policy:

> Many years ago ... our people, proud of their institutions ... altruistic, and sympathetic, entertained the thought that their country was destined by an all-wise providence to serve as the world's great harbor of refuge ... Americans everywhere are insisting that their land no longer shall offer free and unrestricted asylum to the rest of the world.[15]

One observer of the debates of the 1920s noted, with only partial accuracy, that "the passage of the Immigration Act of 1924 marks the close of an epoch."[16] The period did signal the end of the straightforward appreciation of immigrants as a work force at the level of political discourse, and the beginning of an epoch in which the United States increasingly viewed immigration as self-sacrificing at best, and as out of control at worst. But the quotas neither effectively restricted immigration nor ended the role of the immigrant in the U.S. economy. In fact, while the immigration policy-making rhetoric has changed, formal and informal immigration policies since the 1920s remain a catalyst for further labor migration.

A brief look at the history of Mexican migration to the United States highlights the importance of U.S. immigration policies in triggering this migration and the paramount role played by economic factors in the policy-making process.

Mexican Migration as a Backdoor Labor Source

Mexican immigration to the United States gained momentum in the pre-World War I period, as policymakers and even some employers reassessed the costs versus the benefits of European

---

[15] Albert Johnson, Foreword in *Immigration Restriction*, by R.L. Garis (New York: MacMillan, 1927), pp. vii-viii.
[16] J.B. Trevor, "An Analysis of the American Immigration Act of 1924," *International Conciliation* 202 (1924): 5.

immigration. The European immigrant was a reputed troublemaker who frequently became a permanent member of American society and was increasingly the backbone of labor strikes.[17] In 1911, the Dillingham Commission, responding to these concerns, noted the special advantages of Mexican migration:

> Because of their strong attachment to their native land ... and the possibility of their residence here being discontinued, few become citizens of the United States. The Mexican migrants are providing a fairly adequate supply of labor.... While they are not easily assimilated, this is of no very great importance as long as most of them return to their native land. In the case of the Mexican, he is less desirable as a citizen than as a laborer.[18]

The most significant restrictions of the early twentieth century exempted Mexicans from their orbit. A response to warnings from Southwestern growers that successful harvests depended on abundant Mexican labor excluded Mexicans from the literacy test requirement of 1917 for the duration of the war. As World War I came to a close, the labor secretary and immigration commissioner extended the exemptions. As a result of these policies and employers' recruitment efforts, legal immigration from Mexico soared from eleven thousand in 1915 to fifty-one thousand in 1920.[19] Industries as far north as Chicago drew labor from this back door. By 1926, 35 percent of Chicago Inland Steel's labor force was Mexican.[20]

The passage of the quotas in the 1920s again exempted Mexicans. The argument against restricting Mexican immigration was strong:

> The Mexican, they pointed out, was a vulnerable alien living just a short distance from his homeland.... He, unlike Puerto Ricans or Filipinos ...

---

[17]Kitty Calavita, *U.S. Immigration Law and the Control of Labor: 1820-1924* (London: Academic Press, 1984), pp. 103-120.
[18]U.S. Congress, Senate Immigration Commission, *Immigration Commission Report*, pp. 690-691.
[19]F. Ray Marshall, "Economic Factors Influencing the International Migration of Workers," in *Views Across the Border*, edited by Stanley Ross (Albuquerque: University of New Mexico Press, 1978).
[20]Herbert Gutman, *Work, Culture and Society in Industrializing America: Essays in American Working-Class and Social History* (New York: Alfred A. Knopf, 1976), p. 8.

could easily be deported. No safer or more economical unskilled labor force was imaginable.[21]

The shift from European to Mexican migration as a source of labor did enhance flexibility, as evidenced by the repatriation of thousands of Mexican workers and their families during the depression of the 1930s. As World War II refueled the U.S. economy, the United States again needed and used Mexican contract laborers imported through the Bracero Program, whose formal and informal policies contributed to the rise of the undocumented nature of Mexican migration that characterizes the contemporary period. The program attempted to institutionalize the primary virtue of this labor supply, its flexibility.

The Bracero Agreement of 1949 provided that "illegal workers, when they are located in the United States, shall be given preference under outstanding U.S. Employment Service Certification."[22] Illegals, or "wetbacks," were "dried out" by the U.S. Border Patrol which escorted them to the Mexican border, had them step to the Mexican side, and brought them back as braceros. Employers often accompanied their undocumented workers back to the border and contracted them there as legal workers. In some cases, the border patrol "paroled" illegals directly to employers. In 1951 the President's Commission on Migratory Labor estimated that between 1947 and 1949 the United States legalized more than 142,000 undocumented Mexicans in this way, while recruiting only 74,600 new braceros from Mexico.[23]

In addition to these more or less official policies of encouraging illegal migration, Immigration and Naturalization Service (INS) district chiefs enhanced, at their discretion, the supply of undocumented workers for seasonal employment. The chief inspector at Tucson, for example, reported to the President's Commission on Migratory Labor that he "received orders from the District Director at El Paso each harvest to stop deporting illegal Mexican labor."[24]

---

[21]Mark Reisler, paraphrasing the 1929 hearings of the House Committee on Immigration in *By the Sweat of Their Brow: Mexican Immigrant Labor in the U.S., 1900-1940* (Westport, Conn.: Greenwood Press, 1976), p. 181.
[22]Ernesto Galarza, *Merchants of Labor: The Mexican Bracero Story* (Charlotte, N.C.: McNally and Loftin, 1964), p. 63.
[23]President's Commission on Migratory Labor, *Migratory Labor in American Agriculture: Report of the President's Commission on Migratory Labor* (Washington, D.C.: U.S. Government Printing Office, 1951), p. 53.
[24]Peter Kirstein, *Anglo over Bracero: A History of the Mexican Worker in the United States from Roosevelt to Nixon* (San Francisco, Calif.: R and E Associates, 1977), p. 90.

In other cases, Border Patrol officials told agents to stay away from designated ranches and farms in their district.[25] The implicit message from Congress to the Border Patrol was consistent with this laissez-faire approach. Congress was "splendidly indifferent" to the rising number of illegals during the bracero period, reducing the budget of the Border Patrol just as undocumented migration increased.[26]

By the time the United States terminated the Bracero Program in 1964, the symbiosis between Mexican migrants and employers in the Southwest was well entrenched, the product of over fifty years of formal and informal policy-making.[27] Almost five million Mexican workers had been brought to the United States as braceros; more than five million illegal aliens were apprehended during the same period.[28]

While policies associated with the Bracero Program were instrumental in enhancing the appeal of illegal migration from the migrants' point of view, a key congressional decision immunized employers from any risk involved in their employment. In 1952, the McCarran-Walter Act made it illegal to "harbor, transport, or conceal illegal entrants." An amendment to the provision, referred to as the Texas Proviso after the Texas growers to whom it was a concession, excluded employment per se from the category of "harboring." Whether or not "knowing" employment of undocumented workers would constitute harboring remained ambiguous despite congressional discussion.[29] Nonetheless, the amendment was interpreted by the INS as carte blanche to employ undocumented workers.[30]

Of course, the U.S. attitude toward Mexican migrants has not been unequivocal. Mass expulsions and roundups of Mexican workers and their families during Operation Wetback in 1954 and

---

[25]Manuel García y Griego, "The Importation of Mexican Contract Laborers to the United States, 1942-1964: Antecedents, Operation and Legacy," Working Papers in U.S.-Mexican Studies, no. 11 (La Jolla, Calif.: Center for U.S.-Mexican Studies, University of California, San Diego, 1981), pp. 24-25.
[26]A. Hadley, "A Critical Analysis of the Wetback Problem," *Law and Contemporary Problems* 21 (1956): 334.
[27]For a detailed discussion of the combined impact of employer recruitment and U.S. policies on migration patterns, see Wayne A. Cornelius, *Mexican Migration to the United States: The View from the Rural Sending Communities*, monograph no. 3 (Cambridge, Mass.: Center for International Studies, 1976).
[28]Gerald López, "Undocumented Mexican Migrants," p. 707.
[29]*Congressional Record*, 82nd Congress, 2nd Session, Senate, 1952: 794.
[30]For a discussion of this INS interpretation, see Sheldon Greene, "Public Agency Distortion of Congressional Will: Federal Policy toward Non-Resident Alien Labor," *George Washington Law Review* 40 (1972): 453-455.

1955 were reminiscent of the depression policies of the 1930s. In part, these mass deportations reflected the militaristic approach of the new INS commissioner, Joseph Swing, a former U.S. Army general known within the INS bureaucracy as "The General," in apparent reference both to his former military career and to his leadership style.[31] More generally, however, they represented the long-held view of Mexican labor as eminently flexible—welcomed during periods of high demand and deported when the demand had waned. In any case, such periodic deportations neither significantly interrupted the now-institutionalized patterns of migration nor reflected any fundamental change in the perception of Mexico as a backdoor source of labor.

Having set the stage for high levels of documented and undocumented migration from Mexico, U.S. policies in the post-bracero period have perpetuated the entrenched pattern largely by default. In 1965, the Immigration and Nationality Act imposed ceilings on the Western Hemisphere for the first time, and in 1976 an amendment was added to limit annual immigration from any given Western Hemisphere country to twenty thousand (a restriction that had applied to the Eastern Hemisphere since 1965). These limitations "not only increased the backlog of visa requests by Mexicans but has also contributed to the multiple pressures that cause illegal migration."[32]

Budgetary decisions have effectively eliminated the counter-pressures to that migration. As the congressional subcommittee that holds the purse strings of the INS put it in 1981, the agency "has been chronically underfunded, undermanned and neglected."[33] During the 1950s, congressmen from the states bordering Mexico pared down the budget of the Border Patrol to ensure a plentiful supply of labor.[34] The INS budget did not fare much better in the 1960s and 1970s. While the number of apprehended illegal aliens went from about 23,000 in 1960 to 345,000 by the end of the decade, the number of permanent INS positions remained constant at approximately 69,000.[35] By 1978, the number of annual

---

[31]Interview with former general counsel of the INS, Washington, D.C., September 1986.
[32]Briggs, *Immigration Policy*, p. 67.
[33]Quoted in Edwin Harwood, "Can Immigration Law Be Enforced?" *Public Interest* 72 (Summer 1983): 108.
[34]Galarza, *Merchants of Labor*, p. 61.
[35]Congressional Research Service, *History of the Immigration and Naturalization Service: A Report for the Use of the Select Commission on Immigration and Refugee Policy, U.S. Senate* (Washington, D.C.: U.S. Government Printing Office, 1980); U.S. Immigration and Naturalization Service, *Annual Report: Immigration and Naturalization Service* (Washington, D.C.: U.S. Government Printing Office, 1978), p. 49.

apprehensions had risen to more than one million, while total INS personnel reached barely ten thousand.[36] In 1980 the Border Patrol allotment for policing almost six thousand miles of border was only $77 million, less than the budget of the Baltimore police department and less than half that of the Philadelphia police—$95 and $221 million, respectively.[37]

Taken together, these policies confirm both the role of U.S. decision-makers in institutionalizing the current pattern of Mexican migration and the perception on the part of policymakers that Mexican labor is beneficial to the U.S. economy. A number of recent studies validate this perception. One of the most detailed studies of the economic impact of Mexican migration in the contemporary period evaluated the effects of this migration on the California economy, concluding that "the widespread concerns about Mexican immigration are generally unfounded" and that "overall, the immigrants provide economic benefits to the state."[38] In particular, the study's authors argue that these immigrants perform an important labor function in the California economy and, contrary to the widespread perception, "contribute more to public revenues than they consume in public services."[39] The study points out that some local communities may bear a "disproportionate share of the public service burden,"[40] but it nonetheless confirms the benefits of the migration for the state as a whole. Another study of Mexican migrants in California concurs with these findings, highlighting the overall economic advantages of the immigration.[41]

The New Nativism

While the pattern of U.S. immigration policies over the past decades has, either actively or by default, been the catalyst for illegal Mexican immigration, a new round of nativism has accompanied this migration. Now, as in the past, the new immigrants

---

[36]Congressional Research Service, *History of the Immigration and Naturalization Service*, pp. 76, 90.
[37]Michael Teitelbaum, "Right Versus Right: Immigration and Refugee Policy in the United States," *Foreign Affairs* 59:1 (1980): 55.
[38]Kevin F. McCarthy and R. Burciaga Valdez, *Current and Future Effects of Mexican Immigration in California: Executive Summary* (Santa Monica, Calif.: Rand Corporation, 1985), p. vii.
[39]Ibid., p. vii.
[40]Ibid., p. 40.
[41]Thomas Muller and Thomas Espenshade, *The Fourth Wave: California's Newest Immigrants* (Washington, D.C.: Urban Institute Press, 1985).

are blamed for every social ill of modern American society. And, as in the past, because immigrants supply a cheap labor force (i.e., precisely that which policymakers have appreciated), they provide an easy target for backlash by domestic workers and wary taxpayers.

This new nativism, however, is by no means identical to that earlier in the century. For one thing, the new ideology of immigration—as something that is being done to us—compounds it. Second, the predominantly illegal nature of the flow, compared to that of the early twentieth century, both strengthens the force of that ideology by enhancing the conviction that we are no longer in control, and exacerbates the backlash against those who personify this loss of control.

In one more respect the new round of nativism is unique. Nativism and xenophobia are frequently correlated with high unemployment rates.[42] Indeed, each serious recession since the mid-nineteenth century brought reconsideration of immigration benefits and varying degrees of blaming immigrants for economic downturns. The apparent irony of today's restrictionism is that, while it is rooted in the "stagflation" of the 1970s, its heightened pitch in the mid-1980s occurs at a time of declining unemployment.

This is not to say that the new nativism is unrelated to economic factors. Indeed, beginning in the late 1970s, the increased dislocations and transformations in the U.S. economy that have accompanied restrictionism significantly eroded the average U.S. worker's standard of living. Individual wage and salary income fell 10 percent from 1973 to 1985, and the proportion of households with incomes of less than $20,000 a year increased by 8 percent in the same period.[43] As the heavy manufacturing sector has contracted and the service sector expanded, an increased proportion of new jobs appeared in the less desirable secondary labor market. One study prepared for the Congressional Joint Economic Committee estimates that close to 60 percent of the workers added to the labor force between 1979 and 1984 earn less than $7,000 per year.[44]

---

[42]Wayne Cornelius," America in the Era of Limits: Migrants, Nativists and the Future of U.S.-Mexican Relations," Working Papers in U.S.-Mexican Studies, no. 3 (La Jolla, Calif.: Center for U.S.-Mexican Studies, University of California, San Diego, 1982).
[43]Shilling, "America's Dwindling Middle Class," Los Angeles Times, 26 May 1987.
[44]Gordon, "Minimum Wage Hike's Real Payoff," Los Angeles Times, 12 May 1987.

In the past, the increased unemployment that triggered immigrant scapegoating simultaneously reduced temporarily the need for immigrant workers, hence slowing the influx. In contrast, today's economic transformations, which reduce the standard of living and intensify immigrant scapegoating, simultaneously increase immigration as the proportion of minimum-wage, unskilled jobs proliferates. In other words, the structural changes in the economy which fuel undocumented migration are the same transformations that generate restrictionist sentiment, as U.S. residents and citizens blame immigrants for the declining standard of living. Unlike the past, economic forces enhance the need for immigrant workers as they simultaneously generate demands for their restriction.

Using IRCA as a case in point, the following section argues that much of the confusion surrounding immigration is a product of the myth of unilateral benefits described above, compounded by this new nativism.

IRCA and the New Restrictionism

The Immigration Reform and Control Act of 1986 is clearly a product of the new restrictionist mentality, in terms of its origins and the symbolic message of control that it transmits to the American public, if not in terms of its actual impact.

The roots of this latest attempt at immigration reform can be traced to the early 1970s. In 1971, Representative Peter Rodino chaired a five-part series of hearings on "illegal aliens" before the House Judiciary Committee's Subcommittee on Immigration and Nationality. These hearings marked the beginning of efforts to enact a federal employer sanctions law. INS Commissioner Leonard Chapman provided the sense of urgency necessary to gain support for such a measure when in the mid-1970s he estimated that there were as many as twelve million undocumented aliens in the United States, constituting a "vast and silent invasion."[45]

IRCA, with employer sanctions as its most visible centerpiece and with hefty budget increases to the Border Patrol, is at one level a restrictive measure, as INS Commissioner Alan Nelson pointed

---

[45]Leonard Chapman, "Illegal Aliens: Time to Call a Halt!" *Reader's Digest*, October 1976, p. 654.

out.[46] As such, it is the progeny of the mythology of immigration outlined above and the restrictive demands generated by that mythology.

However, a curious paradox emerges from a close analysis of the provisions of IRCA. For while the law has its roots in restrictive mandates, it will predictably increase the flow of immigration. Aside from the inherent difficulties of effectively enforcing employer sanctions, a number of central provisions of the law are specifically designed to enhance the supply of immigrant labor.

The provisions for agricultural labor are noteworthy. The Special Agricultural Workers (SAW) program provided for the legalization of any alien who could establish that he worked in agriculture in the United States for at least ninety days between May 1985 and May 1986. Over one million immigrants applied for legalization under the SAW program.

The Replenishment Agricultural Workers (RAW) program supplements the law and monitors the movement of these SAWs, once they become legal residents, from their agricultural employment to the urban economy. Under this program, beginning in 1990, the Departments of Agriculture and Labor will jointly construct a formula that reflects the shortage of agricultural labor in any given year. On the basis of these formulas, additional workers will be imported annually to work in agriculture for at least three years, after which they can apply for permanent resident status. Because the Department of Agriculture is an equal partner in determining the numbers to be admitted under this program (unlike the H-2 program in which the Department of Labor provides the certification of labor need), it is widely perceived that the formulas will be generous.[47]

In addition to these two programs, a new category of temporary agricultural worker is established—the H-2A worker. This new temporary worker program streamlines the application for regular H-2 workers. Southwestern growers are notoriously reluctant to use the old H-2 program, given the ready availability of undocumented workers and the time and paperwork required in the H-2 application process. This new guest-worker program—in

---

[46]Alan Nelson, presentation to the Seventh Annual Press Briefing, Center for U.S.-Mexican Studies, University of California, San Diego, La Jolla, California, July 9, 1987.
[47]Interview with INS official, Washington, D.C., June 1987.

conjunction with the SAW and RAW programs and the limitations of employer sanctions, to be discussed later—can increase significantly the supply of documented and undocumented labor to agriculture.

One upper-level INS official in Washington in an October 1986 interview cited IRCA as a classic example of "Christmas-tree legislation," with "ornaments of every color" representing all of the special interests involved. It is, according to this depiction, the embodiment of pluralism at work. Upon more careful consideration, however, this pluralist characterization of the polyglot law breaks down. For while the reform effort was decisively propelled by Americans' fear of an "alien invasion" and restrictionist demands embodied in the employer sanctions provision, significant portions of the law specifically increase the supply of immigrant labor.

In other words, IRCA pulls both ways. Later sections of this essay argue that employer sanctions will deter neither employers nor aspiring immigrants and that IRCA's greatest impact will be significant increases in the immigrant work force. The more fundamental argument here is that this reform effort has suffered from a confusion of what the immigrant problem is. With the myth of unilateral benefits and the new nativism as its underpinnings, the debate is mired in a Catch-22 of its own making. As immigration reform ideology clashes head-on with the reality of immigrants as a work force, immigration policymakers are left with the hopeless task of restricting immigration without restricting the flow of immigrant workers.

EVALUATING THE ALTERNATIVES

In the course of the immigration debate of the last decade, a wide variety of proposals have been put forward. From the foregoing discussion, a number of guidelines emerge that help in evaluating these proposals.

- First, and most generally, a rational approach to immigration policy requires official recognition of the mutual benefits that immigration provides.

- Second, a workable approach requires that logistics and feasibility play a central role.

- Finally, U.S. immigration policies must be compatible with the underlying values of a liberal democratic society.

Keeping these criteria in mind, the following analysis examines the merits of specific proposals, beginning with the most restrictionist—militarizing the U.S.-Mexico border.

Militarization of the Border

No other proposal so thoroughly embodies the restrictionist mentality as the periodic suggestion that military personnel and/or resources fortify the border with Mexico. Having diagnosed the "immigration problem" as a relatively porous southwest border which permits clandestine entry by undocumented Mexicans, a significant minority of restrictionists conclude that the problem can be solved only by constructing an impermeable barrier.

Using military force at the Mexican border is not a new concept,[48] but in the months prior to the passage of IRCA, militarization seemed to be gaining advocates. At the local level, San Diego County Supervisor Paul Eckert, in televised comments during his election campaign, recommended using Marines on the Mexican border, explaining, "I think we are going to take a very, very strong position to close the border ... to illegal aliens."[49]

Such proposals are not confined to the local political arena. The Federation for American Immigration Reform (FAIR), a national organization of private citizens linked by their mission to restrict immigration, engaged in a dialogue with INS officials in 1986 aimed at securing the agency's support for the militarization approach.[50] Officials in Washington and on the border already have plans to use some military personnel and equipment to seal the border.[51]

---

[48]According to INS Commissioner Joseph Swing's testimony before the House Subcommittee of the Committee on Governmental Relations in 1956, militarizing the border was seriously considered in 1953 just before he launched Operation Wetback. He reported that "in a meeting the Secretary of State, the Secretary of Labor, the Attorney General of the State of California—all these people had concurred that this was the way to close the border" (Swing, House of Representatives, 84th Congress, 2nd Session: 40). The plan, in which four thousand troops would have been involved, was ultimately rejected in favor of Operation Wetback.
[49]Quoted in the *San Diego Evening Tribune*, 28 May 1986.
[50]Interview with Border Patrol official, Washington, D.C., May 1986.
[51]*New York Times*, 26 June 1986.

Assuming for the moment that sealing the border is a desirable goal, advocates of border militarization overlook the practical and logistical problems of such a policy. Besides the obvious issue of cost and the fact that Mexicans make up only 50 to 55 percent of the undocumented population in the United States, important foreign relations concerns must be considered. Mexican officials have been quick to react to this most extreme and blatant form of the new restrictionism. Mexico's foreign minister, Bernardo Sepúlveda, says he is "deeply concerned" about the "voices of darkness" that threaten to militarize the border.[52] While Mexican officials generally are careful to leave U.S. policy-making to U.S. policymakers, the magnitude of the show of force required to modify immigration patterns would no doubt devastate bilateral relations.

Equally important, such a show of force is antithetical to the tenets of a free society. Policymakers sensitive to the symbolic implications of a fortified national boundary often express this concern. As Ray Marshall, former secretary of labor, put it, it is "not our style."[53] The chair of the Select Committee on Population in the House of Representatives, James Scheuer, observed: "I don't think the American public would like to see a twenty-foot high Berlin wall erected ... with submachine guns and police guards and sirens and watch towers."[54]

Most important for analysis, militarization is misguided in its premise. The logical extension of viewing immigration as an "invasion" is that the national boundary must be defended at gunpoint. As noted above, this depiction of immigrants as an invading force is inconsistent with both the historical record and the present reality. Not only is the contemporary flow a product of long-standing policies of U.S. encouragement, but today's immigrants—far from hostile invaders—provide cheap labor in the contemporary U.S. economy.

Employer Sanctions

Employer sanctions is the undisputed centerpiece of current immigration reform efforts, and as such it merits careful consideration. Its broad political acceptability derives from the fact that,

---

[52]Ibid.
[53]Crewdson, *The Tarnished Door*, p. 307.
[54]James Scheuer, U.S. House of Representatives, hearings before the Select Committee on Population, "Immigration to the United States," no. 5 (Washington, D.C.: U.S. Government Printing Office, 1978), p. 139.

unlike militarization, it purports to be a "balanced" approach, particularly in conjunction with IRCA's legalization program. However, in addition to relying on the myth of unilateral benefits which it shares with the militarization approach, employer sanctions presents its own set of logistical and practical difficulties which cripple its deterrent potential—in particular, the inherent difficulty of enforcing employer sanctions laws and the inability of "voluntary compliance" to offset these enforcement problems.

A 1982 General Accounting Office (GAO) report, commissioned by Congress, on the experience with employer sanctions in nineteen countries and Hong Kong documents the enforcement difficulties with this approach. In particular, the report found that in countries where there is no national identification card, such as Canada, "proving that the employer knowingly violated the law can be difficult."[55] In countries where a relatively secure system of national identification cards exists, as in West Germany, "employers have been able to evade responsibility ... by subcontracting for work through firms that obtain illegal aliens on a temporary basis."[56] Furthermore, when employers have been prosecuted, "judges have not considered the hiring of illegal aliens a serious violation" and have often waived fines of up to $40,000.[57]

In 1985, Congress commissioned a second study with the GAO—this one to focus only on countries where there was reason to believe that there had been some improvement since the earlier study. In this follow-up study, five of the eight countries reported that employer sanctions were deterrents; however, in three countries the deterrent effect was reported to be even weaker than in 1982. Interestingly, the number of undocumented immigrants had decreased only in Hong Kong and Austria, and in this latter case, the decline was reportedly the consequence of decreased labor needs rather than employer sanctions.[58]

The United States probably presents the least amenable scenario for effective employer sanctions, given its 2,000-mile border with Mexico, a long history of employer dependence on immigrant labor, and the absence of a national identification-card system. The difficulties of enforcing employer sanctions in the United States without

---

[55]U.S. General Accounting Office, "Information on the Enforcement of Laws Regarding Employment of Aliens in Selected Countries," GAO/GGD-82-86 (August 31, 1982), app. I, p. 4.
[56]Ibid., app. II, p. 14.
[57]Ibid., app. II, pp. 13-14.
[58]U.S. General Accounting Office, "Illegal Aliens: Information on Selected Countries' Employment Prohibition Laws," GAO/GGD-86-17BR (October 1985), app. I, p. 5.

a national identification system have often been observed. Rev. Theodore Hesburgh, chair of the Select Commission on Immigration and Refugee Policy, is said to have commented that employer sanctions without a secure system of identification is "about as meaningful as kissing your sister."[59]

The record of local employer sanctions laws is bleak. Since California passed an employer sanctions law in 1971, twelve other states have enacted similar measures. There have been only a handful of convictions under these laws, and they have precipitated no discernible reductions in either illegal alien employment or undocumented migration.[60]

Recognizing the enforcement difficulties of employer sanctions and the limited budget and personnel available to them, the INS emphasizes the importance of "voluntary compliance" in implementing this IRCA provision.[61] There are at least two problems with expecting voluntary compliance with employer sanctions to reduce undocumented migration.

First, depending on what one means by "voluntary compliance," it may or may not make any difference. The employer sanctions provision requires employers to ask aspiring workers for documents verifying their identity and eligibility to work in the United States (typically a driver's license and a Social Security card). The law further requires employers to fill out an I-9 form attesting to having seen such documentation. If, upon examination by the INS, the documentation presented to the employer "reasonably appears on its face to be genuine," the employer has an "affirmative defense" against prosecution even if s/he happens to have hired an illegal alien.[62]

Preliminary findings from a study in which 177 firms in California were surveyed in 1983 and 1984 suggest that more than half of the employers in these firms already requested some verification of their workers' eligibility to work in the United States. Nonetheless, virtually all firms in the study employed a significant

---

[59]Quoted in Crewdson, *The Tarnished Door*, p. 311.
[60]Carl Schwarz, "Employer Sanctions Laws, Worker Identification Systems and Undocumented Aliens: The State Experience and Federal Proposals," *Stanford Journal of International Law* 19 (1983): 371-405; for the California experience, see Calavita, "California's 'Employer Sanctions'."
[61]INS Commissioner Alan Nelson, Statement to U.S. House of Representatives, 17 December 1986.
[62]U.S. Congress, House of Representatives, "Immigration Reform and Control Act of 1986," 99th Congress, 2d Session, 1986, Sec. 101.

number of undocumented workers.[63] Many of these employers already complied with the terms of the employer sanctions provision. They already requested documentation from their workers, whether or not that documentation later turned out to be fraudulent. Voluntary compliance in this sense, then, is unlikely to alter either the employment practices of such employers or, ultimately, the flow of undocumented workers.

On the other hand, the definition of employer compliance as "refusing to hire aspiring employees whom one suspects are undocumented", is also fraught with difficulties. First, such refusal potentially violates IRCA's antidiscrimination clause. Unless an employer is somehow certain of a worker's undocumented status, there is a fine line between voluntary compliance and discrimination on the basis of foreign appearance. In fact, some employers contend that compliance with employer sanctions inevitably leads to discrimination. As one El Paso employer put it, "I'm discriminating against Hispanics. I screen them more rigidly than others. I know it's not fair, but that's what the law does to us."[64]

Second, widespread refusal to hire the undocumented in the absence of a serious threat of detection and conviction is unlikely in those industries where the undocumented predominate. This is the case both because such a strategy necessitates fundamentally and disruptively restructuring the work force in these industries, and because many of these industries depend for their survival on this supply of cheap labor. While some firms in the primary sector that only occasionally and incidentally employ undocumented workers may attempt to comply with the spirit of employer sanctions, firms where the undocumented predominate are less likely to have either the inclination or the luxury to comply voluntarily. Thus the effect may be increased concentration of the undocumented in industries where they already predominate, rather than an overall reduction in the migratory flow.[65]

The Cornelius study cited above supports the conclusion that voluntary compliance with employer sanctions will be limited.

---

[63]Wayne Cornelius, "Potential Impacts of New Federal Immigration Legislation on Immigrant-Dependent Firms in California," paper presented at the annual meeting of the Association of American Law Schools, Los Angeles, California, January 1987.
[64]Quoted in the *Wall Street Journal*, 4 May 1988.
[65]It follows that discrimination against the "foreign-looking," resulting from such compliance, will be concentrated in sectors where the undocumented do not predominate, i.e. in those sectors offering the best working conditions and most stable employment.

More than half of the employers interviewed in 1983 and 1984 either thought there already was a law against hiring the undocumented or were not sure whether there was such a law; yet approximately 99 percent of these respondents employed a significant contingent of undocumented workers.

While the employer sanctions approach may be politically more palatable than border militarization, both its conceptual roots in restrictionism and its Pandora's box of implementation difficulties eviscerate it as a productive immigration reform. The child of the new nativism, employer sanctions is likely to become little more than a symbolic tribute to the misguided protectionism that spawned it.

Guest-worker Programs

The third policy alternative examined here—guest-worker programs—contrasts with employer sanctions and border militarization in that it explicitly recognizes the importance of immigrant labor to the U.S. economy and thus avoids the conceptual quicksand of these forms of restrictionism. Nonetheless, this alternative is often proposed side-by-side with employer sanctions and thus represents the confused and ill-destined attempt to restrict immigration without restricting immigrant labor. Guest-worker programs are also notoriously difficult to implement and control. Aside from these issues of feasibility, the concept of guest-workers is incompatible with the most basic values of a liberal democratic society.

The first serious recommendation for a guest-worker program in the contemporary period was incorporated in then-president Ronald Reagan's proposal for immigration reform in 1981. The president's proposed plan was relatively conservative, suggesting that fifty thousand Mexican guest-workers be admitted annually in an experimental, state-administered program. His stated rationale was that, "We must ... recognize that both the United States and Mexico have historically benefited from the employment of Mexicans in the United States."[66]

---

[66] Quoted in Terry McCoy, "The Temporary Workers Provisions of the Simpson-Mazzoli Bill: Implications for the State of Florida," in *America's New Immigration Law: Origins, Rationales, and Potential Consequences*, edited by Wayne Cornelius and Ricardo Anzaldúa, Monograph Series, no. 11. (La Jolla, Calif.: Center for U.S.-Mexican Studies, University of California, San Diego, 1983), p. 132.

Since the first Simpson-Mazzoli bill was introduced in 1982, the guest-worker issue has been a central ingredient of the immigration reform debate. Clearly, the Reagan administration favored such an approach. In 1985, after the Congressional Conference Committee failed to reach a compromise on the immigration issue, the INS proposed to do administratively what Congress had failed to legislate. The plan, ultimately rejected, called for reducing the regulations and paperwork required in the H-2 program to increase dramatically the number of temporary foreign workers admitted.[67]

In 1986, Reagan proposed a second foreign worker program, this one designed specifically for agriculture and having no ceiling on annual admissions. The H-2A program incorporated in IRCA is a variation on this approach. Although politically less visible than employer sanctions and the legalization programs, this guest-worker program is still likely to have a significant impact.

It should not be surprising that support for temporary worker programs has resurfaced. Remember that Mexican immigrant labor has been appreciated primarily for its flexibility and marginality to U.S. society. No doubt the appeal of the guest-worker approach is related to the fact that a large part of the Mexican work force in the United States no longer defines itself as temporary. While nativism and the employer sanctions that it has generated represent in part a reaction to this development, guest-worker plans attempt to guarantee that whatever new immigrant workers that society requires will remain marginal. In other words, in the abstract, immigrant guest-workers represent all benefit and no cost. If immigrants have always been welcomed primarily as a work force, immigrant guest-workers constitute the ideal immigrants.

While the logic of the guest-worker approach appears to be faultless, its feasibility is questionable. Both the western European record[68] and the bracero experience suggest that guest-worker programs not only fail to guarantee the temporary nature of this work force, but they increase the flow of the undocumented as well. As Hadley observed of the braceros, "The next year they wanted to repeat their performance and their neighbors wanted to join....

---

[67]*New York Times*, 27 January 1985.
[68]Mark Miller and Philip Martin, *Administering Foreign Worker Programs* (Lexington, Mass.: D.C. Heath, 1984); Thomas W. Simmons, "Foreign Labor in West Germany, Switzerland and the United Kingdom: A Status Report," unpublished report sponsored by the German Marshall Fund of the United States, 1985.

The result was that there were many more Mexicans who wanted to come to the United States than there were certifications of need issued by the Secretary of Labor."[69]

Compounding this problem, the guest-worker approach is based on a view of immigrant labor as a seasonal phenomenon. But "the vast majority of illegal aliens work in nonseasonal, nonagricultural jobs. A new guest-worker program will have to rotate temporary workers through relatively permanent jobs."[70] Thus, a contemporary guest-worker program aimed exclusively at temporary employment would, at best, fill only a small fraction of the labor need and, at worst, constitute a logistical nightmare that would dwarf the difficulties of the bracero period.

More fundamental than these logistical drawbacks, the guest-worker concept violates the basic principles of U.S. society. In the first place, it violates the free labor market principles that underlie a capitalist economy. The logic of supply and demand and the principle of free contract theoretically moderate capitalism. Infusions into the labor market of those who are neither free agents nor have the ability to unionize thus violate the very tenets of capitalism itself and deprive the system of an important check on the free exercise of power by employers. Nor can the establishment of wages and working conditions at the "going rate" overcome these difficulties, for they are inherent in any program which in its very principle deprives workers of the potential to negotiate with the employer, either individually or through a union.

Finally, the underlying concept of a guest-worker program is to bring into the society a category of workers who must, by definition, remain marginal to that society. This deliberate institutionalization of an underclass which is excluded politically and socially from the society in which it is a de facto participant is incompatible with the values of a democratic society. In conjunction with the problems of logistics and economic irrationality discussed above, a concern for normative consistency should strike the fatal blow against guest-worker programs as a viable immigration alternative.

---

[69]Hadley, "A Critical Analysis of the Wetback Problem," p. 344.
[70]Philip Martin, "Commentaries," in *The Gateway: U.S. Immigration Issues and Policies*, edited by Barry Chiswick (Washington, D.C.: American Enterprise Institute for Public Policy Research, 1982), pp: 457-458.

Maintaining the Status Quo

Given the drawbacks of such immigration reform proposals, it is tempting to advocate inaction. This noninterventionist alternative seems all the more appealing once the myth of unilateral benefits and its corollaries have been refuted. However, the de facto admission of hundreds of thousands of undocumented workers each year creates a work force at least as marginal and "captive" as the braceros of the past. A number of policymakers note the sacrifices to rationality and efficiency that such a "shadow work force" exacts. Law enforcement officials in San Diego have long recognized the difficulties of obtaining the cooperation of the undocumented in responding to crime.[71] Doris Meissner, acting INS commissioner at the time, explained it this way to the Senate Judiciary Committee: "The costs to society of permitting a large group of persons to live in an illegal status are enormous. Society is harmed every time an undocumented alien is afraid to testify as a witness in a legal proceeding, to report an illness that may constitute a public health hazard or to disclose a violation of U.S. labor laws."[72]

An extensive literature attests to the magnitude and impact of economic, political, and social marginality on undocumented workers and their families.[73] It is on the basis of this marginality

---

[71]San Diego County Human Resources Agency, "Impact of Illegal Aliens on the County of San Diego" (San Diego, Calif.: County of San Diego, 1977).
[72]Quoted in Crewdson, *The Tarnished Door*, p. 314.
[73]Robert Bach, "Mexican Immigration and U.S. Immigration Reforms in the 1960s," *Kapitalistate* 7 (1978): 63-80; Jorge Bustamante, "Commodity-Migrants: Structural Analysis of Mexican Immigration to the U.S.," in *Views Across the Border* edited by Stanley Ross (Albuquerque: University of New Mexico Press, 1978); Wayne Cornelius, Leo Chávez, and Jorge Castro, "Mexican Immigrants and Southern California: A Summary of Current Knowledge," Working Papers in U.S.-Mexican Studies, no. 36 (La Jolla, Calif.: Center for U.S.-Mexican Studies, University of California, San Diego, 1982); Arthur Corwin and Walter Fogel, "Shadow Labor Force: Mexican Workers in the American Economy," in *Immigrants—and Immigrants: Perspectives on Mexican Labor Migration to the United States*, edited by A. Corwin (Westport, Conn.: Greenwood, 1978); Crewdson, *The Tarnished Door*; Sheldon Maram, "Hispanic Workers in the Garment and Restaurant Industries in Los Angeles County," Working Papers in U.S.-Mexican Studies, no. 12 (La Jolla, Calif.: Center for U.S.-Mexican Studies, University of California, San Diego, 1980); Marshall, "Economic Factors Influencing the International Migration of Workers"; Muller and Espenshade, *The Fourth Wave*; David North and Marion Houstoun, "The Characteristics and Role of Illegal Aliens in the U.S. Labor Market: An Exploratory Study," report prepared for the Employment and Training Administration, U.S. Department of Labor (Washington, D.C.: Linton, 1976); Demetrios Papademetriou and Mark Miller, *The Unavoidable Issue: Immigration Policy in the 1980s* (Philadelphia: Institute for the Study of Human Issues, 1983); Alejandro Portes, "Labor Functions of Illegal

that the undocumented work "scared and hard."[74] While society and individual employers may benefit economically from this arrangement, these benefits are bought at the cost not only of great human sacrifice but also of violation of the same liberal democratic principles that preclude the acceptability of guest-worker programs.

Finally, to advocate maintaining the status quo on the basis of its economic benefits is to perpetuate the hypocrisy and mythology surrounding the immigration debate. On one hand, the de jure policy illegalizes the migratory flow; on the other hand, the de facto policy not only tolerates the flow but assures that the society and individual employers will reap the benefits of its illegalization. The comments of one bewildered citizen when confronted with the facts regarding the economic advantages of illegal migration illustrate the dilemma: "Well then," she said, "how about putting a ceiling on the number of illegals to be admitted each year?"[75]

To advocate institutionalizing a disjunction between de jure and de facto policy is at best counter-intuitive. At worst, it is counterproductive. It continues to confuse the immigration policy debate with contradictory messages. The de jure restriction of immigration

---

Aliens," *Society* 14 (1977): 31-37; and Portes, "Illegal Immigration and the International System: Lessons from Recent Legal Mexican Immigrants to the United States," *Social Problems* 26 (1979): 425-43Robert Bach, "Mexican Immigration and U.S. Immigration Reforms in the 1960s," *Kapitalistate* 7 (1978): 63-80; Jorge Bustamante, "Commodity-Migrants: Structural Analysis of Mexican Immigration to the U.S.," in *Views Across the Border* edited by Stanley Ross (Albuquerque: University of New Mexico Press, 1978); Wayne Cornelius, Leo Chávez, and Jorge Castro, "Mexican Immigrants and Southern California: A Summary of Current Knowledge," Working Papers in U.S.-Mexican Studies, no. 36 (La Jolla, Calif.: Center for U.S.-Mexican Studies, University of California, San Diego, 1982); Arthur Corwin and Walter Fogel, "Shadow Labor Force: Mexican Workers in the American Economy," in *Immigrants—* and *Immigrants: Perspectives on Mexican Labor Migration to the United States*, edited by A. Corwin (Westport, Conn.: Greenwood, 1978); Crewdson, *The Tarnished Door*; Sheldon Maram, "Hispanic Workers in the Garment and Restaurant Industries in Los Angeles County," Working Papers in U.S.-Mexican Studies, no. 12 (La Jolla, Calif.: Center for U.S.-Mexican Studies, University of California, San Diego, 1980); Marshall, "Economic Factors Influencing the International Migration of Workers"; Muller and Espenshade, *The Fourth Wave*; David North and Marion Houstoun, "The Characteristics and Role of Illegal Aliens in the U.S. Labor Market: An Exploratory Study," report prepared for the Employment and Training Administration, U.S. Department of Labor (Washington, D.C.: Linton, 1976); Demetrios Papademetriou and Mark Miller, *The Unavoidable Issue: Immigration Policy in the 1980s* (Philadelphia: Institute for the Study of Human Issues, 1983); Alejandro Portes, "Labor Functions of Illegal Aliens," *Society* 14 (1977): 31-37; and Portes, "Illegal Immigration and the International System: Lessons from Recent Legal Mexican Immigrants to the United States," *Social Problems* 26 (1979): 425-438.

[74]Marshall, "Economic Factors Influencing the International Migration of Workers," p. 169.

[75]Comment offered at the January 1987 meeting of the American Association of University Women.

officially endorses the myth of unilateral benefits. At the same time, the actual benefits to the receiving society are surreptitiously recognized in de facto policy. "The present incoherence of policy has its political attractions, since it leaves difficult value choices inexplicit, allows the most committed interest groups to pursue their interests unimpeded, and yet avoids explicit endorsement of their aims...."[76] But real progress in immigration reform can only begin once the immigration debate is free from such hypocrisy and the confusion it generates.

Conclusion: An Alternative Approach

The immigration policy discussion elicits a curious alliance between liberal advocates for undocumented workers and the self-interested employers who benefit from this cheap labor supply. Implicit or explicit support of the status quo draws these unlikely political allies together. Upon examination, this alliance is apparently a result of the narrow framing of the issue of immigration reform. Immigration, because it represents the movement of a work force, is above all an economic phenomenon. Hence, immigration policy debates should ideally be part and parcel of broader debates over economic policy. When immigration policy discussions are detached, as in the current debate, from those about economic reforms, people interested in advancing human welfare must choose between the lesser of two evils. They can advocate the continued entry of undocumented immigrants into the United States to take jobs so undesirable that U.S. citizens reject them, or they can support withdrawing this option from those who would thus be confined to far worse poverty at home.

However, if the myth of unilateral benefits is dispelled and immigration "reform" is no longer synonymous with immigration restriction, the debate can progress. In light of the long-standing role of immigrant labor in the U.S. economy and its all-too-often surreptitious recognition in policy, any immigration reform proposal must be based on a straightforward rejection of the myth of unilateral benefits. Fashioning a rational and humane immigration policy requires coupling official acknowledgement of society's need for immigrant labor with a recognition of the human, political, and economic rights of those whose labor the society requires.

---

[76]Teitelbaum, "Right Versus Right," p. 48.

Given this dual premise, one viable alternative is to increase substantially legal immigration quotas, particularly for Mexico and other countries from which the United States draws disproportionate numbers of workers. The reactions against such an approach are predictable:

- A temporary labor program is preferable to this more permanent incorporation of immigrant workers into the society.

- This approach precludes the flexibility permitted with guestworkers and undocumented workers.

- It is precisely the illegal status of the undocumented work force that provides most economic benefits.

In the first place, however, as the foregoing discussion has suggested, temporary worker programs are neither logistically feasible nor morally tolerable. Second, the objection that such a legalization of the immigrant flow precludes flexibility overestimates the real flexibility in either the status quo or any conceivable "temporary" labor program. Finally, it is essential to address the concern that legalizing the flow will deprive the U.S. economy of the benefits of an undocumented labor force. This discussion has already presented the counter-intuitive and morally questionable aspects of deliberately fashioning a contradiction between de jure and de facto policies. In addition, however, it is not at all clear that legal immigrants could not substitute for the undocumented at the bottom of the occupational hierarchy, much as their counterparts did at the beginning of the century. What is clear is that they would not be condemned to remain there by virtue of an undocumented status.

Policymakers have periodically recognized that the current legal immigration ceiling of twenty thousand is unrealistically low for countries like Mexico, where a long-standing pattern of immigration to the United States and visa backlogs provide incentive for illegal migration. The staff of the Select Commission on Immigration and Refugee Policy recommended that the total ceiling on legal immigration worldwide be raised from the current 270,000 to 750,000. In apparent reaction to popular demands for restrictions following the Mariel boatlift, the commission settled on a minor increase to 350,000,[77] a recommendation ultimately rejected in IRCA.

---

[77]Ricardo Anzaldúa Montoya and Wayne Cornelius, eds. "The Report of the U.S. Select Commission on Immigration and Refugee Policy: A Critical Analysis," Research Report Series, no. 32 (La Jolla, Calif.: Center for U.S.-Mexican Studies, University of California, San Diego, 1983), p. 23.

In the aftermath of IRCA, the concept of raising legal immigration ceilings has regained credibility as a policy alternative. Of course any attempt to reduce undocumented immigration by legalizing much of the flow would mean more substantial increases than those heretofore proposed. Furthermore, such a development hinges on dismantling the mythology surrounding immigration and immigration policy-making, and on a commitment to the values of a liberal democratic society.

About the Contributors

Jorge A. Bustamante, a sociologist, is President of El Colegio de la Frontera Norte in Tijuana, Baja California, and the Eugene Conley Professor of Sociology at the University of Notre Dame. He is a specialist on Mexican migration to the United States and the Mexico-origin population of the United States. He has written more than one hundred scientific publications on these subjects, and also contributes a weekly column on border issues to the Mexico City newspaper *Excélsior*.

Kitty C. Calavita is a member of the sociology faculty at the University of California, Irvine, and a Research Associate of the Center for U.S.-Mexican Studies at the University of California, San Diego. She is a specialist on the sociology and history of U.S. immigration law and policy. Her publications include *U.S. Immigration Policy and the Control of Labor, 1820-1924*, and *California's "Employer Sanctions": The Case of the Disappearing Law*.

Wayne A. Cornelius is Director of the Center for U.S.-Mexican Studies and the Theodore E. Gildred Professor of Political Science at the University of California, San Diego. His areas of research specialization include international labor migration, Mexican politics, and U.S.-Mexican relations. His forthcoming books include *The Changing Role of Mexican Immigrants in the U.S. Economy: Sectoral Perspectives* and *Los Norteños: Mexican Migration vs. U.S. Immigration Reform*.

Manuel García y Griego is professor and researcher in the Center for International Studies at El Colegio de México. He received an M.A. in demography from El Colegio de México and a Ph.D. in history from UCLA. Among his publications are *El volumen de la migración de mexicanos no documentados a Estados Unidos: nuevas hipótesis*, with Mónica Verea, *México y Estados Unidos frente a la migración de indocumentados*.

Rosario Green is Mexico's ambassador to the German Democratic Republic (GDR). She studied economics and international relations at the National Autonomous University of Mexico, at El Colegio de México, at Columbia University in New York, and at the Instituto para la Integración Latinoamericana (INTAL) in Buenos Aires. She has been a professor at El Colegio de México and, from 1982 to 1988, director of the Matías Romero Institute of Diplomatic Studies. Ms. Green has published ten books, including a prescient analysis of Mexico's foreign indebtedness, *El endeudamiento público externo de México: 1950-1973*, as well as *Estado y banca transnacional en México*, and, most recently, *La deuda externa de México de 1973 a 1988: de la abundancia a la escasez de créditos*. She has written articles for academic reviews and journalistic media in various languages. Ms. Green has been a consultant to the United Nations and to the Sistema Económico Latinoamericano. In 1987, she was executive director of the International Affairs Commission of the Partido Revolucionario Institucional.

Peter H. Smith is professor of political science and Simón Bolívar professor of Latin American studies at the University of California, San Diego. Born in Brooklyn, New York, he graduated from Harvard College in 1961 and earned a Ph.D. from Columbia University in 1966. A specialist on long-run processes of political change, Mr. Smith has written books on Argentina and on empirical methodology. His best-known work on Mexico is *Labyrinths of Power*, a study of elite recruitment and mobility. He has also co-authored a textbook entitled *Modern Latin America*. Mr. Smith has served as a department chair and academic associate dean at the University of Wisconsin and at MIT, and he is past president of the Latin American Studies Association. He was professor of history and political science at the Massachusetts Institute of Technology before joining the faculty of UC-San Diego.

Marta Tienda is Professor of Sociology and Director of the Center for Studies of the Family and the Community at the University of Chicago. She has written extensively on patterns of socioeconomic mobility in the Latino population of the United States. Her publications include *Immigration: Issues and Policies* (1985) with Vernon Briggs; and *Hispanics in the U.S. Economy*, with George Borjas; and *The Hispanic Population of the United States* (1988), with Frank D. Bean.